GOOD AS GOLD

GOOD AS GOLD

How to Unleash the Power of Sound Money

Judy Shelton

INDEPENDENT
INSTITUTE

Cataloging-in-Publication data on file with the Library of Congress

Independent Institute
100 Swan Way, Oakland, CA 94621-1428
Telephone: 510-632-1366
Fax: 510-568-6040
Email: info@independent.org
Website: www.independent.org

Cover Design: Denise Tsui
Cover Image: madmaxer via 123rf, #18953887
Interior Design: Mike Mott

Contents

Preface
Money Is a Moral Contract

THE HEARING ROOM of the Senate Banking Committee is a cavernous chamber with wood-paneled walls and massive bronze lighting fixtures. I was seated at a table covered in green cloth facing a semicircle of twenty-five black leather chairs tightly arranged behind an elongated curved wooden desk on an elevated rostrum. It was February 13, 2020, and the members of the committee were convened to consider my nomination to the Board of Governors of the Federal Reserve System.

The hearing was called to order by Chairman Mike Crapo, who delivered opening remarks that included a cordial welcome to the friends and family of the two nominees before the committee that morning, Christopher Waller and myself.[1] It was a nice way to start. Besides my husband and son, another seven members of my family, including my mother, had flown in from Los Angeles the previous day.

But there was an early clue that things could get rough—at least for me. Chairman Crapo announced that he was entering into the record an article from the *Wall Street Journal* in support of my nomination. It was entitled "The War on Judy Shelton."[2]

It had certainly started to feel like war in the days leading up to the hearing. I felt supremely grateful for that *Journal* editorial, which I had read aloud to my husband the prior afternoon as we were driving north toward Washington on I-95 from our rural Virginia home. "Ms. Shelton is clearly qualified for the Fed role," the editorial declared. "The caterwauling over her nomination confirms why her intellectual diversity is needed at the Fed." The editorial cited with approval my academic research on historical eras during which economies backed their currencies with gold, noting that it revealed contrasts with "the catastrophic misfires of our era of floating rates." Staunchly contradicting accusations that I had abandoned my belief in monetary discipline for political reasons, the *Journal* affirmed that my long-argued views were intellectually consistent. "The inconsistency and confusion rest with her critics and the prevailing monetary establishment and are dangerous for the U.S. economy."

The *Journal* editorial concluded with the observation that the Fed was straying into uncharted territory in extending its low-rate regime with no well-defined plans for extricating itself from quantitative easing: "If Senators harbor even a sliver of doubt over whether Ms. Shelton's critics know what they're doing, that's all the more reason to confirm her as a distinctive voice in such crucial debates."

Was I ready to be that distinctive voice at the Fed that would add intellectual diversity to monetary policy discussions? In some ways, I had been preparing for the role for nearly four decades. My work as a doctoral student concentrated on money and banking, international finance and economics. An article I wrote in 1981 won the Trefftzs Award for outstanding scholarly achievement from the Western Finance Association and was subsequently published in the *Journal of Financial and Quantitative Analysis*. When I was granted a postdoctoral fellowship by the Hoover Institution at Stanford University, I used the opportunity to focus on the internal monetary and financial conditions of the Soviet Union; I wanted to understand how government management of economic resources impacted a nation's budgetary situation and fiscal viability.

The result was a scholarly treatise entitled "The Impact of Western Capital on the Soviet Economy," which became a commercially published book in 1989 with a far more captivating title: *The Coming Soviet Crash: Gorbachev's Desperate Pursuit of Credit in Western Financial Markets.* What I discovered through my research was that the Soviet government had been running a massive budget deficit for years. It was effectively going bankrupt. Should Western banks bail out the failing Soviet economy or allow the dying Soviet bear to quietly succumb to its own afflictions?

My view was that it made no sense to help sustain the nation most responsible for our own nation's heavy defense spending burden. Though my background was in economics, I found myself being consulted by national security policymakers and asked to participate in war-gaming exercises. The nexus between academic theory and political reality became very clear—and I developed an appreciation for the importance of linking those two worlds through clear policy directives.

My second book centered on the importance of sound money and solvent public finances in providing the appropriate foundation for economic prosperity, both at home and abroad. *Money Meltdown: Restoring Order to the Global Currency System*, published in 1994, was praised by conservative statesman Jack Kemp as "a clarion call for a new stable international monetary order." Indeed, drawing on lessons learned from the gold-anchored Bretton Woods system and its antecedents, my goal was to highlight the need for a level monetary playing field to confront the menace of currency manipulation and uphold the principles of free trade.

It seemed surreal to me that my background and qualifications for serving on the Federal Reserve Board—let alone my motives—were now being questioned. Beyond weighing in on the nation's most pressing economic and national security policy challenges as an expert witness testifying before Congress on numerous occasions, I also served as chair of the National Endowment for Democracy. During the 2016 presidential transition, I was designated lead adviser on international financial matters for the team assigned to the Treasury Department. In May 2018, after being confirmed by Congress, I began serving in London as U.S. director of the European Bank for Reconstruction and Development under the Trump administration. The opportunity to take on this new role as a governor on the Federal Reserve Board was presented in July 2019 when President Donald Trump announced his intention to nominate me for the position.

Throughout my career, I have been a steady contributor to the editorial pages of the *Wall Street Journal*, with more than sixty articles published as commentaries. The members of its editorial board know me well. So when they vouch for my intellectual consistency, my expertise on monetary matters, and my willingness to challenge conventional wisdom, it means a lot. The *Journal* endorsement provided a most welcome counterweight to the *New York Times* editorial published a day earlier. "This Is No Way to Run a Central Bank" ran the banner headline—accompanied by a hideous photo—

denouncing me as a "bad choice for a seat on the Fed's board."[3] The *Washington Post* had featured an article that week by one of its columnists labeling me "an opportunist and a quack."[4] While it was hard to tolerate having my views misrepresented, especially by pundits who struck me as somewhat ignorant in matters of monetary economics, I recognized that political allegiances might be affecting their judgment. Still, it seemed a bit ominous that clashing newspaper opinion pieces were playing a prominent role in defining my qualifications for becoming a Fed governor.

Then it was time for Senator Sherrod Brown to deliver his own opening statement as ranking member of the committee. He described me as someone who "has spent her entire career advocating for policies that would make our economy more volatile, give families and businesses even more to worry about in an uncertain world."[5] According to Senator Brown, "a vote for Ms. Shelton is a vote against Fed independence and our nation's reputation as a financial bulwark for the whole world."[6]

Things went downhill from there. Over the next two hours, I was asked to respond to loaded questions—or worse, compelled to remain silent in the face of long-winded statements distorting my beliefs. Later that day, Reuters published an article calling it a "contentious" Senate confirmation hearing.[7] CNBC described it as "blistering."[8]

Over and over again, the senators questioned me about my prior writings on the gold standard. That was hardly a surprise. Shortly after President Trump announced, on July 2, 2019, his intention to nominate Christopher Waller and myself for the two vacant Fed slots, a *Washington Post* columnist described me as a "denizen of the Republican gold-bug circuit." The danger of the doctrine I had consistently promoted for decades, the writer explained, might be difficult for laypeople to decipher "unless you understand the 'sound money' or 'dependable dollar' code of the crank right-wing fringe."[9]

The morning the column appeared in print, I emailed it to Alan Greenspan along with a tongue-in-cheek message about "an almost hysterical antagonism toward the gold standard," echoing the opening sentence of his 1966 article "Gold and Economic Freedom."[10] Greenspan promptly emailed back: "If gold is such a worthless metal, then why does the U.S. Government, and all other major governments, hold so much of it in storage?"[11]

Logical question, yes, but one that never seemed to occur to commentators who were quick to disparage as "radical" my scholarly writings on international monetary systems based on gold-convertible currencies. They seemed unaware that gold is held by central banks around the world precisely to serve as a monetary bulwark—a point readily affirmed by the former chairman of the Federal Reserve.

Thankfully, there was one brief respite during the hearing when I was invited by Senator Mike Rounds to share my thoughts "without being led into any question." Responding to this precious opportunity to expound more fully on my beliefs, I answered:

> I keep going back to the fact that the power to regulate the value of U.S. money is granted by our Constitution to Congress. It is in Article I, Section 8. And in the very same sentence, Congress is given the power to define official weights and measures for our country—because money was meant to be a measure, to be a standard of value.
>
> Money has to work the same for everyone in the economy. It is important that it serve that purpose as a reliable measure so that people can plan their lives. I do not see how you can have a free-market economy if people cannot rely on the most vital tool that makes markets work. It is through money that we transmit market signals. You need clarity of those signals; otherwise, supply and demand cannot figure out what is the optimal solution.
>
> So I think that, what has importance in discussions at the Federal Reserve, is the responsibility to remember that the money has to work for everyone—and that, in a sense, it is a moral contract between the government and the citizens.[12]

Being able to express my deep-seated commitment to sound money brought a level of satisfaction that far outweighed the caustic slights incurred during the hearing. Bringing up the moral aspect of money as a measure should not put someone in the category of right-wing crank. Striving to ensure that money is trustworthy does not constitute a fringe movement. Indeed, having access to dependable money should be deemed a basic human right that deserves broad support. People should be able to use a medium of exchange that performs as a meaningful unit of account and a reliable store of

value. Why are governments permitted to expropriate wealth through inflation while denying the use of alternative currencies? People need money that
preserves their purchasing power and provides an accurate tool for measuring
value across borders and through time.

Before the conclusion of the hearing, Chairman Crapo summed up the
proceedings:

> We all knew that this was going to be a very aggressive hearing
> today, particularly with regard to you, Dr. Shelton. I think you
> have been very solid in explaining and defending your writings
> and your positions. And, by the way, the reason that I introduced
> into the record in my opening statement an article from the *Wall
> Street Journal* entitled "The War on Judy Shelton" was just to help
> make the point that this is an orchestrated, calculated effort. I
> think you have done very well today, and I just wanted to tell you
> that you have explained, I think very capably, the positions that
> you take and the rationale for them.[13]

The assessment of Chairman Crapo was much appreciated. Nevertheless,
I feel compelled to explain my views and the rationale more fully to make
clear how they justify continuing the endeavor. The purpose of this book is to
examine what has worked, what has failed, and what can be done to appropriately calibrate the money supply to meet the needs of an economy devoted
to free-market enterprise and unlimited opportunity. The crux of my position
is that money is meant to be an honest measure. It should provide a reliable
tool for conducting voluntary transactions among individuals; it should not
serve as an economic policy instrument to be manipulated by the government.

I have come to the realization, in retrospect, that the entire nomination process was a positive experience. It proved to be enlightening—even
clarifying. It underscored the importance of not being deterred by aggressive
tactics and helped me comprehend how much is at stake in the pursuit of
sound money.

Introduction
Call to Action

"The ideas of economists and political philosophers, both when they are right and when they are wrong, are more powerful than is commonly understood. Indeed the world is ruled by little else."

John Maynard Keynes, *General Theory of Employment, Interest and Money* (1936)

WHEN ALAN GREENSPAN wrote that "gold and economic freedom are inseparable" some twenty years before he became chairman of the Federal Reserve, the arguments he put forward marked him as both an economist and political philosopher.[1] From an economic point of view, the benefits of having a gold standard and a free banking system include stability and balanced growth for the domestic economy. An international gold standard also "serves to foster a world-wide division of labor and the broadest international trade." The focus turns to political philosophy when Greenspan notes that "government deficit spending under a gold standard is severely limited" and asserts that "in the absence of the gold standard, there is no way to protect savings from confiscation through inflation." From Greenspan's point of view, the incompatibility of the gold standard with chronic deficit spending is the reason welfare-state advocates oppose it: "This is the shabby secret of the welfare statists' tirades against gold. Deficit spending is simply a scheme for the "hidden" confiscation of wealth. Gold stands in the way of this insidious process. It stands as a protector of property rights. If one grasps this, one has no difficulty in understanding the statists' antagonism toward the gold standard."[2]

Having such strong views posed no impediment to Greenspan's confirmation as Fed chairman, nor did it seem to impinge on his fitness to serve as leader of the world's most powerful central bank from 1987 to 2006. One could make the case that holding strong opinions about government's proper role within an economy based on democratic capitalism should be a prerequisite for those serving at the Federal Reserve—where policy decisions put the integrity of the nation's monetary standard at stake. Ideas are powerful, as Keynes observed, both when they are right and when they are wrong.

One thing is clear: the ideas of economists and political philosophers come profoundly into play on the subject of money and exchange rates. Using arguments first vented in the 1930s, modern disciples of John Maynard Keynes and Friedrich Hayek debate passionately over how much influence government should have in determining economic outcomes. Quarrels continue to this day over whether total discretionary authority should be granted to central banks to stimulate economic activity by deliberately reducing interest rates from what would be their market-determined rate—even as menacing inflation undermines the domestic purchasing power of citizens.

Meanwhile, with major central banks around the world exercising different monetary policies to achieve self-interested economic objectives, international trade and investment relations are distorted by currency swings. To the frustration of academics and real-world players alike, we have yet to settle the question whether cross-border monetary arrangements should be based on fixed or flexible exchange rates—decades after Nobel laureates Milton Friedman and Robert Mundell offered dueling opinions in the *National Post*.[3]

The fundamental question at the heart of these issues arouses the passions and convictions of theorists and practitioners across the ideological spectrum: To what extent are political freedom and economic freedom linked? It's a question that should concern every citizen. Those who believe free-market capitalism delivers the best results for society by ensuring individual liberty while delivering shared economic prosperity are not inclined to relinquish to the government whole swaths of national income and private sector development. Whether they self-identify as conservatives or simply embrace the tenets of classical economic liberalism, they prefer to rely on entrepreneurial initiative rather than government-managed industrial policy to foster innovative solutions to problems. On the other hand, those who are doubtful that the profit motive is sufficient to induce private enterprise to address important issues of economic opportunity and social justice are more likely to put their faith in government to equitably redistribute national income and curtail the seeming excesses of capitalism. Embracing a collectivist view of social organization, they see greed in the aims of private sector companies and harbor suspicions about the predatory inclinations of financial institutions.

Political philosophy especially matters when it comes to money because political leaders have a long history of compromising the purely economic functions of money in favor of achieving other objectives. Money is meant to provide a (1) medium of exchange, (2) unit of account, and (3) store of value. When those purposes are subjugated to other aims of government—whether lofty or self-serving—the validity of money as a reliable standard for evaluating goods and services becomes subject to question. When the money cannot be trusted, the price signals it conveys are increasingly perceived as murky. Free-market economies can hardly deliver the appropriate benefits to discerning consumers and reward the legitimate success of efficient producers if the forces of supply and demand are not properly equilibrated through accurate price signals.

Do we want government to have a strong role in defining the value of money? Granting to government the original power to establish the value of the nation's currency unit by specifying its metallic content is one thing. It is quite another to allow central banks to continually alter the value of the currency unit as either an incidental or intended consequence of conducting discretionary monetary policy by exerting control over interest rates. The purchasing power of gold or silver will be responsive to supply-and-demand conditions, but when the metallic content of a nation's currency is stipulated, the money provides a reliable pricing tool that serves as an unchanging standard for measuring value.

Long-brewing tensions over the failure of governments and central banks, using both fiscal and monetary policy, to deliver price stability as the foundation for productive economic growth have reached a level that cannot be ignored by the public. Inflation has impacted citizens in the United States and around the world—causing disappointment and resentment. Yet it is not entirely clear just who is being held responsible. When it comes to inflation, are central banks exclusively at fault? Governments make the budgetary decisions that determine spending levels; when revenues are inadequate to cover expenditures, the resulting budget deficits are financed through the issuance of government debt. The debt represents a claim on future revenues that have yet to be generated. This raises a fundamental question: Is it even possible to have sound money in the absence of sound finances?

The two major approaches the government uses to intervene in the economy—through fiscal policy or monetary policy—tend to be analyzed separately, but both play a major role in fostering inflation. For example, transfer payments from the government that go directly into the pockets of recipients serve to augment consumer spending power, which puts inflationary pressure on the prices of goods and services. For similar reasons, government forgiveness of student loans also has an inflationary impact. From the monetary point of view, conducting expansionary policy "stimulus" through a central bank fuels inflation because it reduces the cost of capital, which induces firms and households to borrow more money, which leads to increased economic activity—likewise putting pressure on the price level.

Merging fiscal theory with monetary policy models, economist John Cochrane offers a framework for bridging both aspects of government involvement through his 2023 book, *The Fiscal Theory of the Price Level*.[4] Cochrane concludes that inflation breaks out when people begin to doubt that the government will ever repay its massive debts by running future budget surpluses.[5] Whether or not such a calculation goes into the thinking of investors and consumers, Cochrane is clearly onto something in suggesting that any serious effort to address the unsustainability of current U.S. policies will require both fiscal and monetary reforms. When central banks purchase government debt, they create new money—injecting fresh cash into the economy—by enlarging the amount of money commercial banks maintain in their accounts at their regional Federal Reserve banks. These reserve balances are further claims on existing goods and services; they can be loaned out by the banks or invested in other assets. By monetizing the debt issued by governments with a keystroke, central banks function as enablers of fiscal recklessness.

The fact that central banks are massive purchasers of government debt further muddies the issue of assigning responsibility for inflation. It would seem to cross ethical lines that central banks, which are agencies of government, stand willing to accommodate the funding needs of government required by federal budget outlays in excess of federal budget receipts. Elected representatives of the people who are authorized to approve government spending should presumably be capable of adhering to the constraint of running a balanced budget. While it could be argued that the lender-of-last-resort function for central banks exists for the precise purpose of providing liquidity under emergency conditions, this should not mean that government expenditures in excess of government revenues should be routinely accommodated.

Since the global financial crisis of 2008 and the advent of quantitative easing—with the Federal Reserve purchasing vast quantities of Treasury debt and mortgage-backed securities guaranteed by the government—it has become a normalized tool for the nation's central bank to bail out deficit spending. That does not make quantitative easing a healthy practice, however. It is inherently political to intermingle the conduct of monetary policy with the financing needs of politicians, whether they serve in Congress or the White House.

Consider that the Federal Reserve remits the earnings derived from the interest payments received on its own portfolio of financial assets made up of those same government obligations—that is, Treasury debt and mortgage-backed securities—back to the Treasury after deducting the Fed's operating expenses. These remittances are counted as revenues in the federal budget. When the Fed was following a near-zero interest rate policy in the post-2008 period and again during the COVID-19 pandemic (and beyond), this practice meant that the central bank was providing a significant rebate to the government—effectively subsidizing its borrowing costs. This denotes a rather blatant conflict of interest between the Treasury and the Fed, with the government's fiscal needs conveniently met under the rubric of discretionary monetary policy.

The other side of that arrangement is equally disturbing. Whereas a period of loose monetary policy featuring near-zero rates provides a budgetary bonus to the Treasury through Fed remittances, a period of tightening monetary policy requires the Fed to pay higher rates of interest on cash accounts held at the Fed by commercial banks and money market mutual funds. The right to pay interest on reserve balances was part of an emergency set of measures approved by Congress in October 2008. The Fed has since made this practice its primary method for setting its benchmark interest rate, called the federal funds rate. In tandem with the interest paid on reserve balances held in depository accounts by commercial banks, the Fed also pays interest on reverse repurchase agreements with money market mutual funds and other financial entities. These transactions allow the participant to earn interest by keeping cash at the Fed overnight, accepting Fed portfolio holdings as collateral to be returned. When the expense of paying interest on both these categories of cash deposits exceeds the amount of interest the Fed earns on its own holdings, the difference is recorded as a deferred asset. Instead of providing remittances back to the Treasury, the Fed accumulates operating losses while the federal budget loses its former revenue source.[6]

Taxpayers in the United States might be prompted to question why the Federal Reserve as an independent government agency provides interest payments to private parties with funds not specifically appropriated by Congress. In 2023, the Fed paid an unprecedented $281 billion in interest expense to commercial banks and money market mutual funds.[7] Public financial statements issued by the Fed do not provide detailed information that would identify what percentage of the Fed's total interest payment expenditures are going to the top five largest banking institutions. Nor does the Fed divulge what percentage of its interest expense is being paid to foreign-owned institutions. Financial journalists who cover the Fed seem remarkably incurious when it comes to asking who are the beneficiaries of payments made by the nation's central bank. Given that these payments were well in excess of the $164 billion the Fed received in revenues from its portfolio holdings in 2023—with the difference paid out of funds that would otherwise be remitted to the U.S. Treasury—taxpayers deserve answers.

One of the factors cited on the Federal Reserve's website to explain its claim that it is "independent within the government" is that the Fed does not receive funding through the congressional budgetary process.[8] Instead, the website proclaims, the Fed pays its expenses out of the interest income it receives on government securities that it has acquired. That is not the case in reality, given that interest expense now exceeds interest revenue for the Fed—a fact that would seem to violate that aspect of central bank independence. Moreover, it is difficult to imagine a scenario over the next few years wherein the returns on the Fed's investment portfolio (which is slated for reduction by allowing holdings to run off, i.e., by not reinvesting all the proceeds of maturing securities) will generate sufficient funds to cover interest payments at today's high rates on the current level of reserve balances held on deposit at the Fed.

The fact that the Federal Reserve has been operating at a loss since September 2022 would seemingly have come into play with regard to the fate of the Consumer Financial Protection Bureau (CFPB), an agency set up in 2011 with the strong support of Senator Elizabeth Warren, to serve as a watchdog against predatory lenders, junk fees, and other perceived abuses inflicted on borrowers by financial lenders. While the agency's website declares that its mission is ensuring that people are treated fairly by banks, lenders, and other financial institutions,[9] it is seen by many conservative lawmakers as a rogue regulator prone to aggressive enforcement actions. The CFPB is not funded through the congressional appropriations process; instead, its budget is drawn from the profits of the Federal Reserve. The constitutionality of this arrangement was challenged by a trade association on the basis that a funding mechanism outside of the congressional budgetary process raised accountability issues for the regulatory agency. A 7–2 decision by the Supreme Court in May 2024, however, rejected the argument that the CFPB's insulation from the annual budget process was a violation of the Constitution's clause regarding the appropriation of federal money.[10] If the ruling had gone the other way, questions about the Federal Reserve's own status as a government agency might have been raised. Because the Fed likewise funds itself out of its profits, the lack of profits since September 2022 would seem to open an avenue for challenging the accountability of the central bank—especially because the Fed's accumulated losses come at the expense of remittances to the Treasury.

Beyond these concerning practices involving the Federal Reserve and the Treasury, which constitute a serious problem of government transparency for the United States, there is also the challenge of reconciling the monetary integrity of the dollar at home with its broader role as the dominant global reserve currency. How can we criticize the debasement of the dollar as a consequence of inflation while also bemoaning the impact of a strong dollar relative to other currencies? We need a dependable dollar—one that does not skew profits and operating models for U.S. businesses engaged in exporting or based in foreign countries.

The irony of confronting these monetary problems comes from the realization that they are not new dilemmas. We have much to gain from analyzing how past monetary systems functioned, both domestically and internationally. Even as central bankers around the world proclaim that their most important task is to promote stable prices, generally referring to cost-of-living measures related to the needs of average consumers within their own nations, those same monetary authorities are responsible for the volatile interest rates that wreak havoc on international trade and financial outcomes. One of the great features of the classical gold standard was that it reconciled the stability of the national currency for domestic citizens with monetary stability in the international context. That is why it is worth studying.

Instead of rejecting consideration of prior systems with a demonstrated track record of success, we should be actively striving to incorporate the most desirable features into current monetary arrangements. We must be willing to acknowledge the shortcomings of central banking concerning safeguarding purchasing power. The fundamental challenge is to forge a path to monetary reform that can deliver the stable foundation needed for productive economic growth. Money should function as a meaningful unit of account across borders and a trustworthy store of value through time. International trade should be based on a level monetary playing field. Global competition would be conducted more fairly if there existed a common unit of account for measuring value—a benchmark that could be meaningfully interpreted by all participants. Future money should perform as good as gold. Or better. The challenge is to match or improve on past results.

People who contest existing monetary arrangements face the twofold task of making the case for change while also proposing specific actions to be taken. If it is possible to reach agreement about what we believe—and, importantly, what our beliefs imply—concerning current monetary arrangements, we will see more clearly how to proceed to lay out a viable path toward sound money. The first part of the book thus seeks to build the necessary intellectual consensus that will provide the groundwork for implementing an innovative approach based on lessons learned. In the second part of the book, we move from the world of theory to the world of action.

The three chapters that make up Part One take a closer look at general assumptions about how economies best serve the needs of society—that is, how they function optimally. People can differ in defining what is meant by "optimally" and how to measure optimal functioning. But the goal of Part One is to examine assertions that are widely acknowledged as having been proved beyond question—and yet somehow suspended when applied to status quo methods for conducting monetary policy. If nearly everyone can find agreement on certain definitive statements concerning economic performance and what has proved historically to make it better or worse, then it should be straightforward to apply these broadly held views to examining the conduct of monetary policy and discussing the proper role of central banks.

For example, one of the main lessons from the past century is that central planning doesn't work. The great philosophical divide between the United States and the Soviet Union was essentially a disagreement over how best to generate and distribute economic resources. Marxist doctrine argued that private ownership of property should not be allowed, that it encouraged greed and exploitation, and that it would eventually be overthrown as people rose up to demand economic equality. Capitalism relies on private ownership of the means of production not only for reasons of efficiency but also as an expression of individual economic freedom. In a capitalist system, buyers and sellers voluntarily conduct transactions in an open marketplace where prices are determined by the forces of demand and supply. Free competition ensures that consumers will seek the best product for the least amount of money; producers will accordingly endeavor to provide the best value.

Chapter 1 will address this essential issue: if we believe that central planning of prices and government allocation of credit don't work—with the most striking example of this ineffectiveness being the failed Soviet experiment, which led to internal bankruptcy and collapse—then we should question our willingness to permit central banks to control the price of loanable funds and influence credit markets in pursuit of government economic objectives. It seems unwise and anachronistic to empower a government agency to exert such dominance in determining the performance of financial markets and thereby to reward certain segments of society at the expense of others.

Second, it's time to address the stunning disconnect between real economic growth and the growth of financial assets measured in diminished monetary units. Chapter 2 will present the historical evidence for affirming that stable money fosters productive growth. It is vital to comprehend what has been lost in terms of potential growth and higher living standards as a result of today's monetary dysfunction at home and abroad. We need to clarify what we mean by "stable" in defining money. We need to explain what we mean by "productive" in measuring growth. Economists can debate these terms, even if members of the general public inherently understand their meaning. The more contentious issue for mainstream economists might be the assertion that stable money encourages the sort of economic activity that leads to genuine prosperity. Much of the logic behind Keynesian models is based on the notion that people respond to money illusion rather than real gains or losses. Such an assumption insults the intelligence of ordinary citizens, who are somehow presumed to act in accordance with money illusion even when they fully understand they are deliberately being duped as part of official government policy.

Another question: Does it matter to what extent economic activity is centered on the financial sector versus manufacturing or service-oriented pursuits? The notional amounts outstanding of over-the-counter financial derivatives as of June 2023 added up to more than $700 trillion, with 97 percent of them representing contracts linked to interest rate differentials or foreign exchange movements.[11] Should the value of those financial instruments be considered a measure of productive economic activity? While they may generate huge rewards for sophisticated traders, the existence of such speculative opportunities indicates that activist central banking behavior creates a niche for arbitrageurs that exploits the inherent monetary dissonance under status quo arrangements and leads to excessive financialization of the economy.

In Chapter 3, we examine yet another widely accepted precept that seems incongruent with the current international monetary regime. This is the notion that we have a global economy. If ours is truly an open global economy—and we believe in the idea of comparative advantage as the logical corollary for maximizing the gains of trade—we must recognize the need for a common unit of account for measuring value on both sides of a cross-border transaction. Those who decry tariffs as an abrogation of free trade should be among the first to support the need to measure the impact of currency swings in distorting the prices of imported goods and services. The magnitude of a shift in the exchange rate between currencies can easily dwarf the effect of a tariff aimed at addressing differing labor or environmental standards. Consider that the dollar in October 2022 was at its highest level since 2000, having appreciated 22 percent against the yen, 13 percent against the euro, and 6 percent against emerging market currencies since the start of that year.[12] Meanwhile, the average world tariff rate was 2.6 percent, last measured by the World Bank for 2017 using an integrated database that included information from the World Trade Organization.[13]

While all unfair trade practices are an affront to the notion of real competition in an open marketplace, this book focuses on the blatant abuse of free trade that occurs when a nation deliberately manipulates its currency to achieve a trade advantage. The exchange rate regime matters greatly if we are to preserve the benefits of international trade—which is why the role of central banks in causing exchange rate movements needs to be examined. It makes no sense to talk about the world economy in terms of free-market mechanisms unless prices for competing goods and services are meaningfully conveyed across borders without being altered by currency movements. Robert Mundell, whose work on supply-side economics and international exchange rates led to his being awarded the Nobel Prize in Economics in 1999, has long stated, with regard to reconciling monetary arrangements with the notion of a unified global market, that "the only closed economy is the world economy."[14]

Based on rational analysis and historical experience, we should be able to find agreement on the three assumptions presented in Part One: (1) We know that central planning doesn't work. (2) Stable money fosters productive growth. (3) We need a meaningful measure of value across borders and through time—one that encapsulates stable purchasing power. These concepts underscore the importance of developing new monetary arrangements that will reconcile the disconnect between real and nominal economic growth. They clarify the need for serious domestic monetary reform as well as reform of international monetary arrangements. By all the criteria put forward in the first three chapters, status quo arrangements are shown to be at odds with our fundamental beliefs about how best to maximize economic opportunity and increase prosperity.

If heads can nod in agreement that central planning does not work, it opens new policy avenues for revamping the process that enables central banks to manage whole economies. Why allow a small committee to set the price of loanable funds? If we can likewise agree that stable money fosters productive growth, we can proceed to question existing monetary policies and practices that encourage financial engineering rather than productive growth, confounding the aspirations of individuals in favor of achieving government-defined goals. Finally, if it is true that the only closed economy is the world economy, it is only logical to consider options for defining a common monetary benchmark to serve as a unit of account. This in no way implies any kind of global central bank or sovereign monetary authority; to the contrary, having access to a reliable measure of value across borders and through time empowers individuals to flourish.

All these points of agreement dovetail into a single imperative for action to radically transform current monetary arrangements. We cannot move from the current monetary disorder to a genuinely new approach for stabilizing exchange rates without uprooting the existing mess. As Jacques de Larosiere, the distinguished former managing director of the International Monetary Fund, noted in 2014, "If one reflects on the monetary setting of those last fifteen or twenty years, one cannot just say that it amounted to a 'non-system.' It was actually much worse: It amounted to an 'anti-system.'"[15]

If we are to start building an orderly and ethical international monetary system for syncing currency values across borders to provide consistent and re-liable price signals for comparing the value of competitive goods in the global marketplace, we will need to designate a universal monetary unit of account. If we are to achieve success in raising productive economic growth—the kind that improves people's lives because it raises living standards—we must enact fundamental monetary reform that will deliver exchange rate stability instead of pandemonium.

Once a critical mass of consensus is achieved regarding the necessity of working out new currency arrangements to achieve a sound monetary founda-tion for truly competitive free trade, it will enable the next step toward taking action—which requires a strategic plan. That plan should be based on key insights gained from prior experience, because the first step toward designing a new system is to evaluate what has worked in the past.

We can derive extremely useful insights and lessons by studying interna-tional monetary systems from the past—specifically, the classical gold stan-dard and the Bretton Woods system—with an eye toward addressing the shortcomings of our existing anti-system. The first chapter in Part Two of the book does precisely that. Chapter 4 analyzes both these prior approaches for determining exchange rates among different currencies, seeking to identify their strengths and weaknesses. It is important to identify what has worked in the past. We also need to assess what caused these systems to break down or be abandoned. The objective is to maximize the gains from studying these two earlier monetary regimes while evaluating the effectiveness of a gold anchor. Taking time to learn from historical experience will enrich efforts to find a new approach for bringing order to international monetary relations.

Chapter 5 follows directly from this analysis, formulating a blueprint for taking action. It presents a strongly detailed proposal for transitioning to a new international monetary system based on lessons from the past. The outstanding feature of both prior approaches is the link between money and gold—which served to ensure the monetary integrity of the U.S. dollar from the time of our nation's founding. Under the gold standard, there was scarcely a difference between money and gold: gold was money itself. More recently, the former Federal Reserve chairman designated the "greatest central banker who ever lived,"[16] stated that gold is not only money but the world's leading currency. According to Alan Greenspan, "gold is a currency. It is still by all evidence the premier currency where no fiat currency, including the dollar, can match it."[17] Even when monetary systems based on gold are no longer functioning at an official level, the residual appeal of gold coins has still made them viable as a currency. Gold sovereigns, a legacy of the British empire when paper money was backed by gold, were included in the survival kit of agents carrying out special operations during World War II. More recently, during the 1991 Gulf War, gold sovereigns purchased from the Bank of England by Britain's Ministry of Defense were provided to Royal Air Force crew members and special forces members of the British Army for "escape and evasion" purposes in the event they were captured behind enemy lines.[18]

Modern gold coins are generally not used in everyday transactions because their metallic value is considerably higher than the nominal value imprinted on the surface; for example, a one-ounce gold American Eagle listed for sale by the U.S. Mint (May 19, 2024) is shown as available for a price of $3,200, even though it is designated on the reverse side as being worth $50. No one would use such an expensive coin to pay for a $50 purchase despite the indicated face value. Still, all American Eagle Bullion gold coins are legal tender. But aside from this largely symbolic relationship between the face value of U.S. official coinage and its metallic content, there is no official connection today between the dollar and gold.

It is long past the end of the system that reigned during the Bretton Woods era, when foreign central banks could redeem dollars for a specific amount of gold from the U.S. government—even as individuals could not. There are reasons not to resurrect the Bretton Woods system as it was originally structured, with its singular reliance on the United States to maintain stable exchange rates among participating nations. Nevertheless, it could prove useful to utilize gold as part of a new international monetary order. A dollar convertible into gold at a fixed price presents an alluring and powerful concept that could provide the catalyst for transitioning to stable exchange rates. A universal benchmark establishing a measure for value that provides accurate price signaling across borders for tradable goods and services, as well as financial investment opportunities, would greatly improve the efficiency of international trade and capital flows.

In Chapter 6, the narrative goes from presenting an explicit policy initiative that would lay the cornerstone for building an orderly international monetary system to identifying the indispensable element for launching a new approach with profound implications for productive economic growth: political leadership. Making the transition from today's world of central bank activism will most certainly require it. A confident and visionary leader will recognize that establishing a stable monetary foundation for achieving optimal economic performance—and granting access to participating trade partners willing to abide by its tenets—would serve as a testimonial to free markets and free people.

Economic liberty is a fundamental aspect of democratic capitalism. Sound money as a moral precept should guide the quest for meaningful reform to ensure that America's founding principles can serve as a model for the world. The essential purpose of this book is to lay out a path for restoring the integrity of America's money unit. We need a measuring tool that can be trusted. The real economy deserves real money to reach its full potential for maximizing prosperity. To unleash the power of sound money, we should be prepared to launch a bold initiative that will make the U.S. dollar the most trustworthy currency in the world.

PART ONE

Building Consensus

I

Central Planning Doesn't Work

"Problems snowballed faster than they were resolved. On the whole, society was becoming increasingly unmanageable. We only thought that we were in the saddle, while the actual situation that was arising was one that Lenin warned against: the automobile was not going where the one at the steering wheel thought it was going."

Mikhail Gorbachev, *Perestroika: New Thinking for Our Country and the World* (1987)

IN THE WANING days of the Soviet Union, as the economy lurched spasmodically between reforms intended under General Secretary Mikhail Gorbachev's "perestroika" restructuring program and obdurate adherence to moribund economic practices, it became increasingly apparent that the model was collapsing. The Soviet political and economic system was based on top-down management: the government made decisions in the presumed best interests of citizens through centralized planning and centralized control. This approach to generating and redistributing resources was rooted in Lenin's revolutionary ideas for nationalizing sources of wealth—including land, industry, and business—to foil the exploitative behavior of rich individuals. Social justice and equality could be obtained only by granting power to the state to expropriate personal holdings, which could then be redirected toward serving the interests of the proletariat and peasant classes. Lenin hoped that the civil war he started in Russia amid the confusion of World War I would turn into a world revolution to defeat imperialist capitalism.

By the late 1980s, however, the dream of a workers' paradise had failed to match the ideological construct put forward in the 1920s. Soviet citizens were grappling with consumer goods shortages and meaningless wage increases in the face of growing corruption. Stagnation was wreaking havoc with the government's internal budget as productive output languished; at the same time, increasing levels of rubles were distributed to appease disgruntled citizens. Prices were kept fixed by the government, which meant that an increase in the volume of money and credit relative to available goods translated into longer lines, rather than higher prices. Endless queuing for even the most basic items—shoes, clothing, and household goods—compelled people to resort to illegal black-market transactions. Widespread cynicism about the ability of central planners to effectively direct monetary resources toward increasing productive output spawned a growing distrust of party officials.[1]

The fundamental problem with central planning: nobody is that smart. No matter how well-intentioned, no single individual or small committee of government officials can anticipate the countless interactions that take place among economic variables under dynamic circumstances—let alone apportion them efficiently. Friedrich Hayek, who received the Nobel Prize in Economics in 1974, was particularly adept at explaining how efforts by government officials to engineer society by allocating economic resources are doomed to fail. As Edwin Feulner, who founded the Heritage Foundation, writes:

> Hayek employed economics to investigate the mind of man, using the knowledge he had gained to unveil the totalitarian nature of socialism and to explain how it inevitably leads to "serfdom." His greatest contribution lay in the discovery of a simple yet profound truth: man does not and cannot know everything, and when he acts as if he does, disaster follows. He recognized that socialism, the collectivist state, and planned economies represent the ultimate form of *hubris*, for those who plan them attempt—with insufficient knowledge—to redesign the nature of man. In so doing, would-be planners arrogantly ignore traditions that embody the wisdom of generations; impetuously disregard customs whose purpose they do not understand; and blithely confuse the law written on the hearts of men—which they cannot change—with

administrative rules that they can alter at whim. For Hayek, such presumption was not only a "fatal conceit," but also "the road to serfdom."[2]

When government officials presume that they can make better decisions on behalf of citizens than those individuals can make for themselves— following their own hearts and minds—the result is to thwart individuals from seeking to achieve their personal dreams. Instead, they are transformed into wards of the state. The double whammy of central planning, then, is that it proves both inefficient and inimical to individual liberty. It's hard to imagine two outcomes more at odds with American values.

That is why it seems scarcely possible that so much power to control the economy would be granted to a U.S. government agency—even an "independent government agency," as the Federal Reserve defines itself. Although it was originally established in 1913 with the relatively modest task of providing an "elastic" currency to meet seasonal liquidity demands, the Fed has transmogrified into a much more powerful entity. Tasked with steering the U.S. economy toward stable prices and maximum employment through its interest rate decisions, and authorized to supervise and regulate the nation's banks, our central bank today is the dominant force behind movements in financial markets. Investors are attuned to every nuanced statement coming from Fed officials; analyzing their veiled intentions is a strategic aspect of portfolio management. When Federal Reserve Chairman Jerome Powell indicated at a March 2024 press conference that members of the Fed's policymaking committee were still projecting three rate cuts later in 2024 despite stubborn inflation, stocks jumped: the S&P 500 went up 0.7 percent and the Dow Jones Industrial Average went up roughly 1 percent following his remarks that afternoon.[3] Not unrelated to the Fed's increasingly powerful role is the fact that our nation's central bank is the largest single holder of publicly held U.S. government debt.

It is important to note that the Fed's assumption of such powers has taken place with the implicit consent of Congress—that is, in the name of protecting the independence of monetary policy from political influence, Congress has mostly granted free rein to Fed officials to conduct monetary policy using whatever "tools" they deem appropriate. In the process of exercising these discretionary powers, the central bank allocates credit across an array of borrowers by impacting interest rates for maturities that affect particular sectors. For example, when the Fed purchases mortgage-backed securities, it directly increases the price of those securities. Higher prices mean a lower interest rate on mortgage debt, which increases the flow of credit toward the housing sector—and away from other parts of the economy—as private investors reallocate their portfolio holdings.[4]

This seems very different from the intent of the Founding Fathers, who had experienced the chaos and degradation of paper claims issued by irresponsible government authorities. Congress was granted the power to "regulate" the value of money in the Constitution (Article 1, Section 8) in the same context in which Congress was granted the power to fix the standard of weights and measures for the new nation. Indeed, both of these duties are authorized in the same sentence. The power "to Coin money, regulate the value thereof, and of foreign Coin" was strictly disciplined by defining the U.S. dollar in terms of a specific weight of gold or silver. As Thomas Jefferson wrote in 1784, "if we determine that a Dollar shall be our Unit, we must then say with precision what a Dollar is."[5] The Coinage Act of 1792 fixed the value of the dollar at 371.25 grains of pure silver or 24.75 grains of pure gold.

Recognizing the potential for excessive monetary issuance through paper currency or credit, the government was not empowered to emit "bills of credit" that citizens would be obligated to accept as legal tender. This prohibition seemed to be violated in 1862 when the federal government authorized the creation of paper money—not redeemable in gold or silver—to finance the Civil War. Indeed, the Supreme Court ruled in 1870 that Congress lacked the power to make "greenbacks" legal tender. That decision was reversed a year later, however; it was ruled that such action was a justifiable government act because of a national emergency. Constitutional scholars may still beg to differ.

In any case, it is sobering to compare the original intent in granting the power to Congress to regulate money by specifying the value of the dollar in precious metals with the modern power of central banks to use monetary policy as an instrument for exerting government influence over economic outcomes. Instead of allowing money to perform its primary functions as a medium of exchange, unit of account, and store of value, Federal Reserve officials seek to manage interest rates to achieve the central bank's so-called dual mandate of maximum employment and stable prices. The traditional labeling of Fed policymakers as either "hawks" or "doves" relates to whether an individual is more inclined to impose tighter monetary policy through higher interest rates to stem inflation or instead is willing to tolerate more inflation for the sake of increasing employment. With higher inflation, though, every dollar is worth less. To pursue the goal of maximum employment by lowering interest rates and expanding the money supply, the task of achieving stable prices becomes a lower priority. Maintaining the value of the nation's money unit is subjugated to the perceived greater cause of achieving a government economic objective—even as it results in collateral damage to the integrity of the dollar.

The U.S. central bank cites the Federal Reserve Reform Act of 1977 as providing its guiding instructions from Congress. The legislation establishes *three* key objectives for monetary policy: maximum employment, stable prices, and moderate long-term interest rates. The first one, ironically, is inherently problematic for members of the Federal Open Market Committee to achieve through their monetary policy formulations. As the Fed acknowledges on its website:

> The maximum level of employment is a broad-based and inclusive goal that is not directly measurable and changes over time owing largely to nonmonetary factors that affect the structure and dynamics of the labor market. Consequently, it would not be appropriate to specify a fixed goal for employment; rather, the Committee's policy decisions must be informed by assessments of the shortfalls of employment from its maximum level, recognizing that such assessments are necessarily uncertain and subject to revision.[6]

Meanwhile, the problem with the "stable prices" part of the mandate is that the Fed wants to preserve its ability to stimulate economic activity by reducing interest rates. Therefore, it seeks room to maneuver by keeping the nominal interest rate elevated above the real interest rate, where the difference reflects the impact of inflation—that is, as American economist Irving Fisher long ago expressed through the equation that bears his name:

$$real\ interest\ rate = nominal\ interest\ rate - inflation\ rate$$

If there is zero inflation, there is no difference between the real interest rate and the nominal interest rate. The absence of inflation poses an operational problem for monetary policymakers, however, which helps to explain why the Fed's standard for achieving its "stable prices" mandate is oxymoronic.

Because the Fed's basic model relies on money illusion to accomplish its objectives, the goal of price stability has been interpreted to mean achieving 2 percent inflation over the longer run—that is, Fed officials seek stable *inflation* rather than stable *prices*. The rationale for utilizing money illusion comes from a "grease-the-wheels" argument that is a trademark of Keynesian economics. It suggests that some low level of inflation is better than zero inflation because workers and firms resist wage cuts even when the economy has slowed; if inflation obscures price signals, employers can reduce real wages without having to cut nominal wages. For example, if there exists 2 percent inflation, firms can even give workers a 1 percent increase in nominal wages while still effectuating a 1 percent cut in real wages.

Even for major central banks that emphasize price stability as their main policy objective, granting secondary status to other social goals, the practice of targeting an inflation rate higher than zero has become the norm. For example, the European Central Bank (ECB) refers to Article 127(1) in the Treaty on the Functioning of the European Union in declaring that its primary object for monetary policy is to maintain price stability. That task is defined as "aiming for 2% inflation over the medium term" by its Governing Council.[7] The ECB also seeks to "support the general economic policies in the Union with a view to contributing to the achievement of the objectives of the Union" as laid down in Article 3 of the Treaty on European Union: "These objectives include balanced economic growth, a highly competitive social market economy aiming at full employment and social progress, and a high level of protection and improvement of the quality of the environment—without prejudice to the objective of price stability."[8]

Both the Federal Reserve and the ECB, the two most powerful central banks in the world, thus imbue their governing boards with discretionary authority to conduct monetary policy for purposes of achieving goals that might be described as somewhat nebulous—albeit politically correct. It is cold comfort to realize that Europe's central bankers are directed not only to bring about "full employment and social progress" but are also charged with improving the quality of the environment. Fed officials have also ventured into the realm of addressing climate change.[9] The assignment of such beneficent objectives to political appointees vested with inestimable powers smacks precisely of that fatal conceit that Hayek warned against.

The Myth of Monetary Omniscience

Government control of the money supply appears especially vulnerable to the hubris of central planning. Building on the Soviet model, it's interesting to note how much Lenin's plans for managing economic resources, both human and capital, relied on distributing financial capital through the banking system:

> *Without big banks, socialism would be impossible.* The big banks *are* the "state apparatus" which we *need* to bring about socialism, and which we *take ready-made* from capitalism. … A single State Bank, the biggest of the big, with branches in every rural district, in every factory, will constitute as much as nine-tenths of the socialist apparatus. There will be country-wide bookkeeping, country-wide accounting of the production and distribution of goods; this will be, so to speak, something in the nature of the *skeleton* of socialist society.[10]

This vision became reality with the establishment of the Gosudarstvennyy Bank, which was commonly known as Gosbank (meaning "State Bank"). Gosbank was the sole issuer of cash and maintained supervisory authority over credit operations in the Soviet Union. Gosbank officials would advance funds to state-run enterprises and organizations by providing a noncash emission of credit; that is, Gosbank simply made a bookkeeping entry to increase the funds available to the firm as shown in its deposit account.

So long as the enterprises utilized the working capital productively, meeting the output quotas assigned to them by the Soviet government, the financial resources advanced by Gosbank were in keeping with Lenin's use of the banking system to carry out the goals of socialism. There was an inherent problem with central planning conducted through central banking, however: Gosbank officials had more motivation to accommodate the government than to ensure that productive economic activity was actually taking place. Even when funds made available through the banking system to state-run firms were not efficiently utilized to raise productive output (or even maintain current levels), the central bank continued to provide credit by raising the level of funds available to those firms.

In short, Soviet firms had massive sums of working capital available to them but became increasingly less capable of contributing to productive output. Since the firms were required to provide revenues to the central government, they became adept at channeling funds provided by Gosbank back to the federal budget as "receipts." The availability of credit from Gosbank meant that the system was awash in liquidity and could meet any required nominal financial targets. But real activity had become disconnected from the financial system as Gosbank circulated funds that performed no role in supporting productive new enterprises or investment projects.

What happened to the Soviet Union was more than just a financial failure. Massive corruption led citizens to lose faith in government promises. Under Soviet rule, the needs of consumers were subjugated to the prioritization of military spending. Following the demise of the Union of Soviet Socialist Republics, Gorbachev told interviewers: "The Soviet model was defeated not only on the economic and social levels; it was defeated on a cultural level. Our society, our people, the most educated, the most intellectual, rejected that model on the cultural level because it does not respect the man, oppresses him spiritually and politically. ... That is why the most important for us [was] everything connected to freedom."

In rejecting a model that was perceived as oppressive, citizens were expressing an inherent need to believe in an economic and social approach that was both efficient and moral. Even as government administrators fabricated numbers indicating that quotas were being met, the economy had become a cumbersome burden. Centralized state planning was stymied with the co-operation of Gosbank—which had its own reasons to camouflage national economic shortcomings. Gorbachev called for fundamental economic reforms in 1987 to reverse the damage, but the internal budget of the Soviet Union was already in shambles. The nation's official financial statements testified to a balanced federal budget with government expenditures precisely equal to revenues. The unexplained entries defined loosely as "receipts from the socialist economy," however, turned out to be phantom revenues. Recycled credit advances from Gosbank were being used as a "plug" figure to equalize budget expenditures. In reality, the Soviet government was running a huge internal budget deficit. The nation was effectively going bankrupt.[11]

We can infer useful lessons from the Soviet experience about the role of central bank involvement in perpetuating unproductive activity. An unhealthy symbiosis between banking and government develops when banks are so involved in financing government deficit spending that loanable funds are more readily made available to the government—crowding out potentially productive loans to the real economy. For example, in the wake of the 2008 global financial crisis, the Federal Reserve embarked on a series of large-scale purchases of U.S. Treasury debt from commercial banks and other financial institutions. To conduct such transactions, the Fed simply credited the depository account of the seller through a bookkeeping entry that increased its reserve account balance at the Fed.

Congress had meanwhile granted to the Fed, as part of the emergency package passed in October 2008 in response to the financial debacle, the right to pay interest on excess bank reserves. This appears to have incentivized banks to maintain high depository accounts at the Fed rather than engage in traditional lending to the private sector. The danger in paying commercial banks to keep money sitting sterile at the Fed is that it changes the risk/reward parameters of their business operating model. It becomes too comfortable for them to passively receive interest on cash that is exposed to no risk. By inducing private-sector financial institutions to "invest" their funds in a riskless asset that does not serve to finance productive activity, the Fed turns them into government utilities for its own purposes. The Cleveland district bank of the Federal Reserve System issued a report in February 2015 noting that total reserves in the banking system grew from $1.9 *billion* in August 2008 to $2.6 *trillion* in January 2015. The report asked, "Why are U.S. banks holding the liquidity being pumped into the economy by the Federal Reserve as excess reserves instead of making more loans?" The answer turned out to be that, with the Fed paying interest on excess reserves and with low returns on loans, it had become "both easier and more attractive for banks to hold huge amounts of excess reserves."[12]

Since then, the reserve balances kept on deposit at the Fed by commercial banks have increased still further; they amounted to $2.7 trillion in January

2015 and stood at $3.3 trillion in April 2024.[13] Even more dramatically, the rate of interest being paid on these balances has increased; in January 2015, it was just 0.15 percent, but it was raised by more than 500 basis points to 5.40 percent by July 2023, where it has since remained (as of April 2024).[14] When banks can earn substantial interest rate income by keeping reserves sitting dormant in Fed depository accounts, they are apt to become less interested in consumer and small business borrowers. In March 2021, the twenty-five largest U.S. banks held 45.7 percent of their assets in loans and leases, down from 54.1 percent a year earlier. Meantime, their year-over-year holdings of Treasury and agency securities increased 33.5 percent. This shift reflected tougher standards for borrowing and reduced loan demand, but it also revealed a subtle change in how banks operated—indicating that they were pulling back from private-sector lending in favor of engaging more directly with the Fed.[15]

Our nation's banking institutions are at risk of becoming complicit instruments of the federal government rather than functioning as credit-granting companies serving free enterprise. By paying interest on reserves, the Fed is effectively borrowing from the private sector and directing a larger share of financial resources to the government. While such practices hardly mean our central bank has taken on the characteristics of Gosbank, it's nevertheless a sad development when banks are turned away from lending to private-sector borrowers, drawn instead to buying Treasury debt that may well end up being purchased from them by the Federal Reserve.[16]

Individuals must have access to financial capital if democratic capitalism is to survive. If the comparisons between the Soviet banking system and our own cause discomfort, it is because we sense that the trend is moving toward increased domination of the banking system by the Federal Reserve. One might wonder how our own central bankers have largely managed to escape condemnation from their fellow American citizens, who are presumably opposed to central planning. As economic scholars Steve Hanke and Kurt Schuler have observed—with particular reference to nations prone to fiscal deficit spending—"central banking is central planning in money, and central planning works as poorly in money as it does in agriculture or in industry."[17] That observation alone provides a good reason to have a simple and transparent monetary system that cannot be compromised by high-level bureaucrats.

One thing very evident from the Soviet experiment was that fixed prices made it even more difficult for planners to estimate the appropriate levels of capital that should be dedicated to various economic tasks. Without the information conveyed through price signals, there was no way to know how much a product was worth or whether an enterprise was utilizing its capital and labor appropriately. No wonder it became impossible for the Soviet government to identify its core economic weaknesses for so long. When the internal rot was finally revealed, recovering from the accumulated losses proved an insurmountable task.

Yet now we have reverted to a failed economic approach—central planning by a small coterie of government officials—to essentially fix the most important price that exists within a free-market capitalist economy: the interest rate on loanable funds. By artificially setting the benchmark policy rate using its tools, the Fed exerts its influence across the entire spectrum of current and future interest rates, both short-term and long-term, which in turn affects overall financial conditions, including stock prices and the exchange rate of the dollar relative to other currencies. Decisions of households and businesses are impacted by monetary policy, with changes in the Fed's benchmark rate affecting overall spending, investment, production, employment, and inflation. Distortions from what the interest rate on loanable funds would be if determined by free-market forces rather than through the Fed's intervention efforts are thus disbursed throughout the economy.

In short, when monetary officials exercise discretionary powers to deliberately move the target interest rate higher or lower than its natural level, they sow market confusion and obscure the real value of underlying assets represented by financial instruments. Investors must rely on the hedged statements of central bank officials to glean vital market signals, instead of being able to observe interest rates determined by supply and demand. It is damaging to free-market capitalism when decisions about whether to consume today or invest for the future are more influenced by monetary officials with the power to alter the cost of short-term funds than by private market interactions based on authentic price signals.

Central banks substitute the collective thinking of a small committee for the aggregate wisdom of private individuals acting on their own behalf. Instead of basing decisions on the rational calculations of an entrepreneur seeking to run a profitable business—by saving or borrowing funds, hiring labor and purchasing inputs, creating a product and then selling it—people instead seek to fathom the intentions of the committee members who decide the price of capital. Real returns generated by genuinely productive activity become less relevant than purely speculative plays, as investing becomes a game of second-guessing the next move from the Federal Reserve or European Central Bank.

Central banks' displacement of free-market outcomes may one day breed the same sort of cynicism that caused the Soviet approach to collapse. Even as disenchanted citizens were repulsed by the irrational consequences resulting from central planning aimed at fulfilling communist ideals, they found ways to adjust. If it pays to abide by the words and deeds of central bankers rather than concentrate on demand-and-supply price signals for capital, then investors will respond accordingly. "Don't fight the Fed" has long been the credo promoted by Wall Street analysts—with good reason.

Stock markets all around the world were breaking records in the post-2008 years due to central bank intervention aimed at stimulating economic activity through quantitative easing and zero interest rate policies. The Fed infused more than $3.6 trillion into credit markets by purchasing securities, expanding its balance sheet from some $850 billion in assets in 2008 to nearly $4.5 trillion in assets by the end of 2014. Fueled by cheap money, the main stock market indices for the United States, the United Kingdom, Germany, and Sweden all experienced their highest levels ever, with Japan's stock market also reaching near-record levels, after investors interpreted statements made by Fed chair Janet Yellen in February 2015 as a sign that rates would not be going up until mid-2015 at the earliest.[18] "I love these central bankers, they've been very good to the stock market," quipped financial market strategist Ed Yardeni during a CNBC interview the following month. "This is not about investing, this is all about the central bankers. These markets are all rigged, and I don't say that critically, I just say that factually."[19]

The efforts of central banks to get companies and individuals to put financial resources into assets that would raise economic activity and increase employment proved extremely lucrative for investors, though certainly not as effective as the Fed or ECB had anticipated. After more than six years of experimenting with aggressive monetary stimulus programs, economic growth in the United States remained sluggish. Wealthy investors raked in profits—even as overall economic growth performance proved disappointing. Meanwhile, the extraordinarily activist role of central banks was imposing considerable damage on other participants in the economy.

A 2015 report by the company Swiss Re, the world's second-largest reinsurance company, estimated that the near-zero interest rates imposed by monetary policymakers had cost U.S. savers alone some $470 billion dollars in lost interest income. The report noted that "financial repression" had taken its toll not only on savers but also on insurers such as the firm itself—with worrying consequences for capital market intermediation. "Crowding out investors due to artificially low or negative yields will reduce the diversification of funding sources to the real economy, thus representing a risk for financial stability and economic growth potential at large," said the reinsurer's chief investment officer, Guido Furer.[20]

Disaffected savers would be justified in asking why they had to absorb the negative consequences of monetary policy decisions that failed to produce intended results aimed at benefiting the economy as a whole. If suppressing market-determined interest rates through central bank intervention tactics in accordance with the thinking of Fed policymakers does not actually stimulate economic growth, it suggests that faith in the omniscience of central bankers is sorely misplaced—and not just misplaced, but part of the problem. Discretionary authority to formulate and execute monetary policy subjects the notion of a stable dollar to the ad hoc decisions of the Federal Open Market Committee. How, then, can monetary integrity be safeguarded?

The answer would seem to require the imposition of a rules-based approach to constrain the behavior of monetary officials whose collective discretionary judgment has proven all too fallible. Yet according to George A. Selgin, director emeritus of the Center for Monetary and Financial Alternatives at the Cato Institute, it is folly to believe that a rules-based approach would constitute an effective restraint:

> The truth is rather that central banks are inherently discretionary institutions or, more precisely, that central bankers cannot resist exercising discretion. Like a married bachelor, a rule-bound central banker is a contradiction in terms, for both the background

of central bankers and the incentives they confront, combined
with the inescapable imperfections of even the most carefully
crafted of monetary rules, will inevitably tempt them to tinker
with the money stock.[21]

This temptation to tinker persists despite the poor performance of monetary authorities, which means more fundamental reforms are required before the next major debacle takes place. "For it should now be clear, in case it wasn't long ago," Selgin further notes, "that central banks generally, and the Federal Reserve in particular, not only are unable to prevent financial and monetary catastrophes, but are unable to resist pursuing policies that inadvertently help to *cause* such catastrophes."

We have seen little willingness among monetary authorities to tolerate restrictions on the scope of their decisions or operations. Instead, there has been steady resistance to any such notion. While it is an important question to ask whether monetary policy should be determined by a formal rule or the caprices of discretionary policies, there is no sign that an answer is forthcoming. It has been three decades since economics professor John Taylor of Stanford University published his oft-cited paper entitled "Discretion Versus Policy Rules in Practice."[22] But so far, discretion is winning. Janet Yellen, speaking as the Federal Reserve's top official, stated before the House Financial Services Committee in 2015, "I don't believe that the Fed should chain itself to any mechanical rule."[23]

Thus, the monetary policy decision-makers of the world's most important central bank remain free to influence the value of the world's most important currency relative to other currencies; to direct capital flows throughout the global economy by manipulating interest rates, and thereby exchange rates, through the conduct of monetary policy, using tools that distort the functioning of financial markets; to reward sophisticated investors who correctly anticipate the monetary policy actions of the Federal Open Market Committee aimed at achieving its target policy interest rate; to cheat holders of bank savings accounts by orchestrating interest rates lower than those that would be determined by the market—in short, to thwart the normal demand-and-supply mechanisms governing the rate of return on loanable funds by intervening in credit markets. All of this power is held by a government agency with twelve unelected officials whose decisions are meted out eight times a year, approximately once every six weeks, following a two-day meeting. Nothing could be further from a rule. Nothing could better define autocratic monetary authority.

It speaks volumes that the former Fed chairman known as "The Maestro" was more inclined to cite the virtues of a gold standard—with convertibility serving as the ultimate monetary rule—than to rely on his own innate judgment for calibrating the money stock to the needs of the economy. When Congressman Ron Paul, known as a "hard money" advocate, asked Alan Greenspan at a 2001 congressional hearing to explain how central bankers determine the proper level of interest rates in the absence of any monetary policy rule or self-disciplining mechanism for regulating the money supply, the answer was revealing. According to Greenspan, "so long as you have fiat currency, which is a statutory issue, a central bank properly functioning will endeavor to, in many cases, replicate what a gold standard would itself generate."[24]

In other words, the highest level of performance to which a central bank could aspire would be to match the economic interactions and results that would likely occur under a gold standard. Lest anyone doubts the sincerity of Greenspan's respect for the gold standard—long after he wrote about the connection between gold and economic freedom in the 1960s—consider his spontaneous response in October 2007 to a television interviewer's question, "Why do we need a central bank?"

> Greenspan: Well, the question is a very interesting one. We have at this particular stage a fiat money, which is essentially money printed by a government and it's usually the central bank which is authorized to do so. Some mechanism has got to be in place that restricts the amount of money which is produced, either a gold standard or currency board or something of that nature, because unless you do that, all of history suggests that inflation will take hold with very deleterious effects on economic activity. And there are numbers of us, myself included, who strongly believe that we did very well in the 1870 to 1914 period with an international gold standard.[25]

The reason that the perspective of an individual who headed the Federal Reserve for more than eighteen years needs to be taken into consideration is that it carries a powerful message of authenticity. Greenspan had a seat at the table—literally, at the head of the table—around which monetary policy decisions were discussed and debated in meticulous detail by intelligent, knowledgeable, well-qualified, and well-intentioned central bankers. Much was riding on every policy choice they made, with interest rate decisions affecting the stability of global equity markets as well as whether a young couple would be able to finance a new home. Greenspan's declaration that he believed the world did very well under an international gold standard testifies to the conclusion that the collective wisdom of a small committee of government officials has not proved to deliver better results for monetary and financial stability than what was achieved during an epoch that provided for gold convertibility of currency.

The message embodies more than the mechanism of gold convertibility itself; the aspect of economic freedom embraced in Greenspan's earlier article comes into play with the realization that the right to convert is held by the individual who holds the currency. Money supply is not determined by government policymakers sitting around a table but rather by the actions of countless individuals making decisions for themselves and their businesses. It is the aggregate impact of these choices, arising from personal assessments and intuitive judgments—against a backdrop of dynamic economic developments and an ever-changing array of financial opportunities—that calibrate the supply of money and credit. Importantly, the convertibility privilege also stands in the way of those who would confiscate wealth through deficit spending and redistributionist policies.

Distorted Outcomes: Bad Is Good

When investment returns are determined by correctly anticipating the future decisions of central bankers rather than carefully analyzing potential returns from opportunities to finance productive endeavors, market reaction to economic news is often skewed. For example, an improving employment outlook would normally be seen as a positive economic development; if more jobs are being created, one would assume that economic growth is improving. One might even expect stock markets to rise on the prospect of increased output. Economic growth increases prosperity and raises living standards—which should be welcome news.

When equity markets are fueled by easy money, however, the pronouncements of central bankers can become more important than the underlying performance of the real economy. When the Federal Reserve pursues extraordinarily accommodative monetary policies to spur the economy, inducing investors to purchase riskier assets, the result is often surging equity markets. So long as loose financial conditions reign, the returns from arbitraging rising stock prices against the cost of borrowing make for incredibly profitable investment strategies. The only real threat to investors arises when the Fed decides to switch gears and begins to raise interest rates. For those who formerly had access to low-cost funding, the end of accommodative monetary policy means the end of a highly lucrative trading scheme.

No wonder investors respond in what seems a bizarre manner to the seemingly good news of a rise in employment. When an encouraging jobs report comes out, the impact on equity markets is likely to be negative if investors are concerned that it increases the chances of a Fed rate hike. When monetary officials look at low unemployment numbers and take the position that preemptive rate hikes are needed to stave off future inflation, it undermines the growth dynamic that was otherwise gaining momentum. Good economic news becomes bad news for financial markets when central bank actions, rather than real economic developments, determine investment returns. By deliberately seeking to stifle economic activity through restrictive interest rates in the absence of inflation, the Fed unnecessarily curtails growth— illustrating how government intervention can thwart free-market capitalism.

The whole point of using price signals to alert market participants about potentially successful investment projects is that investors should be able to assess risk and reward based on a valid monetary unit of account. When the validity has been compromised by central bank manipulation so that money is not calibrated properly to the credit and liquidity needs of an economy—that is, more has been issued than is warranted by real economic activity—the price-signaling function of money is distorted. It should be cause for concern that central banks deliberately alter price signals. When they do so, individuals and companies are lured into making different investment decisions than they otherwise would have pursued.

Distorted price signals lead to misallocated economic resources and misdirected financial capital. Producers and consumers in the marketplace should be able to depend on money to provide an accurate unit of account, which allows them to evaluate the relative value of goods and services by comparing prices. Transactions will tend to occur at the point where the highest quality can be obtained for the lowest price, which depends on the relative levels of supply and demand. Markets are said to "clear" at the optimal value, with those wishing to purchase an item doing business with those wishing to sell that item at the right price. For some goods and services, quantity may be more important to the buyer than quality; in such cases, demand and supply are mostly driven by price alone. For the consumer, this means, "the cheaper I can get it, the more I will buy." For the supplier, it means, "the cheaper I can produce it, the more I will sell."

When goods and services are price-sensitive, it is particularly important that price signals are clear. If they do not clarify relative value, mistakes are made that cause economic inefficiencies. If buyers suffer an unexpected loss of purchasing power due to inflation, they cannot maintain earlier consumption levels without going into personal debt; this may cause consumer demand to drop. If suppliers have to raise prices to stay even with inflation, they may end up with excess goods or unsold services, impacting profitability. The key is to bring supply and demand into balance—that is, to reach equilibrium. Free-market pricing makes it possible: it's the mechanism through which the interests of buyers and sellers are reconciled at optimum levels. Even if buyers might wish to pay a lower price, and sellers might wish to receive a higher price, the interplay of demand and supply determines the actual price at which transactions occur. Free-market pricing—with genuinely competitive markets and different choices available—is the key to enabling the process that accrues to the benefit of all participants.

The fact that free-market pricing actually works is a testament to the power of price signals. The economic aspirations of millions of individuals work themselves out in the marketplace as sellers and buyers resolve their needs and desires. Prices convey the relative values of goods and services by sending concise messages about demand and supply at various levels of quality. All those messages are transmitted through one vital instrument: money. Money is the means of communication for price signals, and it functions as a two-way channel. Prices not only broadcast information to potential buyers but also provide feedback to sellers about whether they should increase quantity through higher production, improve quality through innovation, or both.

So it is vital that money speaks in a clear language. It must communicate with precision the current state of demand and supply. And just as the market for any good or service requires accurate price signals to optimize transactions among buyers and sellers, the same is true for financial markets. Clear price signals make it possible to synchronize the independent financial choices of millions of people as they direct loanable capital into investment opportunities, seeking to maximize economic returns. Most wondrous of all is that no conscious coordination or central plan is needed to make this process work.

The magnificent mechanism of free-market interactions, so compatible with our belief in individual freedom and economic liberty, should cause us to question why we permit central banks to distort the signaling mechanism that so efficiently conveys value. It goes against founding values and common sense to utilize central planning to tweak the validity of the money unit—deliberately making it more plentiful (through monetary stimulus), or less available (through restrictive interest rates) to alter economic outcomes in pursuit of government-directed objectives. The political philosophy that underpins democratic capitalism, buoyed by historical experience, would find it anomalous to assume that a small committee of individuals can better decide how to steer the economy than the economic participants themselves. Substituting the perspicacity of designated monetary authorities for the shared acumen of hundreds of millions of people carrying out voluntary transactions to facilitate their daily needs and future dreams is akin to selecting the path to serfdom.

If such hubris delivers superior results, one could argue that it is justifiable. This would require evidence that central bankers make better decisions—that they are better managers of economic activity—than the invisible hand that guides individual consumers and producers, savers and borrowers, into making their own choices. But what is the record? No proof exists that a central planning approach to imposing a benchmark policy rate of interest on loanable funds through market intervention by a government agency produces better results than would have occurred under a different sort of monetary regime. In an age when central banks have become openly activist and experimental in their behavior—when the public utterances of monetary authorities have more sway over financial markets than meticulous valuations of underlying economic value—it is reasonable to question whether central banks do more harm than good.

Consider: No other government institution arguably had more influence over the creation of money and credit in the lead-up to the devastating 2008 global meltdown than the Federal Reserve. Yet in testimony before the congressional Joint Economic Committee in April 2008, then-chairman of the Fed Ben Bernanke stated: "We expect economic activity to strengthen in the second half of the year, in part as the result of stimulative monetary and fiscal policies; and growth is expected to proceed at or at a little above its sustainable pace in 2009, bolstered by a stabilization of housing activity, albeit at low levels, and gradually improving financial conditions."[26]

Janet Yellen, who headed the San Francisco regional Fed bank at the time and would replace Bernanke in 2014, scarcely performed better in predicting the approaching financial calamity. According to the transcript from the Fed's monetary policy committee meeting held in April 2008, Yellen estimated a 1.5 percent growth rate for the second half of the year. While Yellen acknowledged the "gloom of the credit crunch," she added, "I do see a possible silver lining in that it may amplify the effects of the fiscal stimulus package, and this is part of the reason that my forecasted downturn is a little milder than the Greenbook's"—referring to the compilation of economic projections and indicators prepared by Fed staff in advance of meetings.[27]

So much for the omniscience of monetary authorities—which, of course, could never be expected from mere mortals whose discernment capabilities do not reach the level of accumulated knowledge held by those actually participating in the economy. Moreover, the Fed's response to the meltdown, which included making large-scale purchases of government debt securities and then paying interest to commercial banks on the increased reserve balances created in the process, exacerbated the damage by lowering the incentive for banks to fund private-sector growth.[28] Broadening the analysis to global considerations prompted by central bank failures, a report published in 2011 by the Bank of England advocating for reform of the international monetary and financial system takes a comprehensive look at how current arrangements have performed in comparison to prior monetary regimes. It concludes that today's system has functioned poorly relative to the gold standard and the Bretton Woods gold exchange system, noting "the key failure—as evidenced by the extraordinary severity of the 2007–09 global financial crisis—has been the system's inability to achieve financial stability and minimise the incidence of disruptive sudden changes in global capital flows."[29]

The potential for future such disruptions in global capital flows is sufficient cause for taking a closer look at the consequences, unintended or not, of interest rate machinations engineered by central banks. Both the Federal Reserve and the European Central Bank, the two most influential central banks, use quantitative easing to stimulate economic activity as an important tool in their monetary policy toolbox. That is, both central banks deliberately seek to suppress market interest rates by purchasing massive amounts of government-guaranteed debt. By increasing the price for government securities, the rate of return is decreased—that is, interest rates on "riskless" assets are pressured downward. The goal is to bring about lower interest rates to encourage more economic activity and stimulate growth, especially for long-term investment projects.

While the European Central Bank was willing to lower its policy target rate into negative territory, the Federal Reserve was reluctant to do so, choosing to pursue quantitative easing in successive programs after its benchmark policy rate was cut to near zero in October 2008—where it would remain until December 2015. The difference in the subsequent interest rate paths followed by these two major central banks set them up for a contest of sorts that had illogical consequences. Nations belonging to the eurozone, controlled by the ECB, could borrow money to finance their sovereign debt at rates lower than the United States after the Fed raised its policy target rate nine times from 2015 to 2020, while the ECB kept its own policy rate at zero. This was a bizarre situation, given that some of the European countries benefiting from the interest rate differential were considered serious credit risks just a few years earlier; in March 2019, the yield on a 10-year government bond for Italy was 2.5 percent, while the yield on a 10-year government bond for the United States was 2.6 percent.

The legacy would continue through the COVID era and beyond as the Federal Reserve and the ECB pursued different timetables for managing their policy interest rates in the perceived best interests of their nations' economic objectives—with the United States continuing to offer higher yields on its 10-year debt securities than many other nations. In December 2023, the 10-year yield for U.S. government debt was 4 percent, while the 10-year yield for Italy's government debt was 3.9 percent; it was 3.2 percent for Spain, and 2.2 percent for Germany. The United Kingdom has its own central bank—the Bank of England—and its 10-year yield on government debt was 3.8 percent. Meanwhile, the 10-year yield on Japan's government debt was less than 1 percent, a reflection of its own central bank's ultra-loose monetary policy.[30]

In focusing on how major central banks fuel monetary distortions that impact trade and investment flows, a key point is that these institutions announce their interest rate decisions and conduct interventions into credit markets to carry out monetary policy directives in accordance with their own particular meeting schedule of national or regional central bank officials. Since the world's major central banks operate on different calendars, communiqués and press conferences revealing their decisions exert differential effects that reverberate in global financial markets and wreak havoc on exchange rates. Each central bank acts according to its statutory mandate, enacting monetary policy using its own tools for implementing the actions deemed necessary to achieve its stated goals. Such actions by central bank authorities are not officially coordinated with the actions of other central banks, even though monetary officials are well aware of the impact their decisions will likely have on global financial markets, currency exchange rates, and trade flows. Such international repercussions are passively acknowledged as "spillover" effects—even when they have a significant impact on the economic well-being of other nations.

When two major central banks are operating in different cycles—say, with Fed officials suggesting they may decide to keep interest rates higher for longer to check inflationary pressures while ECB officials hint they may be prepared to drive rates lower to stimulate economic activity—the consequences of currency movements greatly complicate financial and economic decision-making in the private sector. The higher interest rate trajectory engineered by the Fed increases demand for the U.S. dollar, raising its exchange rate value against the euro and other major currencies, as foreign investors seek the higher returns available in dollar-denominated financial instruments. Conversely, for countries whose currencies are regulated by a central bank prepared to keep interest rates lower for longer, the effect is to lower the value of their currency against the dollar. In April 2024, markets were roiled by uncertainty and volatility following comments by Federal Reserve Chairman Jerome Powell indicating that the U.S. central bank would likely hold off on plans to cut rates; meanwhile, European Central Bank President Christine Lagarde said the ECB was on course to cut interest rates in the near term, subject to any major shocks. The expectation that Europe would move sooner than the United States to reduce rates pushed Treasury yields higher and caused a rapid advance in the U.S. dollar index.[31]

Central bankers may insist that they are not deliberately trying to influence trade or capital flows by targeting currency exchange rates through monetary policy. Claiming that a decision to lower interest rates is motivated solely by domestic monetary policy goals, however, should provoke skepticism. A purposeful attempt by a central bank to weaken its currency is rightly seen as an aggressive move aimed at enhancing exports through competitive devaluation. It should be identified as an unfair practice—a direct refutation of free-trade principles. To be clear: If a central bank enacts monetary policy decisions that will have a predictably negative impact on the value of its currency, it is not enough to assure the world that the *intent* is not to devalue. The offending central bank—and the government (or governments) it represents—should be held to account.

Accusing a central bank of engaging in competitive depreciation risks heightening tensions among trade partners. This sensitivity may explain the new term for beggar-thy-neighbor monetary policy that was coined in a 2015 *Financial Times* article suggesting that central banks around the world were instead engaged in "competitive easing" to bring about a widening transatlantic interest rate gap. Citing the dollar's steep rise against the euro as the European Central Bank sought euro weakness through quantitative easing, the article took aim at the trade distortions imparted by differing central bank actions: "The volatility and uncertainty created by transatlantic divergences is in itself damaging—to economies as well as investors."[32] When central banks were fairly united in pushing down interest rates in the aftermath of the 2008

40 | *Good as Gold*

global financial meltdown, foreign exchange markets were relatively tranquil. But with the Fed seeking "liftoff" in its efforts to normalize monetary policy in 2015 while the ECB was engaged in quantitative easing through its huge bond-buying plan, substantial turmoil was unleashed in currency markets. For spectators, it was a bonanza, as the dollar and euro began to move in opposite directions—with every subtle comment from a central banker on either side of the Atlantic providing an opportunity to stake a currency bet. A huge rally in the dollar could be halted by a single dovish statement from a Fed official. The euro might surge against the dollar for a day, only to resume its slide the next day. "The sheer speed of the round trip in the euro-dollar exchange rate—the world's most heavily traded currency pair—left traders and investors reeling," according to the *Wall Street Journal,* forcing them to cover positions in near panic.[33] A similar episode of currency turmoil may be spawned, as 2024 unfolds, by the pending variance between the intentions of monetary policy officials on either side of the Atlantic—and the differential timetables for carrying out those intentions.

The "accidental currency wars" that are launched under such conditions can plant the seeds for a new global financial crisis. Central banks are required to act when financial markets seize up; that is part of their lender-of-last-resort obligations. But it is critical to recognize that the very global financial emergency that is seen to justify massive central bank intervention itself may have been spawned by destabilizing currency swings caused by divergent actions among central banks. A report issued by the Bank for International Settlements in December 2022 warns that foreign exchange swap markets are highly vulnerable to funding squeezes—as evidenced during the 2008 global financial crisis and again in March 2020 during the COVID-19 pandemic. "Payment obligations arising from FX swaps/forwards and currency swaps are staggering," the report notes, citing the difficulty of anticipating dollar rollover needs and cautioning that "policies to restore the flow of dollars would still be set in a fog."[34] Currency chaos leads to miscalculations by central banks themselves. The Federal Reserve was surprised in March 2020 when the ten-year Treasury yield skyrocketed by sixty-four basis points in less than ten days as U.S. government securities were dumped for cash, prompting the Fed to intervene at unprecedented levels. In the first quarter of 2020, the Fed bought more than $1 trillion in Treasury debt—more than it had purchased during any of its three earlier programs of quantitative easing following the 2008 global financial crisis.[35]

Meanwhile, the impact of shifting currencies on profits spells trouble for American companies that generate sales abroad when the dollar rises in value against other currencies. U.S. exports become more expensive in other countries, and the value of foreign revenue is diminished when it is converted back into dollars. Multinational corporations can be caught off guard by the speed of the dollar's rise—dramatically reversing anticipated gains and subverting corporate planning. The impact of currency shifts resulting from conflicting monetary policies among central banks forces internal accounting and operational adjustments that disrupt and distort normal business decisions. For example, a company with branch operations in a foreign nation with a depreciating currency now has to pay more for needed components from outside that nation. These adjustments may require increased allotments for working capital, purely to accommodate the increased cost of conducting business as a result of unanticipated exchange rate movements.

One might argue that "currency hedging" provides a way for companies to protect themselves from movements in exchange rates affecting their business profits. It's possible to hedge against risk exposure from exchange rate fluctuations by purchasing financial contracts—but in doing so, the company gives up a portion of the return it otherwise would have achieved. For large companies, the cost can be quite significant. Coca-Cola, for example, earned 66 percent of its $38.6 billion in annual sales outside the United States in the first quarter of 2022; to protect profits from currency risk, it held notional foreign exchange cash flow hedges of $7.5 billion, or some 27 percent of its foreign sales.[36] For smaller companies, the hedging option is simply too complex or too expensive to be considered. Currency risk is enough to sink plans for pursuing future business opportunities before they can even get underway.

Former chairman of the Federal Reserve Paul Volcker took note of the distortions imposed by fluctuating monetary signals across borders in his book *Changing Fortunes*, coauthored with Toyoo Gyohten:

> Increases of 50 percent and declines of 25 percent in the value
> of the dollar or any important currency over a relatively brief
> span of time raise fundamental questions about the functioning

of the exchange rate system. What can an exchange rate really mean, in terms of everything a textbook teaches about rational economic decision making, when it changes by 30 percent or more in the space of twelve months only to reverse itself? What kind of signals does that send about where a businessman should intelligently invest his capital for long-term profitability? In the grand scheme of economic life first described by Adam Smith, in which nations like individuals should concentrate on the things they do best, how can anyone decide which country produces what most efficiently when the prices change so fast? The answer, to me, must be that such large swings are a symptom of a system in disarray.[37]

Beyond the cost of hedging, then, it is this more fundamental blow to business and investment planning that reflects the true price tag of our muddled world of international monetary arrangements. The current dysfunctional approach discourages entrepreneurship by distorting—at times, utterly confounding—the signals that would provide free-market incentives to reward those who wish to "concentrate on the things they do best" if they were conveyed through sound and stable money. What is the cost of having to constantly revamp business plans in response to changing expense calculations due to currency shifts? Or worse, what is the opportunity cost for having forgone a potentially viable project because of currency risk? The uncertainty associated with foreign trade or establishing business ventures in foreign countries due to gyrating exchange rates dampens the entrepreneurial spirit and imposes a social loss from reduced economic output.

Finally, among the perverse outcomes caused by monetary distortions engineered through central banking, we must consider volatility in financial markets—and those who welcome it. For market traders who thrive on profits attained through speculative derivatives trading or the $7.5 trillion daily turnover in foreign exchange markets, the riskier the trading, the more lucrative it is. Even if currency volatility fuels global financial market instability, threatens international lending, and menaces global economic performance, those traders still win. As long as nimble traders in the world's preeminent financial centers are racking up profits for their companies and bonuses for themselves, they have little incentive to seek a stable monetary system.

Meanwhile, the risk of a sudden liquidity crisis in foreign exchange markets looms large. Seismic intraday fluctuations and destabilizing spikes can lead to panic as foreign exchange market participants rush to unwind positions at crucial moments. The foreign exchange market is the world's largest market; currency movements that spread alarm among traders provide the kindling that can ignite global financial turmoil, causing banking and credit channels to seize up. Herd behavior is the plague of financial markets, as skittish investors scramble to dump positions—with market mayhem the inevitable result.

Still, we can expect market traders who speculate with derivatives linked to currencies and interest rates to welcome every opportunity to increase profits, despite the danger. The option pricing model used to specify payout parameters assigns a positive value to risk. The prospect of sudden market tightness and reduced liquidity leading to destabilized financial markets may keep central bankers up at night, but it's a rewarding strategy for a well-positioned trader. Banking soundness may be threatened by widespread trading in complex derivatives—but those same financial institutions derive a huge portion of their own profits from currency and interest rate strategies. No wonder foreign exchange and derivatives portfolio managers operate on a hair trigger.

Monetary Policy That Plays Favorites

The goal of monetary policy should be to calibrate the supply of money to the needs of the economy in such a way as to maintain a stable unit of account. Monetary policy per se should not seek to distort the composition of that economy. That is, the structure of the economy should not be warped by actions directly attributable to central bank intervention that create variances among different segments of society in terms of access to credit. If interest rates are deliberately suppressed by Federal Reserve monetary policy decisionmakers, some people stand to benefit, while others stand to lose.

For example, borrowers gain when interest rates are manipulated downward. The largest borrower in the world is the U.S. government.[38] Indeed, the U.S. Treasury reaps the benefit of borrowing through the issuance of sovereign debt at a reduced cost when interest rates are held down. Who else benefits from low interest rates brought about through the Fed's monetary policy directives? Large corporations listed on major stock exchanges are beneficiaries of Fed largesse when they can borrow money cheaply to buy back their own shares in equity markets. By increasing the earnings-per-share ratio, they raise the price of their stock. Because many top managers have compensation packages linked to their companies' share price, this maneuver rewards them.

Individual investors with large financial portfolios are especially well positioned to benefit from "accommodative" monetary policy. So long as they can borrow funds through their brokerage firms at extremely low interest rates (which are made available to wealthy, well-qualified clients), they can arbitrage high returns from pumped-up equity markets against a low cost of borrowing. This bonus enriches those who can take advantage of it—that is, those who are already wealthy. Brokerage firms are protected, because if the borrower's capacity to repay is threatened by a decline in the value of the portfolio, that borrower will receive a "margin call" requiring that shares be sold immediately to maintain adequate coverage of the loaned amount.

All of this begs the question whether ordinary citizens would approve of monetary policy decisions that benefited certain entities within the economy if they truly understood what was happening. Central banking actions can seem mystifying to those not directly involved in the world of finance—and perhaps that gives some cover to monetary policymakers. It seems doubtful that people would knowingly authorize central bank officials to intervene in financial markets to channel low-cost money to the federal government, large publicly listed corporations, and wealthy investors unless they were quite confident that the benefits of "monetary stimulus" would accrue to themselves as well. When that is not the case, lower-income and middle-income members of the population have reason to question why they should have to subsidize those same policies. People who keep their retirement nest egg in a bank savings account receive an artificially suppressed interest rate—lower than what markets would have determined—as a direct consequence of loose monetary policy.

Monetary favoritism is the unspoken consequence of activist central bank intervention aimed at increasing investment and economic activity through low interest rates. If the goal is to expand growth and lift employment, one might argue that an element of perceived unfairness is acceptable. Some early beneficiaries of cheap money can take advantage, while others have to wait their turn, perhaps—but won't an improved economy ultimately benefit everyone? That is the basic question. If a central bank's monetary policy decisions do not succeed in stimulating real growth across the economy, citizens have a right to ask why they should bear the brunt of actions that mainly empower big government and big business—and further enrich people already at the top.

The years of activist central bank intervention following the 2008 global financial crisis were characterized by subpar economic growth. As observed in a *Wall Street Journal* editorial in 2015, "the great paradox of this expansion is that the monetary policy that is supposed to spur faster growth hasn't spurred faster growth."[39] But instead of acknowledging that monetary policies have not proved successful in stimulating faster growth, central banks seem prepared to keep following the same flawed theoretical constructs. This happens even though the Fed and other major central banks tend to overestimate economic growth in their projections.

The danger is highest when chronic economic weakness causes monetary authorities to delay moves that would start to end the bizarre effects of suppressed interest rates. Even as growth predictions were confounded, central banks stubbornly pursued near-zero or negative interest rates for years. Bank resources were increasingly diverted into government debt obligations, which counted as riskless assets, while large corporations continued to utilize cheap funds to purchase their own shares. Wealthy investors continued to take advantage of booming equity markets as asset prices continued to rise.

Meanwhile, who bore the costs of the unconventional monetary policies doggedly pursued by the world's major central banks? While the interest rate manipulations of monetary policymakers offer up a speculator's paradise for those who can grab quick profits by trading derivatives and currencies, these manipulations make life considerably harder for people who must function in the real economy. Banks are reluctant to finance consumer purchases or make small business loans when the future path of interest rates cannot be ascertained. Would-be entrepreneurs can scarcely put forward credible plans for new ventures when the cost of capital won't be known until the next monetary policy meeting—or the one after that, or the one after that. By exacerbating market uncertainty over future interest rates, central banks inhibit economic growth. They quietly kill off confidence in a more prosperous future and willingness to work for it—the animal spirits that form the vital wellspring of productive endeavor.

When monetary policy slants financial rewards to one segment of society at the expense of others, it does a grave injustice to the principle of equal treatment. In her 2021 book, *The Engine of Inequality: The Fed and the Future of Wealth in America*, financial consultant Karen Petrou explains:

> Ultra-low rates fundamentally eviscerate the ability of all but the wealthy to gain an economic toehold; instead, they lead investors to drive up equity and other asset prices to achieve their return-on-investment objectives, but average Americans hold little, if any, stock or investment instruments. Instead, they save what they can in bank accounts. The rates on these have been so low for so long that these thrifty, prudent households have in fact set themselves back with each dollar they save.[40]

There is no justification for channeling inordinately large rewards to those who are already in the top income brackets on the presumption that those in lower income brackets will eventually benefit. The notion is that spurred economic growth will lead to more job offerings, and a tighter labor market will give workers more leverage to push for higher wages. But what if those higher wages don't materialize? When results don't turn out as expected—when the promised benefits of monetary stimulus fail to materialize for the bulk of the population—it's reasonable to question central bank authorities about the effectiveness of their monetary strategy for promoting economic growth.[41] The economic crisis that followed the 2008 financial collapse was deep and protracted. Weakness persisted long after the recession officially ended in June 2009. According to the Federal Reserve's own assessment of the "Great Recession" and its aftermath, "economic growth was only moderate—averaging about 2 percent in the first four years of the recovery—and the unemployment rate, particularly the rate of long-term unemployment, remained at historically elevated levels."[42]

It is not the role of the central bank to guarantee economic outcomes or attempt to allocate credit in pursuit of social justice. Indeed, when government officials focus on "equity" instead of "equal rights" as the policy objective, they lose sight of the fundamental mission. It is easy to be falsely lured through government statistics into calling for redistributionist policies; income and wealth inequality numbers deserve careful scrutiny.[43] But for the Federal Reserve, it needs to be made clear that the mission is to ensure monetary integrity in the form of stable purchasing power. Distorting the value of the dollar and skewing financial market performance in ways that benefit certain groups at the expense of others is antithetical to the notion of equal treatment. Monetary policy should serve the interests of all citizens.

While the Fed and other central banks remain sensitive to criticism that causes the public to demand greater accountability, they seem reluctant to abandon monetary policy experiments—even when they fail to solve the problem of economic stagnation. Instead, Fed officials argue in favor of enlarging the role of government in the economy by enhancing the powers of central banks. In his 2022 book, *21st Century Monetary Policy: The Federal Reserve from the Great Inflation to COVID-19*, former Fed chairman Ben Bernanke advocates for quantitative easing—large-scale purchases of government debt securities—as a basic element of the policy tool kit, which should be utilized "not only in crises but whenever additional stimulus is needed." He notes that the Fed's powerful tools "may not always be enough" and urges that "monetary policymakers therefore continue their search for new tools and strategies."[44]

It is quite telling to recall how Bernanke responded to criticism in 2015, after years of near-zero interest rates and quantitative easing, that Fed officials had proved to be consistently too optimistic about growth. Acknowledging that the Federal Open Market Committee's projections of economic growth had been too high since the financial crisis, Bernanke suggested it was because productivity gains had been slow. "But nobody claims that monetary policy can do much about productivity growth," he stated.[45]

This assertion needs to be powerfully challenged. Monetary policy should always be aimed at providing a solid foundation for productive economic growth. Growth based on monetary illusion ends up creating worse problems down the road by misallocating capital and distorting financial outcomes. If central bankers fail to recognize the negative impact of their policies on productive economic growth, it does not make sense to grant them yet more control over the economy.

Even more damaging than the undermining of long-term economic growth is the harm done to American values when monetary policy is perceived as playing favorites rather than working equally for everyone by providing a reliable monetary unit of account. When citizens believe the system is "rigged" to reward those who are already at the top in terms of wealth and income, this belief feeds an attitude of resentment and cynicism. The "Wall Street versus Main Street" mentality is reinforced when the actions of monetary policy authorities are seen to punish ordinary savers while providing increasing returns to big government, big corporations, and big investors.

It is blatantly inconsistent with founding principles to allow monetary authorities to deliberately debase the dollar to achieve a goal of "price stability" that is actually defined as 2 percent perpetual inflation. It makes matters worse when monetary policy is perceived as violating the notion of equal treatment under the law, as evidenced by growing wealth inequality. Nowhere in the Constitution does it say that money shall be regulated in such a way that some groups benefit more than others in accordance with decisions made by the nation's central bank.

It's worth delving briefly into the monetary history of the United States to examine the intentions of the Founding Fathers. Modern observers of monetary policy might assume that their forebears did not understand the complexities of currency management. On the contrary, America's early leaders had personally experienced the destabilizing and dispiriting impact of currency depreciation issued by individual colonies—and were determined to prevent it at the federal level. James Madison, a primary author of the Constitution, cited the unfairness of changing weights and measures in his notes for an address before the Virginia Assembly in 1786.[46] He argued that unreliable money had the effect of "destroying the confidence between man and man, by which resources of one may be commanded by another." Madison denounced non-interest-bearing credit notes issued by the government—paper money—as being "unconstitutional" because a depreciating currency "affects the rights of property as much as taking away equal value in land." Americans forced to contend with the consumer price inflation that began to meaningfully erode purchasing power in the post-COVID era—reaching an apex of 9.1 percent in June 2022, a record forty-year high—fully understand the sense of personal loss in both financial and psychological terms. Taking away the value of one's earnings by diminishing the value of the unit that denominates their worth is an act of deceit. To deem as "money" the credit notes issued by the government at the federal level was to grant the government power to expropriate property through overissuance. America's founders did not wish to compound the mistakes that states had made earlier. If the founders refused to draw the proper lessons about the risks of government profligacy, their refusal would undermine the cohesion needed to form a strong new nation answerable to its citizens. Alexander Hamilton, destined to serve as the first U.S. secretary of the treasury, argued that monetary abuse was inconsistent with the aspirations and principles of the people. In his resolutions for the U.S. Constitution, he wrote: "To emit an unfunded paper as the sign of value ought not to continue a formal part of the constitution nor ever hereafter to be employed; being, in its nature, pregnant with abuses, and liable to be made the engine of imposition and fraud; holding out temptations equally pernicious to the integrity of government and to the morals of the people."[47] Hamilton's reference to the "integrity of government and to the morals of the people" shows that even those who favored a strong central government with autonomous powers thought it would be anathema to the cause of self-government to permit the issuance of federal credit notes to serve as legal tender.

Thomas Jefferson wrote up his own parameters for establishing an official money unit for the United States that would serve as a common currency across the newly independent states. In his *Notes on the Establishment of a Money Unit*, Jefferson called for a fixed unit of money that would (1) be convenient for use in daily life, (2) have easily calculated proportions, and (3) be consistent with the value of familiar and trusted coins.[48] America's money would be based on a decimal approach to simplify transactions; commerce should not be burdened with complex arithmetic and awkward units of measurement.

Jefferson was firmly convinced that U.S. money should provide a dependable and unchanging standard of value; indeed, he hoped it might one day establish a worldwide standard. As secretary of state, Jefferson submitted to the House of Representatives his "Plan for Establishing Uniformity in the Coinage, Weights, and Measures of the United States," aimed at achieving universal standards that he believed should be unchangeable and also "accessible to all persons, in all times and places."[49] President George Washington reinforced Jefferson's ideas by informing Congress that "a uniformity of weights and measures is among the important objects submitted to you by the Constitution" and that it should be "derived from a standard at once invariable and universal."[50]

The founders had a rigid interpretation of the limited money powers granted to the government by the Constitution. "Regulating" the money meant specifying the definition of the U.S. monetary unit of account in precise weights of gold or silver. As expressed in Article I, Section 8, the constrained monetary authority granted to Congress is "to coin Money, regulate the Value thereof, and of foreign Coin and fix the Standard of Weights and Measures." American money was to provide a standard of value—specified in terms of the metallic content of the money unit—as dependable and constant as the standards for weights and measures. By the exercise of this authority—in combination with the prohibition, in Article I, Section 10, against states making "any Thing but gold and silver Coin a Tender in Payment of Debts"—the new common currency of the United States was established.

We have drifted far away from beginning principles regarding the need for reliable money to unite the independent states into a sovereign nation. It is sad that such an unambiguous commitment to meaningful money, deserving of the trust of American citizens, has become an anachronism. The moral aspect is more pertinent than ever because the integrity of the dollar not only impacts the financial well-being of those who live and work in the United States but also greatly influences economic prospects for the world. Roger Sherman, a signatory to the Declaration of Independence as well as the Constitution, believed that a changeable medium of exchange was "no better than unjust weights and measures" and thus "condemned by the laws of God and man."[51] It's a sobering thought.

Yet we have somehow come to accept the purposeful debasement of the dollar through inflation targeting by the Federal Reserve. Congress does not question the Fed's strategy for achieving its monetary policy objectives, even when the mechanisms used to carry out the directives of its decision-making committee result in unequal treatment of citizens. The widening income and wealth disparity among U.S. households foments dissatisfaction and social discord; according to a Pew Research study in 2020, about six in ten U.S. adults say there is too much economic inequality in the country. Among that group, most say that significant changes to the country's economic system would be required to address the problem.[52] Yet such dissatisfaction seemingly prompts no changes in how the Fed views the legitimacy of its monetary framework—despite its disparate effects—or the impact of its mechanisms for altering its policy interest rate to achieve a targeted level of inflation.

Paradoxically, former Federal Reserve chair Janet Yellen cited the rise in the concentration of income in the top few percent of households during a 2014 speech and observed, "I think it is appropriate to ask whether this trend is compatible with values rooted in our nation's history, among them the high value Americans have traditionally placed on equality of opportunity."[53] What she neglected to mention was the Fed's own culpability in disbursing unequal financial rewards across American households. The Fed's zero interest rate approach to stimulating economic recovery had mainly benefited the wealthiest Americans, who had access to cheap credit, while leaving behind those unable to capitalize on low-cost financing.

The motivations of central bankers to do good may be sincere—they are undoubtedly well-intentioned public servants—but the presumption that a small committee of officials can substitute their own judgment about what the cost of capital should be for a market-based economy is troubling. Seeking to thwart free-market outcomes based on supply and demand in favor of stimulating or restricting economic growth seems a disingenuous practice. Such a government-knows-best mentality goes against the grain for those who believe in economic freedom and individual rights.

Hayek was particularly aware of the dangerous tendency to subordinate individual liberty to government oversight under the spell of a crumbling monetary standard. He warned that monetary distortions engineered through central banking would inevitably lead to more demands for government economic intervention:

> For this reason, all those who wish to stop the drift toward increasing government control should concentrate their efforts on monetary policy. There is perhaps nothing more disheartening than the fact that there are still so many intelligent and informed people who in most other respects will defend freedom and yet are induced by the immediate benefits of an expansionist policy

to support what, in the long run, must destroy the foundations
of a free society.[54]

It is time to explicitly recognize that central planning by way of central
banking does not deliver optimum results. Nor does it conform with historical experience regarding the best path to prosperity for whole nations. On
the contrary, central bank manipulation of interest rates in defiance of free-
market mechanisms has a destructive and demoralizing impact on the ideals
of democratic capitalism because it exalts government-defined objectives
above the hopes and aspirations of individual citizens.

2

Stable Money Fosters Productive Growth

A STABLE MONETARY foundation provides the appropriate platform for maximizing real economic growth. The statement has inherent validity; it doesn't make sense to construct a strong home on quicksand. Still, the fact that monetary stability is sacrificed in pursuit of other government policy objectives suggests that not everyone believes it is worth preserving at all costs; certainly, not all economists do. To understand the presumed trade-offs between stable prices and other monetary policy goals, we need to examine the negative consequences of money that cannot be trusted. Uncertainty over the value of money breeds financial dysfunction and economic dislocations, both domestically and internationally—and highlights the need for meaningful monetary reform.

To measure economic growth, we start with a baseline assessment of an economy's size. A broad measure of an economy's size, commonly used in comparative studies, is expressed by quantifying its output. We ask: How much is produced by a country in terms of goods and services, calculated at market value? Gross domestic product (GDP) is defined as the value of all goods and services produced within a particular nation during a given time period. Determining the GDP number is a starting point for studying the economy of the United States and weighing various policy options. According to the Bureau of Economic Analysis at the U.S. Department of Commerce,

> GDP is one of the most comprehensive and closely watched economic statistics: It is used by the White House and Congress to prepare the Federal budget, by the Federal Reserve to formulate monetary policy, by Wall Street as an indicator of economic activity, and by the business community to prepare forecasts of

economic performance that provide the basis for production, investment, and employment planning.[1]

But what does this all-important "measure" actually measure—and how accurately does it portray the true condition of a nation's economy? When we talk about the health of an economy, we clearly derive valuable information from the GDP number. But we must go beyond the top-line numbers to get a fuller understanding of what is happening. For example, a seemingly healthy economy might be indicated by a low rate of unemployment. If, however, that low unemployment rate is not due to robust business demand for hiring new workers but instead reflects a lack of interest or incentive on the part of employable people, that same low unemployment number could have decidedly negative implications.

In other words, economic information expressed by the GDP number and other frequently cited statistics may not capture the most important information for evaluating the performance of a nation's economy. We need to understand the formulations behind the statistics to gain additional insights about potential developments—especially when they suggest contradictory trends. How can we have low unemployment yet still have so many people out of work? The simultaneous occurrence of low unemployment and low economic growth could suggest that traditional patterns of behavior are changing; the economic impact could be significant and perturbing. Such a situation should prompt us to dig deeper and seek to ascertain what might be happening within the economy to discourage individuals from seeking gratifying employment commensurate with their skills and desires. We need to consider whether certain government policies—fiscal, monetary, or both—may be contributing to a work environment that does not provide adequate incentives for participation. When the workforce is less than optimal, the level of productive economic output is constrained to subpar results.

Indeed, defining "productive" output in economic terms lies at the heart of the statistical muddle. People in the economics profession all too easily become fixated with numbers. Most theories about how to improve economic performance through government policies begin with quantitative formulas or linear regressions using multiple variables to represent the unemployment rate, inflation rate, interest rates (on riskless government debt, the "bank prime loan rate," or both), and other factors. Then it becomes a matter of plugging in appropriate numbers for the time period under consideration. Whether the calculations about how the variables interact within the econometric construct or the behavioral assumptions imputed to the analytical paradigm actually reflect the interplay of financial and human influences leading to an economic outcome is questionable. And even if such formulations indicate a correlation between certain variables and economic growth, the inferences for government policy may not be so clear.

Fiscal directives and monetary policy decisions geared to maximize output, as measured by GDP growth, may provide a sense of dealing expediently with developing trends to steer an economy in the right direction—but they can also camouflage underlying problems. Instead of chasing purely nominal results in defining how much an economy has grown, we should focus on whether perceived increases can be deemed *productive* growth. Policy prescriptions based on formulas engineered to pump up a numerical construct for capturing growth dynamics may be inserted into federal budgeting forecasts, or used for monetary targeting purposes, with the promise of achieving higher GDP. Yet policies based on such formulations may not actually contribute to improved living standards for the bulk of people who live and work within that economy.

Economics, after all, is a social science. Humans tend to be aspirational. Many people long to be better off materially or seek a brighter future with more options for their children. Many have dreams of richness defined in terms of their own personal journey through life. What matters is the perception that conditions have genuinely improved for attaining success. In the Declaration of Independence, the "pursuit of happiness" is included among the natural rights that exist outside of any man-made system of governance because humans are "endowed by their Creator" with an inherent claim. Thomas Jefferson described these rights as "certain unalienable Rights, that among these are Life, Liberty and the pursuit of Happiness" and ascribed to government the duty to protect and preserve them in accordance with the consent of the people.

We do not need to dump conventional numerical measures of economic well-being in favor of some "happiness index" expressed in parameters linked to ambiguous concepts of social welfare or social justice. The goal is rather to emphasize the need for a more meaningful statistic than simply numerical GDP growth as an accurate measure of economic performance. It would be useful, too, to acknowledge that having to differentiate between "nominal" GDP (measured at current prices) and "real" GDP (adjusted for inflation) is an exercise that readily captures the psychological dissonance caused by unstable money. Although real GDP is the most common measurement used for determining the economic growth rate without the distorting effect of inflation, economists often use nominal GDP to gauge the level of consumer purchasing power. Comparing the two measures can reveal the extent to which perceived economic growth is due to increased prices rather than an actual increase in production. Nominal GDP would seem to provide a dodgy number for evaluating the true condition of a nation's economy because it conjoins the rate of inflation with the real growth number and thus could end up masking the simultaneous occurrence of rising inflation with decreasing real growth.

The main purpose of focusing on productive growth is to highlight the outsize influence of income derived from the financial sector. Although financial intermediation plays a vital role in channeling financial capital toward its most efficient use, excessive speculation in financial markets can negatively impact access to capital for manufacturing and other economic activities. It is important to consider the trade-off between achieving genuinely productive growth and merely increasing the size of the financial sector relative to the overall economy.

For that reason, we need to analyze the relationship between stable money and economic performance. Uncertainty about government policies, fiscal and monetary, has a detrimental effect on real growth. Indeed, when erratic movements in the cost of capital exacerbate uncertainty and weaken confidence in the business environment, the result is that innovation, entrepreneurial initiative, and productive risk-taking in the private sector are stultified. In the context of the global marketplace, we need to consider how the lack of a stable exchange rate system impacts the decisions of companies that manufacture in one country while selling to retail markets in another country. In short, we need to highlight how much productive economic endeavor is undermined—how much potential prosperity is lost—due to misguided monetary policy decisions and volatile exchange rates.

Focusing on the Real Economy

A methodical reassessment of the relationship between finance and growth suggests diminishing economic returns from a runaway banking and financial services sector. This should not be surprising; there is clearly an economic impact if financial intermediaries are motivated to seek profits by engaging in speculative activities that are removed from providing capital resources to fund more traditional long-term investment opportunities.

Before proceeding to corroborate the essential relationship between stable money and productive growth, let us be permitted the intellectual indulgence of considering an alternative definition of real economic progress—one that might resonate with those who value basic human rights above more materialistic concerns. The Happy Planet Index measures how well nations are doing by ranking their performance based on three variables: (1) life expectancy, (2) well-being, and (3) ecological footprint.[2] The concept is that countries should be assessed based on "how efficiently they deliver long, happy lives using our limited environmental resources," instead of using measures that focus solely on economic activity to denote national progress—that is, how much is produced or consumed.

Here are the top 10 highest-scoring countries out of 152 ranked by the Happy Planet criteria using 2019 data:

- Costa Rica
- Vanuatu
- Colombia
- Switzerland
- Ecuador
- Panama
- Jamaica
- Guatemala
- Honduras
- Uruguay

Most people would likely dispute the notion that every one of these nations offers a social and economic model that deserves to be emulated. Suffice it to note the high rate of emigration from Guatemala and Honduras as citizens flee gang violence and extreme poverty. It seems pertinent here to acknowledge that providing access to a stable monetary platform arises as a political imperative for poorer nations as well as rich ones—especially because one of the compelling arguments in favor of sound money is that it empowers citizens to pursue their own definition of life, liberty, and happiness. Panama and Ecuador have adopted the U.S. dollar as their official currency (as have El Salvador, Zimbabwe, the British Virgin Islands, the Turks and Caicos, Timor-Leste, Bonaire, Micronesia, Palau, and the Marshall Islands). For those nations, it is a step up from central bank abuses of their own domestic currencies, which have inflicted decidedly unhappy consequences.

Happiness is a subjective measure, of course, that can hardly be compared across individuals—let alone countries. But there is doubtless a correlation between happiness and economic prosperity when the latter translates into a more comfortable and stress-free life. Individuals commonly pursue material wealth as well as happiness, with one reinforcing the other, for themselves and their families. Whole nations dedicate their policy agenda to achieving more economic growth and development. That is why we should analyze the impact of monetary dissonance in providing the financial capital needed to fund projects that increase prosperity and raise living standards.

It is important to determine to what extent a rapidly expanding financial sector can displace more productive economic growth. A 2012 analysis by Stephen Cecchetti and Enisse Kharroubi at the Bank for International Settlements examined the impact of the size and growth of the financial system on aggregate economies and concluded:

> First, as is the case with many things in life, with finance you can have too much of a good thing. That is, at low levels, a larger financial system goes hand in hand with higher productivity growth. But there comes a point—one that many advanced economies passed long ago—where more banking and more credit lower growth.
>
> Our second result comes from looking at the impact of growth in the financial system—measured as growth in either employment or value added—on real growth. Here we find evidence that is unambiguous: faster growth in finance is bad for aggregate

real growth. One interpretation of this finding—one to which we subscribe—is that financial booms are bad for trend growth.

Finally, in our examination of industry-level data, we find that industries that are in competition for resources with finance are particularly damaged by financial booms. Specifically, we show that manufacturing sectors that are either R&D-intensive or dependent on external finance suffer disproportionate reductions in productivity growth when finance booms.[3]

The study shows that financial sector size has an inverted U-shaped effect on productivity; there is an optimum point on the curve at which the size of the financial sector maximizes economic productivity. This is analogous to the Laffer curve relating tax rates to total tax collections. If the tax rate is zero, tax collection is zero; if the tax rate is 100 percent, tax collection may also be zero, because there is no incentive to work. An optimum point on this curve represents the level of taxation that yields the highest amount of revenues, after which there are diminishing returns to total tax revenues collected by the government. The study by Cecchetti and Kharroubi likewise shows that at either extreme of the curve—that is, if a country had no finance sector or if the finance sector were 100 percent of the economy—the size of the country's financial system would have no impact on its productivity growth. In short, there is a point after which further enlargement of the financial system can reduce real growth: "more finance is definitely not always better."[4]

So we have the dilemma of using a GDP number that includes the "output" of the financial sector in its measurement of gross domestic product, even though a fast-growing financial sector can negatively impact total productivity growth. This is particularly true for advanced economies, where the finance sector competes with the rest of the economy for scarce resources—including the human capital of bright minds drawn to the sophisticated and lucrative world of global finance. A follow-up Bank for International Settlements (BIS) working paper by Cecchetti and Kharroubi posits that when skilled labor is attracted to the finance sector, the real economy pays a price because well-educated and adept human resources are drawn away from computing, aircraft manufacturing, and other R&D-intensive industries.[5]

The way monetary policy is currently formulated and implemented, however, feeds the finance industry, enlarging the power and influence of banking and financial services ("Wall Street") at the expense of manufacturing ("Main Street"). This is especially damaging for industries requiring the long-term commitment of resources, human and financial, to conduct research and development over an extended period before producing final results. These efforts should be able to attract both talent and investment capital; they are investment projects that ultimately raise the quality of life for society. We need to consider the ramifications of a money system that compensates day traders for arbitraging the quick profit opportunities presented by offhand remarks from central bank officials more generously than it rewards scientific researchers committed to fighting diseases and extending human life.

No one disputes the value of financial intermediation when it channels investment resources to useful purposes. But having an incentive structure that rewards those who are quick to exploit the divergent interest rate policies of central banks, which are part and parcel of current monetary arrangements, seems an economic waste. There is nothing scandalous in the fact that profits from currency trading overwhelmingly accrue to large international banking institutions.[6] There is certainly nothing illegal about making profits from buying and selling currencies so long as these activities do not violate laws against colluding to manipulate prices. Indeed, many clients ask their banks to provide currency hedging services as part of business planning to protect against losses from exchange rate movements. Companies selling products outside their own country wish to avoid getting caught in the crosscurrent of exchange rate fluctuations that wreak havoc with profits.

When foreign exchange activities contribute substantial revenues to banking institutions, however, calculations of economic growth are distorted, because the increased incomes stemming from currency trading profits are conflated with productive output. The U.S. financial sector grew from 10 percent of GDP in 1950 to 22 percent by 2020. In 1950, manufacturing had 40 percent of all profits and 29 percent of the nation's jobs; today, finance has 40 percent of the nation's profits with 5 percent of the jobs.[7] Instead of producing things—increasing the supply of goods, raising living standards for whole societies—part of the increase in incomes reflects the talent devoted to profiting from monetary policy uncertainty. Those who can figure out how to make money by taking advantage of status quo monetary arrangements are simply maximizing their own well-being and cannot be faulted; rather, the governments that have failed to provide stable money deserve to be taken to task.

Although it must be conceded that traditional manufacturing industries have given way to more high-tech activities as a natural response to modernity and changing demand, it also seems apparent that increasing financialization has drawn investment away from firms that require long-term sources of capital. The financial profit opportunities that arise from gaming the differential monetary policies of central banks act to crowd out investment in projects with longer planning horizons. Financial intermediaries may be less inclined to commit funds to long-term private sector borrowers—whose prospects for success are necessarily risky—when it is possible to capture near-instant profits by trading in foreign exchange markets. Monetary instability that fuels an ever-increasing volume of activity in foreign exchange markets constitutes an inefficient use of resources in the sense that it is enabled through irrational currency arrangements and volatile interest rates. Changing expectations about the paths of future interest rates in major advanced economies heightens currency volatility; turnover in global foreign exchange markets reached $7.5 trillion per day in April 2022, a volume that is 30 times greater than daily global GDP.[8] As Jacques de Larosiere, who served as governor of the Banque de France and managing director of the International Monetary Fund, observed in *Putting an End to the Reign of Financial Illusion: For Real Growth*, published in 2022, "an economy cannot function in the long term and for the good of all if investors' choices are oriented (notably because of monetary policy) towards immediate speculative opportunities and gains on valuations, rather than towards long-term growth prospects."[9]

Increasing financialization exerts negative effects on real capital accumulation. It causes capital to be directed into financial assets instead of real assets by changing the incentives of firm management regarding investment decisions. Greater and more immediate financial profit opportunities, when they can be quickly reaped, may be sought at the expense of long-term opportunities. Short-term profits are not inconsistent with maximizing the value of a firm, so management has every incentive to choose its best option. Reducing the planning horizon for providing financial resources may not serve the needs of society more generally, however. A scholarly study by Ozgur Orhangazi concludes that there is a negative relationship between real investment and financialization.[10] Using data from nonfinancial corporations from 1973 to 2003, the analysis suggests that (1) increased financial profit opportunities crowd out real investment by changing the incentives of firm managers and (2) increased payments to financial markets impede real investment by decreasing available internal funds and shortening the planning horizons of firm management.

Another problem with the increasing size of the financial sector as a percentage of the economy is that it draws talent away from more genuinely productive activities that result in higher output or higher living standards. Compensation in the financial services industry was similar to compensation in other industries until the end of the 1970s but began to increase in the 1980s. No one can blame young college graduates for wanting to maximize their salaries by choosing an industry where they can achieve high compensation. Before the global financial crisis in 2008, 47 percent of graduating seniors from Harvard planned to work in finance after leaving campus. The figure dropped as the lure of tech firms started to draw off many students; for the class of 2013, 31 percent of seniors were headed to consulting or finance, while 13 percent were drawn toward engineering and technology.[11] Because the same talents are required for both sectors, a tug-of-war continues to exist between financial services and technology companies for those with strong "quant" skills in mathematics.

The allure of working at high-paying jobs in banking and financial services clearly faded after 2008 as the illusion of stability and coherence in global financial markets was shattered. According to research provided by the Federal Reserve Bank of Cleveland, however, the financial sector had accounted for 20–35 percent of domestic profits in the United States for nearly two decades prior to the global financial crisis.[12] Focusing on the tendency of the banking and finance industry toward excessive risk-taking, the Cleveland Fed study links this propensity to the compensation packages of executives and employees at financial institutions. When short-term performance is heavily rewarded (for example, through bonuses), managers may take opportunities that boost immediate profitability but risk future financial health, reasoning that they may not remain forever with the same firm. The banking and finance industry paid significantly higher bonuses and awarded more restricted stock shares than other industries; top executives in financial institutions earned about 30–40 percent more pay than their counterparts in other industries in 2005, totaling $3.4 million per executive. Bonus pay for workers in New York City's financial securities industry hit a record high of $240,400 in 2021.[13]

Value judgments are not the focus here; individuals are free to decide how best to apply their skills and talents, and toward what purpose. What has sparked controversy and launched heated debates is the implication that even questioning whether an increasingly financialized economy serves the best interests of society is tantamount to criticizing financial intermediation itself. No one who has faith in the virtues of democratic capitalism would minimize the importance of making access to capital widely available. Channeling the loanable funds saved by individuals as needed "seed corn" for investing in projects that have the potential to bring about a greater future harvest is the very essence of financial intermediation—a noble endeavor. But when an increasing percentage of economic activity and resources is devoted to financial market investment as an end in itself, with little connection to any real project or creative new endeavor, we should look more closely. Unhealthy trends can be harbingers of problems; they merit greater research and scrutiny. It would be devastating to an economy based on free enterprise if expanding financialization—fueled by unpredictable monetary policy and disorderly currency arrangements—undermined faith in the capitalist model.

The risk of fomenting such a backlash against democratic capitalism is encapsulated by the critical assessments put forth in a 2013 study entitled "Financialization: Causes, Inequality Consequences, and Policy Implications," which captures a slew of grievances:

> The U.S. is now a financialized economy, where the financial sector and its priorities have become increasingly dominant in all aspects of the economy. We focus on financialization as a process of income redistribution with two faces. The first face is one of rent seeking by an increasingly concentrated and politically influential finance sector. This rent seeking has been successful, leading to the pooling of profits and income in the finance sector. The second face is a shift in behavior of non-finance firms away from production and non-financial services and toward financial investments and services. This shift has had both strategic and normative components and has reduced the bargaining power of

labor and the centrality of production. As a consequence, financialization of the non-finance sector has led to lower employment,
income transfer to executives and capital owners, and increased
inequality among workers.[14]

The danger in ignoring how the lack of a reliable money unit and coherent exchange rate regime have brought about increasing financialization is that the negative economic and social consequences can begin to be addressed from the perspective of a progressive policy agenda of redistribution by the government. This would be a travesty of political philosophy, as support for sound money arises more naturally from the values of classical liberalism: individual autonomy, limited government, and economic and political freedom. America's founding principles uphold equality and individual rights while supporting private property and the rule of law. In seeking meaningful reforms to restore stable money at home and abroad while at the same time reinstating the soundness and fruitfulness of financial intermediation, it is imperative to avoid the sort of remedies propounded by those with redistributionist leanings: "If the solvency of the finance sector is to be insured, some check on their market power should be explored. One solution to this problem is to restructure the incentives and tie the banking sector's profitability to economy-wide growth. Surplus profits could be taxed and redistributed for long-term investments in infrastructure, human capital, and research and development."[15]

The far better solution is to limit the role of the U.S. government, in keeping with the language of our nation's Constitution, to establishing the value of America's money. Context is critical: the enumerated power that grants authority to Congress to coin and regulate U.S. money, including its value relative to foreign coin, and to fix the standard of weights and measures as well, was conveyed for purposes of establishing official standards for the nation. It seems clear enough that America's money unit was intended to serve as a dependable measure of value from the beginning.

Whatever the reason that those lured into the world of high finance and speculative trading in pursuit of quick profits have chosen not to seek a presumed higher calling, the tendency is subject to change. It seems that young graduates from the "millennial" generation, born between the early 1980s and the late 1990s, may have developed a value system different from their predecessors'. As quoted in the *Financial Times*, Simon Collins, U.K. chairman of KPMG, observed: "This generation is looking for meaning in life, which candidly and shamefully I don't think our generation was."[16] For many, the prospect of becoming a tech entrepreneur seemed to hold the allure formerly attached to the lifestyle portrayed in the 1987 film *Wall Street,* which famously put forward the mantra "greed is good."

Even as millennials prioritize finding a balance between their work life and personal time, however, those who aspire to create a successful tech start-up company soon discover there is little "free time" for anything else. And that may be OK. To the extent that personal fulfillment ranks high among millennial objectives, even hundred-hour workweeks can be worthwhile. The dream of creating a breakthrough application or developing a new field of computing holds out tantalizing possibilities. Business school administrators report that students have seen the impact of tech innovations in their own lives and have become increasingly eager to work in such a fast-paced sector. Derrick Bolton, assistant dean and director of MBA admissions at Stanford's business school, says that students are asking: "Where's the place that I can drive innovation? Where's the place that I can have the most impact?"[17]

If the search for a meaningful career in technology has replaced the pursuit of financial intermediation, we should reflect on the reasons. Banking was an entrepreneurial endeavor at one time. In the early 1990s, community banks, often founded by a few individuals who were personally involved in their management, channeled funds from savers to borrowers in an efficient and productive way. Community bankers were primary lenders to businesses in America's smaller cities and towns. The ability to make judgments about the merits of a loan and the dependability of the borrower contributed to the success of a community. The ongoing viability of the bank's portfolio provided a safe repository for the savings of depositors.

But the number of community banks, defined as those with assets of less than $10 billion, declined from just over 8,300 in 2000 to 4,277 as of June 2020; they account for only 18 percent of bank loans.[18] As the number of community banks has decreased, Main Street borrowers have been forced to apply to larger institutions—often to be rejected or asked to meet stiffer terms. For many large banks, extending credit to small companies is not seen as an effective use of their resources because it tends to be difficult to automate, tough to securitize, and expensive to underwrite and service. Making small business loans is very time-intensive because it requires familiarity with the individual client in a way that makes sense only when conducted locally.[19]

Other factors have influenced the trend toward bank consolidation—notably the increasing cost of regulatory compliance. To be sure, the decline in the number of small community banks has been ongoing for decades, explained in part by the pressure from regulation and an uneven lending playing field. Large banks now dominate the industry because they are better able to compete against the small and medium-size banks that used to provide a disproportionately large share of retail and commercial loans. The trend away from local lending, in favor of taking positions in complex derivatives hedging interest rates and currencies, has fundamentally changed the nature of financial intermediation.

As the financial sector increases as a percentage of the economy, the shift does not mean that financial resources are being put to better use. The world's largest banks may be capable of deftly managing speculative positions in financial markets and generating profits through currency trading, but perhaps they are becoming less capable when it comes to channeling investment resources to the most promising endeavors. We need to ask whether monetary policy itself, as conducted through the discretionary actions taken by central bankers, negatively affects the performance of the real economy.

The growing financialization of the U.S. economy appears to mirror the increasing dominance of the Federal Reserve, not only over the banking industry but also over financial markets. It is thus reasonable to consider whether such developments have occurred as the result of having officially severed the earlier intrinsic connection between the value of the U.S. dollar and the real economy. We need to study whether the existence of a rules-based monetary system—when the actions of central banks were constrained by the responsibility to maintain fixed exchange rates of their currencies against the dollar, and the United States was obligated to convert foreign holdings of U.S. dollars into gold at a fixed rate—helped to curtail purely speculative financial activity seeking arbitrage profits resulting from monetary and currency discrepancies.

The end of the Bretton Woods system is plausibly connected to the increased financialization of the American economy, according to Brian Domitrovic, a history scholar and author of *Econoclasts*. Domitrovic asserts that the final loss of the dollar's gold connection after 1971 had major economic repercussions that began in the financial sector. Basically, the effect of disconnecting the dollar from gold was to steer investment away from "real purposes" into monetary speculation: "The primary harms fell upon wage-earners, who are dependent on real investment for jobs and the affordable provision of real goods and services. The primary benefits (which were proportionately smaller than the harms) fell to those who were well-positioned in one place—in the financial sector—to profit from the new status of currency hedges."[20]

By removing the last vestige of gold convertibility required by the strictures of the Bretton Woods international monetary system, the dollar was no longer linked to any kind of commodity with intrinsic value. Whereas gold had functioned as a surrogate for the real economy, the floating dollar was a measure of indeterminate value with only a vestigial connection to quantifiable inputs such as labor or materials. "Suddenly the importance of simply saving money diminished," Domitrovic notes. "Money that was saved also had to be hedged. If you simply saved money after 1971, you stood to get killed as the dollar lost value against things it was supposed to be able to procure in the future."[21]

By allowing the dollar to become less of a precise measure—defined in the Jeffersonian context as an essential tool for evaluating competing goods and services—the U.S. money unit has become a deteriorating asset itself. Access to a meaningful unit of account helps ensure more stable purchasing power and more solid savings. To lose the dollar as an accurate measure and dependable store of value is to violate the purpose of the nation's money.

When the simple virtue of saving is forced to give way to the need to speculate about how best to claw back some of the dollar's deterioration, it is time to reevaluate the role of the nation's central bank and assess both the economic and social damage caused by monetary policy. It is unfair—and a violation of American founding principles such as equal rights and equal treatment under the law—to permit the sort of monetary favoritism that rewards some citizens at the expense of others. Wage earners should not be penalized by monetary decisions that steer investment resources away from manufacturing and service-oriented companies into the pockets of financial institutions. Policies that impact one major sector of the economy quite negatively while ensuring profits for another are inappropriate. The rationale of using monetary policy to maximize growth and employment is confounded when the overall effect of monetary "stimulus" is to discourage loans to small business in favor of financial market speculation.

Worst of all, by concentrating immense powers over credit and capital flows in the hands of a small committee of monetary officials responding to data-driven events on a meeting-to-meeting basis, the logic of long-term business planning is defeated. Rational investors can hardly be expected to finance capital-intensive projects under such conditions. It is sobering to realize that when the international gold standard was in effect, roughly from the late 1870s to 1914, investors willingly purchased bonds issued by railroad companies with maturities of fifty and one hundred years.

Uncertainty Is Paralyzing

The Federal Reserve has gained significant power since its establishment in 1913 as a relatively passive institution for supplying banks with sufficient cash to meet customer demand. Today it exerts immense influence in allocating credit and capital to various segments of the economy. One of the primary tools used by the Fed for influencing market expectations of future levels of interest rates is "forward guidance" to communicate the likely future course of monetary policy. Normally, this is provided by the chairman of the Federal Reserve, most powerfully during the press conference that follows the announcement of the latest decision taken by the Federal Open Market Committee (FOMC) following each of the eight two-day meetings held during the year. But the Fed chief is not the only one who provides forward guidance; hints of future actions can also be gleaned from statements by other Fed officials.

The practice began in December 2008 in the wake of the global financial meltdown as the Fed was embracing near-zero interest rates and other unconventional approaches to stimulate growth and felt pressured to be more transparent in its actions to reduce financial market volatility. Some five years later, Janet Yellen (serving as Fed vice chair) emphasized that clear communication about goals and how central banks intend to achieve them was a key ingredient of her monetary policy framework. She contrasted this attitude with the Fed's earlier practice of providing no such guidance, noting that it "had journeyed from 'never explain' to a point where sometimes the explanation *is* the policy."[22]

But as the metrics for achieving the Fed's desired goals began to diverge and grow more complicated, communicating the Fed's intentions likewise became more difficult. Whereas the Fed had defined an unemployment level of 6.5 percent as the threshold for raising the Fed funds rate, the achievement of that unemployment level was due to discouraged workers abandoning the workforce rather than any real pickup in employment. Meanwhile, based on the FOMC's preference for a cushion against deflation, the secondary target on inflation was moving in the wrong direction. By March 2014, the FOMC was moving away from its earlier commitment to specific numerical objectives, indicating instead that it would consider "a wide range of information, including measures of labor market conditions, indicators of inflation pressures and inflation expectations, and readings on financial developments."[23]

Soon the Fed would be announcing a decision to provide qualitative rather than quantitative guidance in future FOMC statements: Fed officials would not be constrained by statistics but rather allowed to respond to evolving conditions. According to financial journalist Caroline Baum, writing after the Fed's 2015 annual symposium in Jackson Hole, Wyoming, monetary authorities were anxious to see the latest numbers on various economic performance meters before deciding whether to begin raising interest rates for the first time in more than nine years. "What new information in the next two weeks could possibly be instrumental in that decision?" Baum asked. "What exactly would another month of status-quo employment statistics do to convince the Fed to act? And if the report is an outlier in any way, then what? Wait for more data?"[24]

Needing to evaluate the latest statistics before making a decision raises the question whether forward guidance is a useful tool or merely highlights the lack of omniscience possessed by members of the FOMC. Given the Fed's poor record of forecasting, a move away from providing specific forward guidance might be viewed as a nod toward greater humility. But one could also view Fed reluctance to telegraph decisions in advance because they are "data-driven" as a bid by FOMC members to exercise even *more* discretion to make monetary policy decisions. Instead of committing in advance to any particular course of action aimed at expanding or contracting the money supply, they want the authority to make ad hoc decisions. By refusing to be constrained by earlier parameters for taking specific monetary policy actions, Fed officials undermine their accountability; they can always claim they were making the best decision at the time.

If the logic of providing forward guidance is that it allows markets to anticipate the future cost of capital well in advance, citizens are now being denied a useful information tool. The FOMC has taken the stance that monetary policy decisions will be based on the latest happenings in financial markets and may not accord with previously announced metrics. "We will continue to make our decisions meeting by meeting," Fed chair Jerome Powell stated in July 2022, noting the need to "be nimble in responding to incoming data and the evolving outlook."[25]

So it appears that the Fed's once-vaunted tool of forward guidance no longer has validity in terms of preparing markets for likely Fed actions on monetary policy. A speech by Fed governor Michelle W. Bowman in October 2022 indicated that forward guidance might now be expressed in vague terms with little actionable information for market participants:

> To be considered forward guidance, a statement does not need to be explicit about future policy actions or the timing of potential actions. It may be more qualitative in describing likely policy actions that may be taken in the future and, in some cases, may only describe how the FOMC will be thinking about its future decisions rather than signaling the likely future direction of policy actions.[26]

Such a lack of specificity, however, seems inconsistent with Bowman's assertion in the same speech: "Let me stress here that I view clear and transparent communication with the public from the Federal Reserve as crucial to enable a better understanding of and to reinforce the effectiveness of our monetary policy actions, all of which help keep us accountable to the public."[27]

If the Fed's goal is to make sure that markets are not surprised by its moves, how can such confusion over using forward guidance as a monetary policy tool possibly be explained? Muddled messages that merely hint at transient sentiments voiced by FOMC members at the latest two-day monetary policy meeting in Washington, D.C., would seem to foment uncertainty more than defuse it.

Economists surveyed in December 2022 about the Fed's intentions on interest rates had differing opinions: 62 percent predicted that the Fed probably would not begin cutting rates until 2024, while 38 percent thought the Fed would hike rates in 2023 but begin cutting them before the end of that year. An investor survey of market participants agreed with the latter opinion, believing that the Fed would have no choice but to cut rates and save the economy from a recession by fall 2023.[28] How can the average chief financial officer—let alone an ordinary citizen whose work does not involve equity or bond markets—make viable plans when even the experts are unable to predict the future cost of capital?

The Federal Open Market Committee has twelve voting members at most (positions can remain vacant for years); it is composed of the seven members of the Board of Governors of the Federal Reserve System, the president of the Federal Reserve Bank of New York, and four of the remaining eleven Reserve Bank presidents. All seven members of the Board of Governors are nominated by the president and confirmed by the Senate for terms of fourteen years. The most influential members of the FOMC are the chair and the vice chair; they serve four-year terms and can be reappointed multiple times. While the president of the New York Reserve Bank is always a voting member of the FOMC, the other four Reserve Bank presidents serve one-year terms on a rotating basis. Nonvoting Reserve Bank presidents attend FOMC meetings, participate in discussions, and give their assessments of the economy. But it is the voting members who make the monetary policy decisions—whether to increase interest rates, decrease them, or leave them unchanged.

One can question whether it makes sense to have so few people exercise discretionary authority over the cost of capital, which is arguably the most important price for an economy based on free-market capitalism. The process for determining the benchmark interest rate is subject to stray remarks by FOMC members at a time when global financial markets are highly vulnerable to alarming swings. No wonder the minutes of past Fed meetings are obsessively gleaned for insights into the thinking of U.S. monetary officials; no wonder every comment is dissected in excruciating detail.

But if ambiguity over the future path of interest rates offers up a speculator's paradise for those who can grab quick profits by trading derivatives and currencies, it makes life considerably harder for people who must function in the real economy. Banks are reluctant to finance consumer purchases or make small business loans when the future path of interest rates is highly vulnerable to erratic monetary policy. Would-be entrepreneurs can scarcely put forward credible plans for new ventures when the cost of capital cannot be known until the next FOMC meeting—or the press conference afterward with the Fed chairman.

By perpetuating uncertainty over interest rates, monetary officials wield a paralyzing effect on economic growth. Confidence in a better future, and the willingness to work for it, provide the vital wellspring for productive endeavor. In a sense, the interest rate measures faith in a better future; it is the fee borrowers pay to nurture the financial seed corn saved by those willing to forgo current consumption. No one would save rather than consume unless they believed the resources made available to an enterprising and hard-working individual would produce a greater harvest. For that, savers provide capital at a price that compensates them not only for delaying consumption but also for taking the risk that the borrower's promises may not be fulfilled. The Latin root of the word "credit"—*credere*—means "to believe." Trust in a better future is an essential aspect of free-market capitalism.

But instead of helping to tamp down the uncertainty that plagues investor confidence in the future, especially during difficult economic times, the Fed often fuels it. During 2022, the Fed raised its benchmark interest rate from near zero to more than 4.24 percent— its highest level in fifteen years—through a series of aggressive monetary policy decisions that included four consecutive increases of seventy-five basis points. Investors were left to scan for hints about future monetary policy by perusing economic data and the minutes from the latest FOMC meeting, hoping to gain insights into Fed intentions and possible actions amid fears of a looming recession. When incoming information provides conflicting signals, economic and investment activity is stymied. "Human nature is that when we feel uncertain, we're much more likely to stay put—and that's what happened in 2022," commented Jay Parsons, a senior vice president and chief economist for RealPage, a real estate service firm.[29] Interest rate volatility is fanned by monetary policy that needs to be corrected by imposing harsh measures. The mistake of keeping rates too low for too long defeats Fed aspirations to achieve price stability; rushing to reverse the damage by curtailing demand through restrictive interest rates does further damage to economic growth.

Uncertainty over the direction of the Fed's monetary policy would increase once more in April 2024, after disappointing readings on inflation in the first three months of the year dampened expectations for a cut in the central bank's target interest rate. Investors had been pricing in three likely cuts for 2024, based on earlier indications that Fed policymakers were anticipating their readiness to be less restrictive. It was even suggested that instead of a rate cut, the Fed might decide to impose a rate increase; analysts were torn by dueling circumstances for the path of U.S. interest rates and mixed signals for the future value of the dollar. "There is loads and loads of uncertainty," according to Benson Durham, head of global policy and asset allocation at Piper Sandler, as quoted in the *Financial Times*. "My base case has been similar to the Fed's base case for the last 18 months, but I can also see them cutting a lot faster under certain scenarios. I can also see them, for various reasons, adding another dollop."[30]

If the outlook for the U.S. economy is difficult to ascertain based on Fed signals regarding the future cost of capital, the exchange rate value of the U.S. dollar relative to other currencies is even more unpredictable. Given that financial volatility can intensify at warp speed, the potential for currency mismatches poses a threat to global financial stability. Because foreign companies that choose to borrow in dollars must repay in dollars, the risks from a strengthening dollar commensurately rise with an increase in dollar-denominated debt. Yet it seems doubtful that the potential for dramatic movements in foreign exchange markets figures prominently into the decision framework for FOMC members, who must decide whether or not to maintain a hawkish position against inflation even if recessionary forces begin to push back. It is only when foreign exchange bets gone wrong lead to widespread panic in currency markets that major central banks feel compelled to intervene—with the Federal Reserve necessarily involved.

An unexpectedly strong dollar could trigger massive defaults for borrowers abroad because it would make it more difficult for them to meet dollar-denominated debt obligations that have grown larger in terms of the local currency. If a foreign company receives most of its revenues in a currency that is depreciating against the dollar, repayment of dollar-denominated debt requires significantly higher revenues in the local currency; the debt becomes more expensive to service. According to the Bank for International Settlements, the total amount of U.S. dollar-denominated credit to non-banks outside the United States stood just below $13 trillion at the end of December 2023.[31] Moreover, additional massive amounts of dollar payment obligations—in the form of foreign exchange swaps, forwards, and currency swaps—do not appear on balance sheets and are missing from standard debt statistics. An alarming BIS report issued in December 2022 notes:

> Non-banks outside the United States owe as much as $25 trillion in such missing debt, up from $17 trillion in 2016. Non-US banks owe upwards of $35 trillion. Much of this debt is very short-term and the resulting rollover needs make for dollar funding squeezes. Policy responses to such squeezes include central bank swap lines that are set in a fog, with little information about the geographic distribution of the missing debt.[32]

When people do not have confidence in the future value of their currency and its impact on revenues—because they purchase inputs in a different currency, or have debts denominated in a different currency—they operate at a tremendous disadvantage. The differential monetary policies conducted by the world's central banks make business planning across borders more perilous. For emerging market competitors, a strengthening dollar that raises the cost of inputs and debt service might erase profits that would have resulted if exchange rates had remained stable. For Americans whose businesses involve selling exported goods in foreign markets, a stronger dollar directly undermines the competitiveness of their product or service; it has become more expensive when priced in the local currency of customers.

Indeed, for all participants who come in good faith to the global marketplace to engage in voluntary transactions, currency movements that compromise the price signals of competitive goods confound the logic of free markets. Mixed messages from central bank officials feature prominently in this type of uncertainty. Currencies can be pushed in different directions in response to market rumors about pending interest rate decisions. Bottom-line calculations of profitability can be wiped out in the aftermath of a press conference or speech given by the head of the Federal Reserve or the European Central Bank.

When Fed chair Jerome Powell stated in November 2022 that the U.S. central bank could scale back the pace of its interest rate hikes, it put the dollar index on track for its worst month since 2010; the dollar index had reached a twenty-year high just two months earlier.[33] Long after the Fed's target interest policy range had reached a presumed peak in July 2023, expectations for lower rates were dashed over concern that the next easing cycle would have to be delayed; it was feared that Fed officials might be forced to consider a rate hike because of insufficient progress on inflation. The fate of the dollar, already strong against the currencies of major trade partners, was left in limbo as markets awaited more data about consumer spending and the robustness of the economy. Whether the dollar would further strengthen was inextricably linked to the discretionary judgment of the monetary policy committee members who were scheduled to meet the next week—a slim reed for upholding a reliable money unit. But this pattern of uncertainty over the next interest rate decision spreading throughout global financial markets, including the market for foreign exchange, has persisted for many years. When former Fed chair Janet Yellen hinted in a speech in September 2015 that a long-awaited rise in interest rates was likely to happen before year-end, investors responded by focusing their attention on how to best position themselves for pending instability amid growing fears of deflationary pressures. "Sentiment is very negative at the moment," commented a bond fund manager to a *Financial Times* reporter. "The rules have changed. The uncertainty on how to assess Fed policy is throwing people into a loop."[34]

An Absence of Rules Begets Irrationality

Most people do not have time to follow every speech by a central bank official, let alone to react quickly to an extemporaneous comment that has market-moving implications. Planning for business or personal reasons is thus made more difficult by the lack of rules governing monetary policy. Only those specialists with enough financial acumen to interpret the prevaricating statements of monetary policy committee members stand to reap gains.

Just as it is not possible to ascertain in advance an interest rate change resulting from a decision made by central bank officials on a given day, it is also not possible to predict the future exchange rate between currencies affected by such monetary policy decisions. When corporate profitability can be undermined by currency effects, advance planning about where to build production facilities is no longer guided by considerations of comparative advantage. An executive who has been burned by currency losses might decide that the wiser strategy is to operate in a country where expenses and revenues are denominated in the same currency. Even if it costs more to produce the item in a country where it otherwise makes little business sense to operate, at least the revenues from selling the item within that same country will prevent losses from unexpected exchange rate movements.

Paul Volcker, whose own experience at the monetary helm as Fed chairman from 1979 to 1987 grants particular relevance to his insights, made the argument years ago that gyrating exchange rates are anathema to the benefits of free trade as envisioned by Adam Smith:

> The economic case for an open economic order rests, after all, largely on the idea that the world will be better off if international trade and investment follow patterns of comparative advantage; that countries and regions concentrate on producing what they can do relatively efficiently, taking account of their different resources, the supply and skills of their labor, and the availability of capital. But it is hard to see how business can effectively calculate where lasting comparative advantage lies when relative swings and prices among countries are subject to exchange rate swings of 25 to 50 percent or more. There is no sure or costless way of hedging against all uncertainties; the only sure beneficiaries are those manning the trading desks and inventing the myriad of new devices to reduce the risks—or to facilitate speculation.[35]

The key concept of comparative advantage is that there are benefits from specialization and free trade: countries gain when they trade the set of goods they can produce at lower cost for goods that can be produced at lower cost by other countries. As Smith wrote in *The Wealth of Nations*, "If a foreign country can supply us with a commodity cheaper than we ourselves can make it, better buy it of them with some part of the produce of our own industry, employed in a way in which we have some advantage."[36]

When the logic of comparative advantage is undone by currency movements prompted by differential monetary policies among central banks, business and investment decisions are distorted. Instead of seeking out the lowest-cost producer, companies adjust to the reality of currency instability by seeking to match expenses and revenues in a predictable way—sacrificing cost savings or higher revenues. To avoid currency mismatches, companies are deterred from rational business planning. Corporate "inversion" becomes a more serious problem for collecting taxes, as profits compiled in an overseas currency are not repatriated to the home country.

If currency stability were guaranteed by a mutually agreed set of rules to bring order to global monetary relations, multinational companies could focus on productivity instead of the cost of currency hedging. Although present at the Camp David meeting that brought about Nixon's decision to delink the dollar from its gold-convertibility obligations under the Bretton Woods agreement, Volcker offered this sober reflection some twenty years later:

> What can an exchange rate really mean in terms of everything a textbook teaches about rational economic decision making, when it changes by 30 percent or more in the space of twelve months only to reverse itself? What kind of signals does that send about where a businessman should intelligently invest his capital for long-term profitability? In the grand scheme of economic life first described by Adam Smith, in which nations like individuals should concentrate on the things they do best, how can anyone decide which country produces what most efficiently when the prices change so fast? The answer, to me, must be that such large swings are a symptom of a system in disarray.[37]

But if Volcker's lament was aimed at suggesting any kind of return to a rules-based exchange rate system, he would not find an ally for that cause in the multilateral organization that was originally established to oversee the Bretton Woods system. The International Monetary Fund (IMF), far from advocating fixed exchange rates, has abandoned the notion of an orderly system with regard to international monetary relations. A visit to the IMF website confirms that the former international monetary system based on fixed exchange rates anchored by gold convertibility is anathema to IMF requirements for member countries:

> Under an international monetary system of the kind prevailing on January 1, 1976, exchange arrangements may include (i) the maintenance by a member of a value for its currency in terms of the special drawing right or another denominator, other than gold, selected by the member, or (ii) cooperative arrangements by which members maintain the value of their currencies in relation to the value of the currency or currencies of other members, or (iii) other exchange arrangements of a member's choice.[38]

Financial stability can arise only from rational and comprehensible monetary arrangements, domestically and internationally. So long as the threat of a monetary breakdown looms over financial markets—causing investors to operate on a hair trigger for fear of being burned by a financial crash—worthwhile investment opportunities will be unable to secure the long-term financing that enables productive capital investment and genuine economic growth.

But calls to address the purely discretionary policy authority granted to central bankers to manipulate interest rates face stiff resistance—from the central bankers themselves. As early as 2015, challenges to the Federal Reserve's powers and its decisions were beginning to be put forward by powerful members of Congress. "One way our economy could be healthier is for the Federal Reserve to be more predictable in the conduct of monetary policy," Representative Jeb Hensarling, Republican chairman of the House Financial Services Committee, told Fed chief Janet Yellen in July 2015. "Today we're left with so-called 'forward guidance,' which unfortunately remains somewhat amorphous, opaque, and improvisational. Too often, this leads to investors and consumers being lost in a rather hazy mist as they attempt to plan their economic futures and create a healthier economy for themselves and for us all."[39]

Pursuing his concern that the Fed had become too powerful and too political, Hensarling held a subsequent hearing in June 2016 at which he stated to Yellen that a better way forward for the nation's central bank would be to ensure a "systematic monetary policy framework that is truly data dependent, consistent and predictable."⁴⁰ Hensarling's legislative initiative to implement several major reforms to the Federal Reserve—known as the Fed Oversight Reform and Modernization (FORM) Act—called for the Fed to improve transparency by choosing a mathematical model for making its policy decisions rather than conducting ad hoc monetary policy purely at its own discretion. If the Fed decided to stop following its policy rule, it could do so provided that it explained its reasoning to Congress. The thrust of the legislation was to gain bipartisan support for reducing uncertainty about the Fed's future interest rate decisions while not overly restricting its policy flexibility.

Stanford economist John Taylor, whose own rules-based model for conducting monetary policy is one of the most prominent frameworks put forward as an alternative to purely discretionary monetary policy, notes that the goal of reformers through history has been to prevent monetary shocks and reduce the chances of inflation, financial crises, and recession. "Their idea was that a simple monetary rule with little discretion could avoid monetary excesses whether due to government deficits, commodity discoveries, or mistakes by government."⁴¹ Citing the goal of determining monetary policy using rules instead of a more chaotic approach—whether the chaos was caused by the discretionary behavior of policymakers or exogenous economic shocks—Taylor suggests that rules-based monetary policy can help to achieve good macroeconomic performance both at the national level and for the global economy.⁴²

Responding to such proposals, monetary officials have voiced concerns that their hands would be tied if required to abide by a single rule. Yellen's response to the initiative put forward by Hensarling that would require the Federal Reserve to choose a rule for conducting monetary policy was decidedly negative.⁴³ Yellen also made it clear that she strongly opposed proposals to audit the Fed, asserting that doing so would constitute an incursion into the central bank's independence.⁴⁴

On the Federal Reserve's own website, the "challenges" associated with using rules to make monetary policy are evaluated in detail. The commentary reflecting the position of the Board of Governors notes that "some academic research on policy rules contends that tying monetary policy to a simple and unvarying policy rule could potentially enhance the effectiveness of monetary policy by helping guide households' and businesses' expectations of future economic and financial conditions."[45] But the Fed response is to state that "the central bank does not have to tie monetary policy to a simple rule to gain the benefits of managing expectations." Instead, according to the Fed note, to achieve the benefits of a policy rule, it is sufficient to indicate a commitment to explicit goals, in conjunction with policy transparency and clear communication that allow the public to understand how the central bank's policy actions relate to its goals.

Defending this position, the Fed commentary asserts that academic research in favor of using a rule to conduct monetary policy depends on numerous assumptions that "are unlikely to hold in the real world" and that such limitations argue against mechanically following any sort of rule:

> For example, this research assumes that the structure of the economy is well understood by policymakers and the public, and that the economy can be represented fairly accurately by a small number of equations. However, the true structure of the economy is not known for certain; it is highly complex, and the simple models used by researchers do not capture that complexity. Furthermore, in the real world, the structure of the economy changes over time, and those changes are not apparent immediately.[46]

The Fed's argument against following rules-based monetary policy actually invites the larger question of whether a small committee should be entrusted with broad powers to impact interest rates and the allocation of capital at all—given that the economy is indeed highly complex, difficult to model, and subject to dynamic changes over time. Former Fed chief Alan Greenspan told Gillian Tett in a *Financial Times* interview in October 2013 that the economic models used by leading financial institutions were seriously flawed; he contended that the 2008 global financial crisis was not anticipated because the models did not properly weight human behavior as a factor. Specifically, he suggested that humans did not always behave rationally: "Fear is a far more dominant force in human behaviour than euphoria."[47]

In his book *The Map and the Territory: Risk, Human Nature, and the Future of Forecasting*, Greenspan elaborates on the "almost universally unanticipated crisis of September 2008" as a time when modeling unequivocally failed.[48] "The Federal Reserve Board's highly sophisticated forecasting system did not foresee a recession until the crisis hit," Greenspan notes. Likewise, the model developed by the International Monetary Fund had concluded as late as spring 2007 that global economic risks had been declining; the U.S. economy was thought to be holding up well, and there were also encouraging signs elsewhere. Greenspan admits that he himself did not foresee the crash even the day before it occurred: "With the crisis less than twenty-four hours away, conventional wisdom had not yet coalesced around even the possibility of a typical recession, to say nothing of the worst economic crisis in eight decades."

Such unpredictability goes to one of the main justifications for having created the Federal Reserve—to have a lender of last resort capable of providing liquidity in the event of widespread financial panic. The awesome power of central banks to respond to this sort of catastrophe no doubt serves as both a relief and a concern to policymakers. Although it is uncomfortable to permit unelected government officials to wield authority over the disbursal of trillions in emergency funding on an ad hoc basis, it is frightening to contemplate what might have happened in 2008 had the Fed and Treasury not taken their unprecedented actions to address a global banking system that had largely seized up.

Having the authorization to perform as the lender of last resort does not require the Fed's constant presence in financial markets, though. The Fed should neither wield unwarranted influence over the banking sector nor play such a prominent role in allocating capital. The decisions taken by the governing board of a central bank exert far too much influence over national economic performance, impacting personal incomes and skewing the accumulation of wealth across society. There is no disputing the notion that the Federal Reserve exercises control over key variables that impact the redistribution of wealth. Monetary policy decisions inordinately reward owners of financial assets when the Fed engages in quantitative easing programs to keep interest rates deliberately repressed—even as those same accommodative financial conditions punish savers who receive low interest payments on bank savings accounts.

A key question is whether monetary policy would better achieve the goal of providing a stable foundation for productive economic growth if it were determined by a strict policy rule instead of relying on the purely discretionary judgment of monetary policy committee members. An excellent summary of this debate is provided by the Cato Institute's Norbert Michel in a February 2015 report wherein he argues that Congress should require the Federal Reserve to institute a rules-based monetary policy to reduce uncertainty:

> The Fed is completely free to judge both the direction of the economy and the appropriate monetary policy response. In general, if the Fed believes unemployment is too high or that there is a danger of deflation (a falling price level), it pursues expansionary policy by purchasing securities. If, on the other hand, the Fed believes unemployment is too low or that there is a danger of inflation, it follows a contractionary policy by selling securities. In any case, the Fed is not bound to implement expansionary or contractionary policies at any particular time using any particular benchmark.
>
> Defenders of this type of discretion-based policy claim that the enormous complexity of the ever-changing economy requires broad discretion, but the nature of the economy actually makes the case for rules-based policy. No one person—or small group of central bankers—can ever be expected to understand and react properly, much less to always act consistently, with respect to changing conditions throughout the economy. Rules-based monetary policy would actually reduce uncertainty because it would anchor people's expectations with respect to what the Fed will do on an ongoing basis.[49]

The argument for a rules-based approach connects back to the main conclusion of this chapter: stable money fosters productive growth. The corollary assertion is that productive growth is more beneficial to society than increased financialization of the economy. Raising the level of economic output, in the form of more goods produced and more services provided, serves to raise living standards for whole nations and enhance prosperity. Speculative investing in financial markets that seeks to profit from the monetary and exchange rate instability caused by discretionary decisions made by central bankers may generate high incomes, but it doesn't increase the size of the economic pie. Monetary policy would better serve the needs of the real economy by providing a dependable measure of value. This would facilitate budgetary calculations and assist in prudent financial planning—not only at kitchen tables but throughout the halls of government.

Life is uncertain enough without complicating the ability of people to survive, let alone thrive, by subjecting them to unpredictable policy decisions that confuse price signals and compromise the integrity of the monetary unit of account. Having access to money that provides a meaningful measure helps to clarify daily decisions. Having access to money that can be trusted helps to indemnify long-term planning. In contrast to being at the mercy of monetary officials who exercise discretionary power over the purchasing power of legal tender, the existence of a monetary rule—straightforward and inviolate— grants protection to citizens from government expropriation of their earnings.

3

Money Should Work Across Borders

HOW CAN THE United States pursue a domestic economic policy agenda that best serves its own interests while also meeting the challenges of international economic competition? We live in a global economy where markets for goods and services, including financial capital as well as commodities, span national boundaries, and rivals can ascend from every corner of the earth. Meaningful reform of the U.S. monetary system cannot take place in a vacuum; it will affect the entire world. The importance of America's money provides leverage to our nation in shaping how a new approach to trade that emphasizes the critical need for a level monetary playing field can lead to better economic outcomes. Propounding the potential gains from international trade while neglecting to address the unfair trade practices that undermine its logic makes for hollow rhetoric. We must first acknowledge how currency manipulation subverts the presumed advantages of an open global marketplace. Then it becomes clear that the lack of coherent monetary arrangements creates opportunities for nations to gain an unfair trade advantage by engaging in currency wars.

Debates in Congress over whether to move forward on trade agreements have foundered in the past on the issue of currency manipulation. Reverting to the imposition of tariffs can seem like the only effective method for countering deliberate currency depreciation by foreign trade partners. Currency manipulation is a bipartisan concern: Republicans team up with like-minded Democrats on whether they can support free trade in the absence of a level monetary playing field. Fervent free traders are pitted against skeptical protectionists in both parties when it comes to the question: Should governments be allowed to manipulate the value of their currencies in foreign exchange markets to achieve a trade advantage? I believe the answer is no. Economists might argue that any such advantage would prove to be only temporary, as the offending nation would ultimately experience domestic inflation over the longer run. But these temporal distinctions are not likely to matter much to the workers displaced by the unfair trade practice of currency manipulation. Manufacturing facilities are moved out of the United States, or factories permanently closed down, long before the impact of currency depreciation brings economic pain to the nation that launched it. According to a *Harvard Business Review* article, "offshore manufacturing is most promising when three conditions hold: the dollar is strong, foreign wages are low, and trade barriers are absent."[1] Surging imports from China and the resulting growing trade deficit with China had a key role in manufacturing job loss between 2001, when China entered the World Trade Organization, and 2018. The Economic Policy Institute, in a 2022 report, places the blame squarely on policy mistakes by the United States:

> The mismanaged integration of the United States into the global economy has devastated U.S. manufacturing workers and their communities. Globalization of our economy, driven by unfair trade, failed trade and investment deals, and, most importantly, currency manipulation and systematic overvaluation of the U.S. dollar over the past two decades, has resulted in growing trade deficits—the U.S. importing more than we export—that have eliminated more than five million U.S. manufacturing jobs and nearly 70,000 factories. These losses were accompanied by a shift toward lower-wage service-sector jobs with fewer benefits and lower rates of unionization than manufacturing jobs. The loss of jobs offering good wages and superior benefits for non-college-educated workers has narrowed a once viable pathway to the middle class.[2]

When currencies misrepresent the true value of goods and services, this misrepresentation makes a mockery of arguments extolling the benefits of free trade. It undermines the basic principles of free-market competition. We should not reject global trade and the economic opportunities it presents simply because we have not managed to work out rational monetary arrangements. The wiser approach would be to fix what's wrong. The debate over trade provides an opening to discuss the need for a rules-based international monetary system. Instead of targeting specific countries for tariffs in retaliation for currency manipulation, or simply applying a uniform tariff against all countries, we need to think bigger. The United States is in a uniquely powerful position to drive home the point that the case for free trade cannot be made without discussing the exchange rate regime.

The time has come to develop a comprehensive approach to international monetary reform that makes exchange rates conform to purchasing power parity—an approach that allows currencies to meaningfully quantify value across borders. If markets are to function properly, money needs to convey accurate price signals. That won't happen so long as exchange rates can be stage-managed by governments. Currency manipulation provides illegitimate access to global markets for duplicitous trade partners. It is time to recognize that "competitive devaluation" is not about competing—it's about cheating. The challenge for monetary reform is to resolve the fundamental dissonance between the principles of free trade and the global monetary disorder that mocks them.

One approach to resolving the problem of exchange rate misalignments would be to create a global currency—or adopt one that has arisen spontaneously, such as Bitcoin—so that all parties to a transaction would be using the same monetary unit of account to value goods and services. Another approach might be to encourage every nation to make its currency convertible at a fixed rate into a single common denominator asset that is universally accepted. The result in either case would be to provide a common currency based on a common reference point for measuring value, which would enable the proper functioning of supply-and-demand mechanisms through price signaling.

There's a sticking point, however, even for those who embrace the concept of leveling the monetary playing field: What guarantee can be put into place to ensure that the system won't be compromised by government intervention? Could an alternative private money come into widespread use without hazarding the imposition of restrictions through increased government regulation and legal tender prohibitions? Then, too, many people are rightly concerned that moving toward a common currency would spur calls for increased global cooperation and enliven a movement toward world government. After all, problems among eurozone member countries often lead to suggestions for more centralization of fiscal resources, which in turn requires more consolidated governmental authority over countries using the euro.

It doesn't have to be that way. Instead of creating powerful new supranational monetary institutions or enhancing the authority of existing multilateral financial institutions, any new approach to defining a common currency unit should empower individuals with genuine monetary autonomy. For the first time since the days of the classical international gold standard, every citizen would enjoy the same benefits of monetary sovereignty as the sovereigns themselves. Just as any individual, prince or pauper, could redeem gold on demand in exchange for the requisite amount of currency, a new common currency approach would accord with rules of convertibility that applied to all. Unlike the Bretton Woods international monetary system, which granted gold convertibility of U.S. dollars only to foreign central banks and governments, a new system would grant convertibility privileges to all participants. Moreover, offering to redeem currency in gold would be neither the monopoly privilege nor the singular burden of any one country.

Such a bold approach assumes that gold convertibility at the option of the money holder would be a necessary feature of any new arrangement. Yet that doesn't have to be the case; it might be possible to merely designate a reference asset as the common denominator acceptable to those utilizing a particular currency. Buyer and seller would acknowledge that at the moment of a transaction, the designated reference asset would serve as the numeraire—a benchmark for comparing the value of similar products or financial instruments—for purposes of expressing prices. If the asset tended to have a stable value, it could perform the store-of-value function of money and also serve as a unit of account and medium of exchange.

The potential to design a more logical system for aligning currencies seems quite promising in the face of today's awkward reality. Transactions for goods and services are conducted across national borders, and financial resources are transmitted instantly around the world, even as people in different countries must wrestle with the complications and increased costs of using different currencies. The Bretton Woods system collapsed some fifty years ago. Some of the great minds in economics have channeled their prodigious talents into contemplating how best to align currencies in keeping with free-market principles and free trade—and they come up with altogether different frameworks. Renowned theorists such as Robert Mundell and Milton Friedman have shaped the academic debate over whether fixed or fluctuating exchange rates among currencies lead to better outcomes, with both approaches seeking to define an exchange rate regime that reaps the gains of comparative advantage in keeping with Adam Smith's model for increasing the wealth of nations. In some ways, it could be said that Friedman prevailed and the world switched to floating exchange rates after the end of the Bretton Woods system. But it could also be argued that Mundell's theory that some regions might be better off using a common currency rather than having each country issue its own currency provided the template for the creation of the euro, which is now used by more than 350 million people across twenty countries that are part of the European Union.

So while both men put forward viable approaches for addressing currency chaos in the absence of a mechanism for convertibility—such as had earlier existed under the classical international gold standard and the Bretton Woods gold exchange system—history has shown that tackling the fundamental problem is not the same as solving it. For all the influence both these economists have exerted over real-world developments, the exchange rate dilemma continues to plague investment and trade relations across borders, for advanced as well as emerging economies. Hybrid solutions that involve deliberate intervention by governments in currency markets violate the basic tenets of a floating rate system and further compound the distortions that arise from monetary disorder and misleading price signals. Central banks have a starring role in the shifting currency narrative that changes the terms of trade among countries—even as monetary policymakers are careful to maintain plausible deniability.

In short, the brilliantly argued views put forth by Friedman and Mundell have provided only partial solutions for the real world, and their efficacy has eroded over time as governments have found ways to avoid the inherent parameters of the model. For example, a government's piling up of reserves for defending the currency negates the premise that free-market forces are determining the currency's exchange value against other currencies—so much for freely floating rates. Consider, too, that a common currency goes further than fixed rates in aligning currencies. So if the euro makes sense for member nations belonging to the European Union, because it eliminates currency risk for internal trade and financial transactions among them, it would seem reasonable to consider whether the same logic for having a shared currency might also apply to the global economy.

Yet for many, including myself, the notion of a global central bank is repellent. Instead of pushing for a global common currency managed by a supranational monetary authority, I would argue that we should move control of the money supply in the opposite direction—granting to individuals the autonomous right to enlarge or contract the money supply through the privilege of gold convertibility. The money supply would expand or contract with each decision by an individual to convert his or her holdings of cash into gold, or vice versa, depending on that person's own sense of whether credit conditions were getting frothy or too restrictive. Convertibility offers a more organic way to calibrate the level of money and credit to the needs of the real economy and has the additional benefit of being the ultimate rules-based approach, with the only rule being the established rate of convertibility that defines the value of the money unit. Convertibility at the option of the holder thus provides a way to avoid the uncertainty of having to decipher the intentions of monetary officials to gain insights about the future value of money. Convertibility provides an alternate route to depending on a small group of monetary policy officials who have been granted discretionary powers to move interest rates and impact the purchasing power of money while lacking full knowledge about the minute-to-minute dynamics occurring within the economy they seek to manage.

Mundell Versus Friedman

The appropriate intellectual background for preparing to meet the challenge of sound money is to gain familiarity with the competing approaches of Friedman and Mundell and to reconcile the points of disagreement that stratified economists into warring camps. The irony, as we will discover, is that these great thinkers would come ever closer to reaching consensus in their later writings. Much can be gleaned, however, from reading their earlier works and analyzing their points of disagreement. Friedman and Mundell conducted a series of debates through email correspondence published by Canada's *National Post* newspaper that is particularly informative in this regard; their differing views provide a touchstone throughout this chapter. The crux of their argument was whether floating or fixed rates better served economic performance in accordance with free-market ideals.

Originally from Canada, Robert Alexander Mundell won the Nobel Prize in economics in 1999 and is considered to have been a visionary in world monetary affairs. The Royal Swedish Academy of Sciences cited his "uncommon—almost prophetic—accuracy in predicting the future development of international monetary arrangements and capital markets."[3] Mundell is often cited for laying the intellectual groundwork for establishing a single European currency. He is also considered the architect of "supply-side" economics, which defined the monetary and fiscal policies implemented during the Reagan administration in the 1980s—and which are credited for the U.S. turnaround from economic stagflation.

These broad theoretical constructs from Mundell have something in common: they are consistent with preventing governments from intervening in the economy. Mundell's scholarly work supported political initiatives with real-world consequences. The goal of creating a common currency was to prevent politicians from indulging in monetary stimulus to temporarily juice growth. "It puts monetary policy out of the reach of politicians," Mundell explained to a journalist.[4] Moreover, creating a common currency would help to curb the government from engaging in regulatory excess and overspending, according to Mundell. "Monetary discipline forces fiscal discipline on the politicians as well."

One can thus see that proposing a new currency for Europe that would prevent governments from engaging in fiscal profligacy through monetary manipulation involves thinking analogous to that behind the basic pillars of "Reaganomics." The goals of Reagan's economic program were to cut the growth of government spending, reduce income taxes, downsize the regulatory burden, and stifle inflation by restricting the growth of the money supply. "Only by reducing the growth of government," affirmed Ronald Reagan, "can we increase the growth of the economy."[5] Prohibiting the use of the monetary printing press to finance deficit spending would motivate politicians to find pragmatic solutions for economic problems while pursuing a balanced budget.

The uncertainty associated with rising inflation had to be addressed to prevent fear of the unknown from paralyzing the private sector.

Mundell came to his policy recommendations by way of a scholarly examination of the interplay of fiscal and monetary policy. Mundell constructed a framework for examining monetary and fiscal policy outcomes under different exchange rate regimes; he focused on how cross-border commerce was affected by the currency exchange rate between trade partner countries. In short, he launched the modern field of international macroeconomics and spurred new thinking on the role of international capital flows in determining economic performance.

The breakthrough fostered by Mundell stems from his academic journal articles in the 1960s, which introduced a model of an economy with two markets: one for goods and services, one for foreign exchange. Mundell then demonstrates through the model that monetary policy is powerful and fiscal policy is powerless in affecting economic output under two conditions: (1) the exchange rate is floating, and (2) there is perfect capital mobility—that is, no capital controls or restrictions. Mundell then goes on to demonstrate that when (1) the exchange rate is fixed and (2) there is perfect capital mobility, fiscal policy is powerful and monetary policy is powerless.

Mundell concluded that countries faced what he called the "impossible trinity," or "trilemma," in combining monetary and fiscal policy options. Mundell's hypothesis states that a country may choose only two out of the three goals of (1) monetary independence, (2) exchange rate stability, and (3) financial integration. Although a floating exchange rate ensures monetary policy autonomy and permits financial openness, one loses exchange rate stability. A fixed exchange rate provides exchange rate stability and is consistent with financial openness but takes away monetary independence, because it restricts the domestic policy options of the central bank. Finally, although it's theoretically possible to have activist monetary policy while maintaining a fixed exchange rate, that combination doesn't work with open financial capital markets.[6]

Imposing capital controls is a perilous route to pursue because it cuts off countries from the benefits of globalized financial capital flows. Economic growth can be enhanced when financial resources flow into a country, augmenting domestic savings, because total factor productivity increases through more efficient resource allocation. Financial openness exposes countries to economic instability, however, as investment money flows in quickly, only to be withdrawn when interest rate conditions change elsewhere in the world. Countries that pursue financial openness thus have to be prepared for potentially rapid capital flight. Many seek to insure against this sort of volatility by accumulating international reserves—in the form of gold and major foreign currencies, mainly the dollar and euro—for intervening in foreign exchange markets. Because the impact of cross-border financial flows can critically impact emerging market economies, nations have become more concerned about having sufficient preventive measures against financial volatility, rather than trade volatility.

But what level of reserves is considered sufficient, and what constitutes excessive reserve accumulation? The definition matters because nations seen to be stockpiling foreign reserves in amounts beyond what is deemed sufficient can be accused of currency manipulation. If countries wish to claim they have a floating rate regime, why should the government accumulate any reserves at all? Theoretically, the free-market interplay of demand and supply for a given currency should be the only determinant of the exchange rate. Yet many countries are afraid to abide by a fully floating approach due to the vulnerabilities imposed by fickle capital flows. Does that mean a country should resort to capital controls when foreign investment threatens to disrupt the nation's economic plans or cause too much financial instability?

The dilemma—or trilemma, in Mundell's parlance—is that fixed rates might be the better option for smaller countries. Whether they fix to the dollar or euro, they could participate in the stability of the larger currency area and enjoy the cross-border benefits without having to wrestle with exchange rate movements. In Mundell's view, the best of all worlds results when both small and large countries adopt fixed exchange rates—as could happen with an improved Bretton Woods system. Mundell asserts that monetary sovereignty is less important than the economic advantages of participating in a stable monetary regime. "There was nothing fundamentally wrong with the kind of monetary system we had in the postwar world," according to Mundell. It is a mistake to encourage countries to move to flexible rates— "balkanizing the monetary world into a ridiculously large number of tiny currency areas."[7]

One could point out that being opposed to having a huge number of tiny currency areas does not mean that only a single global currency is the answer. It was Mundell, after all, who justified the euro through his theory of "optimal currency areas," where high labor and capital mobility and similar business cycles exist. A world that utilized, say, two or three major regional currencies might be seen by Mundell as an improvement over having disparate forms of money put forward by myriad issuers.

Still, the ultimate answer for maximizing the benefits of free trade and unimpeded capital flows would be to have a global currency, Mundell suggested. Trying to separate economic effects from pure currency distortions made no sense for an integrated global marketplace, as he asserted in his 1971 book, *Monetary Theory: Inflation, Interest, and Growth in the World Economy.*[8] Mundell reiterated his viewpoint in a 2010 interview (conducted by me) that was published in the *Wall Street Journal*, stating: "The whole idea of having a free trade area when you have gyrating exchange rates doesn't make sense at all. It just spoils the effect of any kind of free trade agreement."[9]

Milton Friedman also supported the notion that free-trade principles are best served when buyers and sellers conduct transactions on the basis of a unified currency, especially in his later observations following decades of government intervention in foreign exchange markets under the supposed regime of freely floating rates. As Terence Corcoran, who organized the intellectual debate between these two Nobel economists published in late 2000 in the *National Post*, wrote:

> Both are staunch advocates of free markets and free trade, low taxes and less government. But one core issue has divided them for decades: exchange rates. The shorthand version of their disagreement is that Professor Friedman favours the flexible exchange rate regime adopted by Canada; Professor Mundell insists on the merits of fixed rates and currency unification. How can two economists who share so many views hold such different ideas on currencies?[10]

Friedman considered it expedient to let the exchange rate serve as a cushion when internal prices for a nation were unlikely to adjust to external pressures. Friedman thought it simpler to let one thing change—the value of a nation's currency in foreign exchange markets—rather than to force countless adjustments in domestic prices and wages. Friedman explained:

> The argument for flexible exchange rates is, strange to say, very nearly identical with the argument for daylight savings time. Isn't it absurd to change the clock in summer when exactly the same result could be achieved by having each individual change his habits? All that is required is that everyone decide to come to his office an hour earlier, have lunch an hour earlier, etc. But obviously it is much simpler to change the clock that guides all than to have each individual change his pattern of reaction to the clock, even though all want to do so. The situation is exactly the same in the exchange market. It is far simpler to allow one price to change, namely the price of foreign exchange, than to rely upon changes in the multitude of prices that together constitute the internal price structure.[11]

Friedman thought Mundell would likely agree with him about the analogy. But although Mundell was unfailingly courteous, he was not an accommodating intellectual foe. Responding to Friedman, Mundell refuted the notion that an exchange rate is an effective cushion against real shocks. He further argued that exchange rate flexibility is no substitute for price flexibility and called the time zone analogy a "seductive half-truth" that did not apply to economics:

> If wages and prices get out of line, it is argued, it is easier to accept the fait accompli and restore international competitiveness by changing the exchange rate than it is to lower wages and prices, just as it is easier to shift to daylight-saving time than it is to make people adjust their habits by an hour. But the analogy has a fatal flaw. The change in the exchange rate will introduce expectations of future changes and set in motion further wage and price movements that start the country down the slippery slope of inflation The physical universe is very different: setting the clocks back does not change the position of the sun![12]

Mundell took the position that a fixed exchange rate system was better than having currency exchange rates serve as the shock absorber for economic adjustments. He believed that fixed exchange rates could allow monetary authorities to exercise some discretion in their domestic monetary operations but would still permit the adjustment mechanism to work. "A deficit in the balance of payments requires sales of foreign exchange reserves to keep the currency from depreciating, and this sale automatically reduces the money base of the financial system, setting in motion a decline in expenditure that shifts demand away from imports and exportable goods and corrects the deficit. An analogous process occurs in the opposite direction to eliminate a surplus," Mundell explained.[13] He noted that major countries (with the exception of Canada) practiced this system during the Bretton Woods era—specifically citing Germany, Japan, Italy, and Mexico as examples of countries that were able to keep fixed exchange rates in equilibrium for most of the period between 1950 and 1970. Noting that the Bretton Woods system evolved from an adjustable peg system, in its early years, into a "virtual fixed exchange rate system," monetary economist Michael Bordo points out:

> Between 1949 and 1967, there were very few changes in parities
> of the G10 countries. The only exceptions were the Canadian
> float in 1950, devaluations by France in 1957 and 1958, and mi-
> nor revaluations by Germany and the Netherlands in 1961. The
> adjustable peg system became less adjustable because, on the basis
> of the 1949 experience, the monetary authorities were unwilling
> to accept the risks associated with discrete changes in parities—
> loss of prestige, the likelihood that others would follow, and the
> pressure of speculative capital flows if even a hint of a change in
> parity were present.[14]

Mundell argues that a reformed international monetary system in the twenty-first century could work successfully by borrowing certain concepts from the Bretton Woods accord, including the use of gold as a reserve asset. "There was nothing fundamentally wrong with the kind of monetary system we had in the postwar world," he states.[15] Bretton Woods broke down, in his opinion, because the United States was not willing to revalue gold in the wake of excess spending in the 1960s and resultant inflationary pressures; thus, prices stated in dollars in 1971 were no longer in conformance with the earlier rate of convertibility. Mundell believes that if the U.S. had revalued gold, the system might have continued for an additional two or three decades.

It would seem to defeat the notion of a stable international monetary system, however, if the United States could simply revalue gold in terms of dollars. If the original commitment to convert thirty-five dollars into one ounce of gold when so requested by a foreign central bank could be unilaterally altered by the nation that issued the "anchor" currency, the credibility of the international monetary agreement would necessarily be weakened—and confidence in the viability of the system would thereby be undermined.

So what does that suggest about what could be done today to restore some kind of stable international monetary system to facilitate world trade and finance? Clearly, certain requirements would need to be imposed on nations wishing to participate. The world's major currencies were most responsible for wreaking havoc with global economic performance, according to Mundell. He sought to alleviate the disturbances caused by big movements in exchange rates by concentrating on the largest currency issuers. "The most important initiative you could take to improve the world economy would be to stabilize the dollar-euro rate," Mundell believed.[16] Pointing out that the dollar and euro together represented 40 percent of the world economy, Mundell suggested that the European Central Bank, along with the Federal Reserve, should intervene in currency markets to limit movement in the world's single most important exchange rate. Once the dollar-euro exchange rate was stabilized, Mundell thought it would be possible to extend the stable monetary platform to other important currencies, including ones issued by major Asian countries.

In an interview with Bloomberg Television in 2011, Mundell went so far as to propose a role for gold as a reserve asset that could be traded among central banks at a fixed price in "a kind of Bretton Woods type of gold standard" that would capture the discipline of a gold-anchored international monetary system:

> The great advantage of that was that gold is nobody's liability and it can't be printed. So it has a strength and confidence that people trust. So if you had not just the United States but the United States and the euro tied together to each other and to gold, gold might be the intermediary and then with the other important currencies like the yen and Chinese yuan and British pound all tied together as a kind of new SDR [Special Drawing Right] that could be one way the world could move forward on a better monetary system.[17]

One important difference from the Bretton Woods system would be the absence of a singularly powerful nation willing to have its currency function as the central reserve asset for maintaining an international monetary arrangement. The United States fulfilled that role in the post–World War II decades, but Mundell suggested that the power configuration had changed—and it would not be possible to forge a monetary system with the dollar as the key reserve currency. "To be fair, America's position is not nearly as strong now, but what has disappointed me is the reluctance of the U.S. to take into account this big movement in the rest of the world to do something about restoring stability to the international monetary system," Mundell noted.[18] He attributed the policy initiative deficit to a lack of both intellectual creativity and political will. "I don't think the U.S. has any ideas, they don't have strong leadership on the international economic side," he said in October 2010. "There hasn't been anyone in the administration for a long time who really knows much about the international monetary system."

What about the earlier question of how two giants in the field of economics, Mundell and Friedman, could have such different views on what constitutes the best exchange rate regime for the world economy? As it turns out, Friedman eventually conceded that a global economy would best be served by a "unified" currency. Friedman would forever remain suspicious about a fixed exchange rate administered by central bankers; under pressure, he was sure they would always resort to monetary activism and exercise discretionary authority. He favored orthodox currency boards for smaller nations, however, that would fix the local currency to the currency of a large, stable developed country. Friedman endorsed currency unification for newly independent former Soviet bloc nations in the 1990s, fixing to the German mark or the U.S. dollar. He wrote glowingly about Hong Kong's currency board system (introduced in 1983), which operated without any central bank and was fixed to the U.S. dollar.

What Friedman vehemently objected to was any kind of "pegged" rate system requiring (or allowing) government intervention conducted through monetary authorities:

> In my opinion, a system of pegged exchange rates among national currencies is worse than either extreme: a truly unified cur-

rency, or national currencies linked by freely floating exchange
rates. The reason is that national central banks will not, under
modern conditions, be permitted to shape their policies solely to
keep exchange rates at the agreed level. Pressure to use monetary
policy for domestic purposes will from time to time be irresist-
ible. When that occurs, the exchange system becomes unstable.
Pegged rates can be maintained for a time by governmentally
arranged capital flows, by foreign-exchange controls, or by restrictions on international trade, but these are only temporary
expedients and generally lead to the conversion of minor problems into major crises.[19]

Friedman saw the Bretton Woods system as a pegged exchange rate approach, whereas Mundell differentiated it from a system that would allow a
central bank to peg the exchange rate without giving any priority to maintaining equilibrium in the balance of payments. Mundell concurred with
Friedman that fixing the exchange rate in the absence of policy commitment
to maintaining parity was undesirable and left the currency vulnerable to
speculators. Mundell stated that he would never advocate a general system of
pegged rates, because such systems always break down. Still, Mundell believed
that fixed rates could be successfully implemented by larger countries without
resorting to a currency board or monetary union, adding, "and I would say
that the Bretton Woods arrangements proved that, as did the gold standard
in the past."[20]

For his part, Friedman acknowledged in 1994 the virtues of a gold standard and a monetary system controlled by a single independent central
bank, even as he maintained his strong opposition to a system of pegged
exchange rates among national currencies. "A true gold standard—a unified currency—is indeed consistent with free trade," Friedman wrote in an
essay for *National Review* entitled "Free-Floating Anxiety" that coincided
with the fiftieth anniversary of the Bretton Woods conference. Friedman
concluded, "The lesson is that for any group of economic entities to have a
unified currency, there can be at most one independent central bank. ('At
most,' because with a pure commodity standard, e.g., a gold standard, no
central bank is needed.)"[21]

Currency Malfeasance

If the appropriate currency platform to maximize economic gains from international trade is a level monetary playing field utilizing as a reference point some kind of common unit of account, currency manipulation is clearly a suboptimal approach. Yet even as we recognize currency manipulation as a serious abrogation of free-trade principles, the world's major central banks breezily dismiss its impact as an unintended consequence of their domestic monetary policy. It clearly matters whether decisions by monetary authorities cause the value of a currency to sink—or soar—relative to a trading partner's currency. Indeed, such decisions change the terms of trade. And because these decisions do matter, the question is raised whether it is possible to differentiate between deliberate currency warfare and spillover effects claimed to be incidental.

The rationale for fixing exchange rates rather than permitting nations to gain a trade advantage by devaluing their currencies was provided in a 1942 draft memorandum by Harry Dexter White, a senior U.S. Treasury Department official whose concepts had a dominant influence on the design of the Bretton Woods system:

> The advantages of obtaining stable exchange rates are patent. The maintenance of stable exchange rates means the elimination of exchange risk in international economic and financial transactions. The cost of conducting foreign trade is thereby reduced and capital flows much more easily to the country where it yields the greatest return because both short-term and long-term investments are greatly hampered by the probability of loss from exchange depreciation. As the expectation of continued stability in foreign exchange rates is strengthened there is also more chance of avoiding the disrupting effects of flights of capital and of inflation.[22]

When sliding exchange rates undermine the supposed benefits of an open global marketplace, there is much to lose in terms of unnecessary costs as well as lost opportunities. Textbook arguments in favor of free trade and capital flows come up against the reality of currency movements that alter economic outcomes. Yet even though unstable exchange rates have damaging financial effects and subtract value from the world economy as a whole, individual nations seem willing to engage in this practice. The operative word is "seem," because it is difficult to define when deliberate devaluation—as opposed to monetary policy actions that are taken in pursuit of domestic economic objectives—is taking place.

For a U.S. auto worker, the careful terms used by economists and politicians to frame currency manipulation are likely to come across as palaver. American workers who accept the challenge of competing globally are all too aware that exchange rate movements can tilt the sales outlook in favor of producers whose national currencies have weakened. Consider the situation between Japanese and American competitors during the three years from 2012 to 2015, when the value of the yen to the dollar dropped from roughly 80 yen to 120 yen to the dollar. The effect was to boost the price of goods exported to Japan from the United States by some 50 percent while slashing the price of Japanese imports in U.S. markets. "What I know about the auto industry is that they can out-compete any of their competitors," asserted Debbie Dingell, the U.S. representative for a Michigan district that includes a manufacturing hub for the automotive industry. "But they can't out-compete the Bank of Japan and the Japanese government."[23]

Many supporters of free trade are quick to promote sweeping trade agreements that remove tariffs while neglecting to confront the problem of exchange rate movements that impact price competition. Currency manipulation is clearly an unfair practice that undermines the accepted principles and fundamental logic of free trade based on comparative advantage. Automotive workers deserve to compete in foreign markets without having the price of U.S. cars hiked up through monetary sleight of hand. Nor is it fair that cars produced in countries that cheapen their currency appear more competitively priced in U.S. markets.

U.S. lawmakers were caught off guard when, in 2015, the issue of currency manipulation rose to the top of concerns over proceeding toward a major trade agreement that would govern America's relationship with Japan and ten other Pacific nations—a region encompassing some eight hundred million people and roughly 40 percent of the world economy. Efforts to pass legislation, called Trade Promotion Authority, that would simplify congressional approval of future trade agreements went beyond the usual political wrangling, as proposals were linked to satisfy lawmakers seeking worker compensation for those displaced by foreign trade competition. But as different ploys for adopting the trade agreement made their twist-and-turn procedural route through Congress, the issue of currency manipulation kept coming up, as a surprisingly bipartisan concern.

In the Senate, a bill jointly sponsored by Republican senator Rob Portman of Ohio and Democratic senator Debbie Stabenow of Michigan sought to impose enforceable currency rules as part of any future trade agreements. Although the proposed legislation failed in a close vote of 48–51, it caught the attention of the *Wall Street Journal*, which reported that "the deepest and most difficult divide in the congressional trade fight has little to do with tariffs, workers or U.S. policy. Instead, it's all about exchange rates."[24]

Perhaps most remarkable was not just the consensus across party lines on the need to address currency manipulation but also the powerful intellectual arguments that emerged. Arthur Laffer, an American economist strongly associated with the conservative supply-side economic programs enacted under President Reagan, produced a well-researched monograph arguing that countries engaged in currency manipulation "as part of a long-term, export-driven growth tactic" gained an unfair economic advantage at the expense of their trading partners. As a condition for pursuing the Trans-Pacific Partnership trade agreement, which was behind the push for Trade Promotion Authority, Laffer recommended the inclusion of "defined monetary policy standards and a means to identify currency manipulators and enforce violations." He proposed that the following three questions should constitute the test for determining whether a country (over a specifically defined period) has been guilty of currency manipulation:

- Did the nation have a current account surplus over the six-month period in question?
- Did it add to its foreign exchange reserves over that same six-month period?
- Are its foreign exchange reserves more than sufficient (i.e., greater than three months normal imports)?[25]

Despite the fact that Laffer has long been a proponent of free trade and a highly respected policy guru to Republicans, his views closely aligned with

Democratic political leaders such as New York senator Chuck Schumer. Whether Democrats or Republicans held the White House, Schumer asserted that his measure for cracking down on currency manipulators needed to be part of any trade agenda going forward. "What we've got now is a tough currency bill that doesn't require the OK of the administration because both the Bush administration and this administration have refused in this instance to protect the American workers by citing China for currency manipulation, even though everyone knows they're doing it."[26]

The ideal pro-growth economic program definitely includes free trade—but also includes stable exchange rates to ensure a level monetary playing field across borders. This invites the question, How do we identify and prevent competitive depreciation? A nation's direct intervention into foreign exchange markets may be seen as prima facie evidence of tampering with its currency's exchange rate, yet that same nation might argue that it is endeavoring to stabilize its exchange rate with a major trading partner. How can that argument be reconciled with either Mundell's approach or Friedman's? Another nation might forswear actual intervention in the market through buying or selling yet through its activist monetary policy bring about the same result as if it had dumped its own currency in foreign exchange markets.

In any case, when the outcome is a change in the exchange rate from what it would have been without government intervention—whether conducted through the government's Treasury Department, its central bank, or both—it is appropriate to raise the question of currency manipulation. For example, from the 1960s to the mid-1990s, the Fed and the Treasury intervened in currency markets on numerous occasions.[27] The height of intervention occurred in 1985, when U.S. Secretary of the Treasury James Baker pursued deliberate depreciation of the dollar against other major currencies, chiefly the Japanese yen and the German deutsche mark, through the Plaza Accord—a secret agreement to choreograph the massive sale of dollars in currency markets. U.S. manufacturers and agricultural interests at the time were complaining to officials in Washington that they were being unfairly squeezed by competition in world markets because of the strong dollar; it was considered overvalued at 263 yen and 3.44 deutsche marks. The resulting brute force of joint intervention caused the dollar to drop like a stone, with the collusive actions bringing about a shift so dramatic that the United States was compelled to launch another coordinated effort less than two years later to manipulate the value of the dollar in world currency markets. The goal in 1987 was to stop the dollar's further decline from the now prevailing rates of 1.83 deutsche marks and 154 yen to the dollar.

While the immediate effectiveness of the intervention effort through foreign exchange operations seems impressive, many economists and officials remained doubtful that intervention to actively depreciate the dollar could bring about sustained effects on exchange rates or could meaningfully change investment and trade relationships. Yet over time, it has also become apparent that China's massive and sustained intervention to hold its currency down has enabled that nation to maintain large account surpluses for years. In 2015, exactly thirty years after the Plaza Accord, a conference moderated by former Treasury Secretary Baker brought together numerous experts to reflect on currency policy and whether views had changed during the intervening years.[28] Commenting on foreign exchange intervention since the 1980s, Joseph Gagnon from the Peterson Institute for International Economics made the following observation:

> At the time of the Plaza Agreement there was widespread skepticism that foreign exchange intervention was a potent tool for managing exchange rates and current account imbalances. Now we know that intervention is effective—it just takes far larger magnitudes of intervention than anyone (except the Japanese) was willing to contemplate in the 1980s. Massive purchases of foreign assets by governments have been a key driver of the unprecedented current account imbalances since 2000. …
>
> The case for new and forceful rules to limit official flows is persuasive. We need them not only to help counter market excesses, but also to prevent a devastating round of beggar-thy-neighbor devaluations in the next global recession. This is no time for complacency.[29]

For the most part, the United States has stopped intervening directly in the foreign exchange market to reduce or increase the value of the dollar. According to the Federal Reserve Bank of New York, the United States has intervened on only three separate occasions since 1996: a purchase of Japanese yen in June 1998, a purchase of euros in September 2000, and a sale of Japanese yen in March 2011.[30] One might therefore take the position that America does not attempt to manipulate the value of its currency to achieve a trade advantage in the global marketplace. Yet when the Federal Reserve began its successive rounds of quantitative easing—purchasing bonds in massive quantities, flooding banks with reserves, and pumping additional credit into the system through its zero interest rate policy—U.S. trade partners began yelling foul. Brazil's finance minister declared that America and other wealthy countries were engaged in a "currency war" as they sought to mitigate their economic troubles through monetary stimulus. Low interest rates in highly developed nations were driving yield-seeking investors to pour capital into emerging market nations, such as Brazil, pushing up the value of their currencies and making their exports more expensive in foreign markets.

But if direct interventions and aggressive monetary stimulus policies are both potential ways to devalue currency and gain a trade advantage—whether intentionally or as an incidental consequence—what approach is most rational for addressing the problem of currency manipulation? If it were possible to remove these influences from foreign exchange markets, would the resulting interaction between those who wish to exchange one brand of money for another, whether for trade or investment purposes, reflect the interplay of demand and supply? In other words, what is the ideal free-market approach for determining the relative values of currencies?

Let's take a look at the foreign exchange market itself. Currencies are traded in a global decentralized market—also called the forex, FX, or currency market—wherein the main participants are multinational banks. The foreign exchange market is the largest market in the world in terms of volume; turnover in global FX markets reached $7.5 trillion per day in April 2022, a volume that is thirty times greater than the daily global GDP.[31] Trading activity is concentrated in a few major currencies and mostly takes place in the five trading hubs that are major financial centers. The U.S. dollar is the single most traded currency, involved in nearly 90 percent of global transactions; the euro has a share of roughly 30 percent, with the Japanese yen and the British pound also featuring prominently in trades (as two currencies are involved in every transaction, the sum of shares in individual currencies totals 200 percent). Emerging market currencies have risen in recent years, with China's renminbi increasing to a 7 percent share of global FX turnover.[32]

Why do individuals and organizations trade currencies? In the absence of a common global currency, it's evident that cross-border trade requires convertibility between currencies. Sellers generally want to receive payment in the currency they use for their own needs; buyers must therefore convert their own currency into the seller's currency to pay for purchases. Similarly, investors who wish to place financial resources in a country outside their own need to exchange currencies. So it makes sense that a market would exist to facilitate the conversion of one type of money into another type of money— similar to cashing in chips at a casino—to enable parties using different currencies to carry out commercial and financial transactions.

But this task is hardly the reason the foreign exchange market has boomed. The bread-and-butter function of converting currencies for purposes of trade or long-term investment is a relatively minor part of the foreign exchange market. The overwhelming motivation for participating in global FX markets is speculation. The largest players in the foreign exchange market are commercial banks, but central banks also participate through currency interventions—buying or selling their own money in an attempt to make their currency appreciate or depreciate. Portfolio managers, pooled funds, and hedge funds constitute another influential category of foreign exchange market players; they may trade currencies to purchase foreign securities or to engage in purely speculative trades. Corporations use the foreign exchange market both to pay for goods and services and also as a hedge for future transactions; currency hedging helps to protect business plans from foreign currency exposure risk. Individuals round out the group of currency market participants; their volume of trade is extremely low compared with that of banks and hedge funds, but the FX market provides an increasingly popular "investment" activity for day traders.

How well does this immense foreign exchange market comport with our notions of how best to reconcile supply and demand for currencies at any given point in time? One warning sign that something is amiss in the forex market is the fact that five global banks were required to pay more than $5 billion in penalties and plead guilty to criminal charges in May 2015 for colluding to manipulate the price of dollars and euros.[33] Citigroup, Barclays, JP Morgan Chase, and Royal Bank of Scotland Group utilized online chat rooms and communicated in code to influence the exchange rate market benchmarks established twice daily. Brazenly referring to themselves as "The Cartel," the guilty banks extracted higher profits for their own accounts at the expense of customers by executing trades to benefit other members of the group. This was accomplished by withholding pending bids or offers to avoid moving the rate in a direction that would hurt the position taken by a fellow conspirator. The fifth bank, UBS, received immunity in the antitrust case but pleaded guilty to manipulating the London Interbank Offered Rate, or LIBOR.[34]

There are clearly problems with the foreign exchange market. The notion that it functions in accordance with free-market mechanisms to value currencies relative to one another is compromised by central bank interventions—buying or selling directly into the FX market—or through the more subtle influence of monetary policy decisions on exchange rates. Moreover, the world's largest private banks have proved capable of undermining market-determined outcomes through outright collusion. Most foreign exchange trades are not connected to cross-border trade or financial transactions but rather are driven by the quest for speculative profits. Given that the fundamental purpose of money is to serve as a reliable measure so that it provides a meaningful unit of account, it's reasonable to ask whether today's global currency market would even be necessary if more rational international monetary arrangements existed.

The Logic of a Common Money Unit

For those concerned about the ability of financial ministers or central bankers to manipulate the value of the monetary unit of account through intervention in currency markets or monetary policy decisions, the better alternative would seem to be a monetary standard that rests outside the control of government officials. Turning to an outside anchor would permit nations that trade with each other to transcend politics in their currency relations. An outside anchor offers an objective monetary point of reference, as opposed to requiring countries to coordinate economic policies or suffer the financial spillovers resulting from the monetary actions of other nations.

Monetary credibility has historically been associated with economic hegemony. The position of the United States at the time of the Bretton Woods agreement testifies to the role a powerful nation can play within a global monetary system. That power, however, provides no guarantee that a key currency will retain its integrity; the most powerful country is the one most apt to pursue its own economic priorities without worrying about the fallout for other nations. Then again, hegemonic authority tends to shift over time. So if one of the primary goals of having a monetary anchor is to provide a standard of value that has meaning through time—for decades, perhaps a century—it is better not to link it too closely with the political fortunes of empires that can rise or fall.

But why is it necessary to have an objective monetary point of reference? What is the point of having a money unit that functions as a commonly agreed standard of value? In his 2014 book (coauthored with Elizabeth Ames), *Money: How the Destruction of the Dollar Threatens the Global Economy*, well-respected business publisher and economic commentator Steve Forbes suggests that money has three roles in an economy:

1. It is a measure of value.
2. It is an instrument of trust that permits transactions to take place between strangers.
3. It provides a system of communications throughout a society.[35]

These functions are comparable to the traditional purposes of money defined as a unit of account, a medium of exchange, and a store of value.

In the absence of money, people wishing to carry out transactions are reduced to barter. This is a very inefficient way to conduct trade; it requires that the desired object for each party to a potential exchange happens to be precisely what the other one is offering. If they can both agree instead that some other object—a stone, a coin, a gold bar—represents an acceptable store of value, the transaction can be completed to the satisfaction of both the buyer and the seller. Money should be understood as an ingenious human innovation that came into existence long before governments got involved. As a medium of exchange, money eliminates the inconveniences of barter and thus facilitates voluntary economic transactions. Early money tended to rely on commonly used commodities that were acceptable to a wide swath of the population; goods such as cowrie shells, iron, ivory tusks, and rock salt have all been used as money.[36]

Portability is a very important characteristic for a suitable medium of exchange; money needs to be easily transferred from one holder to another without losing its inherent value. The notion of portability comes from the days of hand-to-hand transactions, though one can imagine more modern ideas involving the ease with which money can be moved around. Gold and silver became popular as forms of money because of their natural indestructibility and widespread cultural acceptance as a means of payment. Gold and silver are also divisible, meaning they can be cut into smaller pieces while still retaining their fractional value; they can even be melted down and remolded into an entirely new form that nevertheless holds its value in accordance with its weight. Gold and silver fulfill the main functions of money quite well, providing a unit of account and a store of value.

All these features that define a suitable monetary standard are succinctly described in Sir William Blackstone's *Commentaries*, a treatise on English law published in the late 1770s:

> Money is a universal medium, or common standard, by comparison with which the value of all merchandise may be ascertained: or it is a sign, which represents the respective values of all commodities. Metals are well calculated for this sign, because they are durable and are capable of many subdivisions: and a precious metal is still better calculated for this purpose, because it is the most portable. A metal is also the most proper for a common measure, because it can easily be reduced to the same standard in all nations: and every particular nation fixes on its own impression, that the weight and standard (wherein consists the intrinsic value) may both be known by inspection only.[37]

This statement may well have informed the thinking of Thomas Jefferson, the American Founding Father and future president, who took on the task of defining the money unit for the United States. Jefferson, at age thirty-three, was the primary author of the Declaration of Independence, which was based on the operating principles that all men are equal and that they have natural and inalienable rights that cannot be usurped by government. It's intriguing that the man largely responsible for defining the ideals of a new nation would take on the task of defining the value of that nation's money unit. Why did

Jefferson believe it was important to adopt a common currency for the United States of America?

In the midst of currency chaos and at a critical moment in the birth of a sovereign nation composed of separate states, each using its own hodgepodge of foreign coinage, Jefferson produced twelve handwritten pages on how to establish a unified money unit for citizens of the United States. In these pages, described in the first line as "Notes on the establishment of a Money Unit, and of a Coinage for the United States," Jefferson laid out his analysis and recommendations for how best to create a common currency to facilitate internal trade among the states and forge a shared identity for the nation.

The writing itself rings with clarity, reflecting the author's logical mind. It is notable that Jefferson would use the term "money unit" in formulating the objective; it's a term of reference more likely to be employed by an economist than a political leader. But there can be no doubt that Jefferson was indeed focused on defining a money *unit* that would serve as an accurate and reliable standard of value. Jefferson saw his task clearly: the United States needed its monetary standard to be defined in terms as specific and unvarying as its official weights and measures. For Jefferson, that meant defining the value of America's money unit as a precise weight in both gold and silver that would serve as an unchanging standard of value. "If we determine that a Dollar shall be our Unit," Jefferson wrote in his *Notes*, "we must then say with precision what a Dollar is."[38]

In presenting his parameters for establishing a money unit, Jefferson emphasized three main considerations. Americans must find it convenient to use, easy to understand, and familiar. Jefferson recognized that citizens' needs for commerce should be the primary consideration in adopting a new money unit; it should provide them with a useful measurement tool for the ordinary transactions of daily life. Being able to add, subtract, multiply, and divide using the new money unit is critical, Jefferson pointed out, and should therefore be easy "so as to facilitate the money arithmetic."[39] Jefferson suggested that the easiest ratio for people to comprehend is multiplication and division by ten, which might seem obvious. But approval of Jefferson's recommendation would mark the first time in history any nation officially adopted a decimal coinage system. To keep the new American money unit familiar for its users, Jefferson sensibly turned to the well-known Spanish dollar as the basis for defining the new money, as it was commonly used and "much referred to for a measure of value."[40]

The remaining task was to perform an in-depth analysis of various mintages in current circulation of dollar coins that had been struck at different times and had diverse weights and fineness. Jefferson assigned specialists to assay various coins with scientific accuracy and report back their findings. "We should examine the quantity of pure metal in each & from them form an average for our Unit," he reasoned.[41] Defined as a precise weight in precious metals—371.25 grains of pure silver or 24.75 grains of pure gold—the new U.S. dollar would perform its most important function as a trustworthy measure. Jefferson believed that a dependable monetary standard would empower citizens to make responsible decisions; it would unify the American states and enable the fledgling country to advance. This was a vision consistent with Jefferson's faith in the capabilities of individual citizens to make choices that would benefit themselves and their compatriots, as well as their nation.

Confidence in the competence of people to make good economic and financial decisions based on accurate price signals provided by sound money has been greatly undermined as the United States has transitioned away from a metallic standard. Modern fiat money is managed by central bank authorities with wholly discretionary powers; the value of the U.S. dollar is subject to monetary policy decisions aimed at expanding or contracting the supply of money and credit available to the economy. When the money supply is determined through market forces of demand and supply for loanable funds, and interest rates equilibrate those levels naturally, the amount of cash and credit available to the economy is self-correcting. Price signals are compromised to the extent that Fed actions bring about artificial results, with the central bank's policy interest rate higher or lower than the rate that would have reflected the interaction of market participants.

The Federal Reserve operates with an objective of achieving its desired level of inflation—specifically targeting a specified rate of decline in the value of the dollar. Although the policymaking committee of the Fed is transparent in announcing its inflation goal, the practice contradicts the basic concept of establishing a monetary standard. Moreover, the inflation goal is subject to change. Central bankers are not sufficiently omniscient to know what the price should be to borrow loanable funds. The dollar cannot provide an immutable store of value when its prespecified rate of decline is a matter of human choice subject to temporal criteria. The money unit should not be a deteriorating asset.

No wonder so many people have been drawn into the world of alternative currencies whose main feature is that they are not controlled by central banks. The rise in the popularity of cryptocurrencies since 2009 has been fueled by their seeming capacity to decentralize the governance of monetary. Bitcoin emerged early as a quasi-subversive but increasingly acceptable form of money that generated enthusiasm both for its technological advantages for conducting cross-border transactions and also for its philosophical appeal. The genesis of Bitcoin dates from November 2008, when an author with the name Satoshi Nakamoto posted a paper on the Internet entitled "Bitcoin: A Peer-to-Peer Electronic Cash System." The issuance of this currency, Bitcoin, would be governed by a computer protocol that enabled people to "mine" blocks of Bitcoin through a complex process involving substantial computing facilities and associated expenditures for electricity. What is the appeal of such an approach? In the original paper, the elusive Nakamoto (the name is widely believed to be a pseudonym) explained: "We have proposed a system for electronic transactions without relying on trust."[42]

The reference to trust seems explicitly related to financial institutions as the third party whose involvement in voluntary transactions between buyer and seller is avoided under the Bitcoin system. In seeking a monetary alternative to the status quo, Bitcoin users are expressing a lack of trust in existing money and banking institutions regulated by government authorities. As Gillian Tett observed in the *Financial Times*,

> investors have been putting money into gold for decades, partly because they do not trust governments (or banks). And this mistrust has been rising rapidly in recent years, as western monetary experiments keep gathering pace—hence all those gold bars now sitting in Swiss banks. But what is striking about the bitcoin experiment is that it takes the issue of trust to a new level. Instead of relying on governments and banks to underpin currencies, investors are essentially placing their faith in a complicated software, maintained by a community of volunteers and users with possibly conflicted interests and diverse levels of skill and commitment—

and people have as little knowledge about how it really works as they have about Wall Street financial products or central bank balance sheets. To my mind, at least, that almost makes it seem rational to have faith in gold bars.[43]

The early message sent by users of alternative currencies, along with the establishments willing to accept them as payment for goods sold or services rendered, was that an unfamiliar and untested form of money was deemed a better alternative than relying on fiat money issued by central banks. The soundness of Bitcoin was based on an abstruse computing formula that limits its supply; compared to the discretionary monetary policy framework practiced by central bankers, this was seen as more virtuous. Protecting the privacy of voluntary exchanges of goods, services, or both was also deemed an important advantage of cryptocurrencies. The charge that some individuals had nefarious reasons for wanting to keep their transactions off the radar screen proved valid in some cases—but it's not outside the mainstream to desire some level of privacy concerning personal financial affairs.

The other primary reason for turning to cryptocurrencies is that cross-border exchanges involve no transaction fees or foreign exchange risks. So long as both parties to a transaction are willing to consummate the deal using a common monetary unit of account, there is no need to complicate the process of payment by converting one currency into another. Although there may be substantial fees and exchange rate risk to convert an alternative currency such as Bitcoin back into a conventional currency—the value of Bitcoin has fluctuated wildly against major fiat currencies issued by central banks—there is also a possibility of speculative gain. The price of Bitcoin in U.S. dollars was $0.09 in July 2010 but soared as high as $69,789 in November 2021. In December 2022, it was trading for under $20,000, but the price was more than twice as high in January 2024.

Bitcoin has spawned myriad other decentralized peer-to-peer cryptocurrencies—such as Ethereum, Tether, Binance Coin, USD Coin, XRP, Binance USD, Cardano, and Dogecoin—designed to offer alternatives to government-managed money for use as a medium of exchange. Payments are made using encryption to verify transactions; cryptocurrency is stored in a digital wallet, and transactions are recorded in a public ledger. Many experts dismiss cryptocurrencies as a highly speculative investment rather than a legitimate means of payment. Commenting in January 2023 in the wake of the collapse of the crypto exchange FTX, former Federal Reserve chairman Alan Greenspan said, "With respect to the wider crypto universe—I view the asset class as too dependent on the 'greater fool theory' to be a desirable investment."[44]

Even as Congress is taking aim at regulating cryptocurrencies, however, visionary entrepreneur Elon Musk, owner of Tesla and X (formerly Twitter), appears to be moving toward allowing fintech services such as peer-to-peer transactions, savings accounts, and debit cards on the X platform—even filing to register with the U.S. Treasury as a payments processor in November 2022.[45] Although the system would initially utilize fiat currencies, it would be designed to function with cryptocurrencies in the future. Meanwhile, according to a February 2023 survey, Bitcoin is accepted at such well-known enterprises as Expedia, Microsoft, Domino's Pizza, DISH Network, BMW, Shopify, and the Red Cross.[46] Also worth noting: Senator Ted Cruz (R-TX) introduced a resolution in January 2023 to require food service contractors and vending machine operators in the Capitol to accept cryptocurrency.[47]

Why is there so much interest in nontraditional currencies? Overstock. com was the first major online shopping retailer to commit to accepting Bitcoin as payment in exchange for its products. According to the company's chairman and CEO, Patrick Byrne, the reasons for doing so were both business-related and philosophical. The business reasons included wanting to appeal to large numbers of Bitcoin holders who were eager to patronize firms that would accept this form of payment. Byrne also wanted to avoid the 2 percent cost associated with carrying out credit card transactions—which was roughly equivalent to the company's own net margin on sales. But the other rationale for accepting Bitcoin went beyond normal profit considerations:

> Now, the philosophical reasons: I believe limited government is a better business model for our nation than is unlimited government (and limited government has the additional benefit of being consistent with our Constitution). Among the many vices of authoritarianism is that it can sustain itself only by offering more things to more people than it can actually deliver, and one way it makes up the difference is by debasing its currency. People who share my belief in limited government often favor gold-back

money, because for millennia, mankind's stock of gold has increased at a rate of 2–3 percent per year, and no government mandarin has the power to will additional gold into existence. As a digital currency, bitcoin is, of course, suited to online transactions. In addition, however, it possesses those key virtues of gold: Bitcoin is mathematically constrained such that there can be no more than 21 million (infinitely divisible) units, and the supply will grow in a predictable manner. I am agnostic regarding the future value of bitcoin. I merely feel bitcoin is a viable medium of exchange that Overstock.com should embrace to better serve our customers, and that the U.S. should embrace to create a robust, viable alternative to our current monetary institutions.[48]

The interest in Bitcoin testifies to the ideological appeal of cryptocurrencies to avoid the strictures of intrusive government and assert libertarian principles. Many who oppose debasement of the U.S. dollar by government policies are attracted in particular to Bitcoin because its issuance is mathematically constrained; supply is limited to the rate at which new coins can be "mined," and a final cap of twenty-one million units has long been established. But even if alternative forms of money hold out the promise of providing a currency that satisfies the three chief functions of money—as a medium of exchange, a unit of account, and a store of value (denominated in terms of itself, although the value of the cryptocurrency may vary wildly against the U.S. dollar)—there still exists a legitimacy problem that renders all cryptocurrencies subject to government regulations. Although Bitcoin and other major cryptocurrencies are not prohibited in the United States, they are restricted or banned in some nations. Laws against money laundering and terrorist financing affect the routine use of cryptocurrencies and impose reputational risks. The collapse of FTX in late 2022 was due to liquidity and solvency issues brought on by the discovery of massive fraud in misappropriating customer assets. The event had an explosive impact on the crypto market, shattering investor confidence and causing serious repercussions for alternative currencies.

Is there any way to achieve the benefits of a reliable currency that would be acceptable to national governments as legal tender? Could a global medium of exchange and unit of account be specifically designed for use in cross-border transactions? One can imagine a theoretical construct for specifying a global monetary unit in terms of a basket of leading currencies akin to the Special Drawing Right (SDR) offered by the International Monetary Fund (IMF). The value of the SDR is set daily by summing the values in U.S. dollars, based on market exchange rates, of a basket of major currencies: the U.S. dollar, the euro, the Chinese renminbi, the Japanese yen, and the British pound sterling. The SDR itself is not a currency, according to the IMF's website, but an asset that holders can exchange for currency when needed. The SDR serves as the unit of account of the IMF and other international organizations.[49]

The logic of a common money unit is indeed compelling. But what is the path to a common currency for voluntary transactions throughout the world? It makes sense to have a common frame of reference for determining monetary value, whether for purchases of goods and services or for capital investment purposes. Although the appeal of cryptocurrencies may align with this sort of thinking, it must also be recognized that the government of a nation-state exercises power over the rules that determine the ability of alternative forms of money to compete with government-issued money. Even more important is that currencies issued by central banks—or the world's most prominent forms of fiat money, at least—retain more public trust than privately issued money. If it comes down to a contest between private crypto issuers and central banks for complying with legal tender laws and taxation requirements, the deck is stacked against the former.

That doesn't mean, however, that a new regime for international monetary relations could not tap into the technological advances for settling transactions across borders that blockchain provides by using a distributed public ledger to continuously record transactions. One can imagine a harmonious partnership that harnesses innovative approaches arising from the fintech industry in combination with the familiarity and broad acceptability of the world's dominant currency—perhaps starting with the U.S. dollar. It would not be the first time the United States stepped up to the challenge of restoring international monetary stability in a troubled world. But how can the unit's value be stabilized? Resolving that question is the key to unleashing sound money.

PART TWO

Taking Action

4

Fix What Broke

THIS CHAPTER LOOKS at past international monetary systems to analyze their advantages while also examining why they are no longer in effect. The chapter will not provide an exhaustive study of humanity's every attempt to utilize some object as money—cowrie shells, tobacco, feathers—but will instead take a shortcut by going straight to the two most recent international monetary systems the world has known. The word "system" is used to denote that the prior set of monetary arrangements was a rules-based approach for maintaining stable exchange rates through either (1) a self-disciplining mechanism or (2) the establishment of an international organization to oversee and enforce compliance with the rules. In short, this chapter will look at what has worked.

In defining on what basis a monetary system could be said to have worked to advance economic goals, it makes sense to set parameters. For example, an important aspect of determining a monetary system's success is examining whether it fostered economic growth and whether this growth was *real*—that is, productive. We will look to see whether wages increased along with the higher level of economic performance and will also examine whether economic gains were broadly shared. This last question goes to the issue of income inequality. We have already discussed how monetary policy can channel financial benefits to some members of the population at the expense of others. For example, near-zero interest rates aimed at stimulating economic activity in the wake of the 2008 financial crisis ended up serving the needs of big government, big business, and owners of financial assets, while ordinary savers received almost no return on their savings for more than a decade.[1] Ideally, a foundation of stable money should help facilitate the growth of income and wealth not only on a median basis but across the social spectrum to the benefit of households in all quintiles. We shall see that prior international monetary systems were associated with such laudable results. Correlation is not causation; we cannot automatically link better economic results with the existence of a particular monetary system. But to overlook the role of stable money in determining economic performance would be intellectual negligence.

The main lesson is that prior monetary systems that relied on convertibility, allowing participants to choose between paper money claims and gold, have coincided with impressive economic and financial results. Both the classical gold standard and the Bretton Woods gold exchange system appear to have contributed to widely shared prosperity over lengthy time periods. Building a new monetary system that will endure during times of financial duress requires an understanding of the pressures, both economic and political, that can bring about collapse. What caused those earlier systems to fail? The objective should be to construct future arrangements more resistant to such pressures while also delivering a level monetary playing field. To analyze the efficacy of the classical international gold standard—the international monetary system in operation from the 1870s to 1914—we will seek to determine whether economic performance was impressive in terms of the metrics cited above using available comparable data. What was the economic growth rate per capita? Can we meaningfully apply some measure of productivity? We should also try to ascertain to what extent the full labor force participated in economic gains under the gold standard, keeping in mind that it is desirable for gains to be broadly shared across all sectors of the population rather than being mostly concentrated in the top income-level group.

If opportunity for all is a primary economic objective—providing a decent chance for people to achieve higher levels of prosperity—then it matters whether the monetary platform serves the needs of all members of society. One reason a system may run afoul of public support is that it is perceived to play favorites, spawning accusations of a rigged system. Cynicism among the citizens who must utilize the nation's money unit can undercut any pretense about the benefits of granting full discretionary powers to monetary policymakers. An analogous observation can be made about the international arena as well. If global trade and investment flows are part of the formula for increasing opportunity and maximizing growth, then the international monetary platform should ideally serve to facilitate voluntary trade at some level that results in optimal benefits to participants. It must also conform to standards of fairness and honest competition—not slanting benefits to nations that cheat by depreciating their currencies.

The first section of this chapter will focus on the era of the classical gold standard. The second section will examine the gold exchange system that was established after World War II and remained in effect through August 1971. Currency chaos and bitter trade disputes characterized the interwar period between roughly 1915 and 1944 when official gold convertibility was essentially abandoned. An attempt to restore gold convertibility after World War I did not succeed. In 1925, Britain made the mistake of trying to resume convertibility between the pound sterling and gold at the rate that had been in effect before the war, not taking into consideration the inflation of the nation's currency that had taken place during the war years; Britain stopped using the gold standard in 1931. In the United States, the exigencies of the Great Depression motivated the Roosevelt administration to force the surrender of all privately held monetary gold in exchange for currency in the 1930s and to prohibit international gold payments. The failure of Britain's attempted restoration of the gold standard had caused the Federal Reserve to alternate from trying to preserve the international gold standard to focusing on stabilizing the domestic price level. By 1919, after World War I had ended, the United States was the only country in a position to uphold a gold standard; other major nations had suffered four years of inflation, price controls, exchange controls, and massive loss of gold reserves. The United States was criticized by some economists and politicians for not playing by the strict rules of the gold standard during the 1920s—"dragging her golden anchor" rather than having it attached to the ocean bed.[2] With a gold reserve ratio above 70 percent as gold flowed into the United States from 1921 to 1925, the Federal Reserve had opted to sterilize the effects of gold flows to shift the burden of adjustment of international prices to other gold standard nations.

In short, the 1920s and 1930s were a time of banking crises, currency depreciation, disintegrating trade, and worldwide economic recession. This era of currency chaos paved the way for the new international monetary agreement hammered out by representatives from forty-four nations at Bretton

Woods, New Hampshire. The essential difference between the two systems under study in this chapter was that gold convertibility was a right guaranteed to all currency holders under the classical gold standard, whereas only foreign central banks could redeem currency for a preestablished amount of gold under the Bretton Woods agreement—with that privilege applying only to the U.S. dollar. Other nations were obligated to keep their currencies aligned with the dollar at a stable exchange rate but were not directly responsible for maintaining gold convertibility.

Limiting the analysis to these two international monetary systems makes it practicable to compare and contrast with clarity the advantages and disadvantages of both approaches. Further, this provides a well-defined basis for comparing economic performance under these former international monetary regimes with contemporary arrangements, which is the purpose of the final section of the chapter. Focusing on how best to achieve the optimal combination of benefits while reducing the costs and vulnerabilities of these prior systems facilitates serious consideration—in both theoretical and pragmatic terms—of potential approaches for securing the best of all monetary worlds.

This chapter is thus a forensic exercise to derive lessons from history that might be applied to building a new international monetary system with lasting impact. The fundamental question is whether these two prior systems based on gold convertibility can be said to have "worked" by empowering growth and opportunity through free trade and capital flows over an extended period of time. That both systems—the classic international gold standard and the Bretton Woods gold exchange standard—were eventually abandoned serves as a cautionary lesson in itself. Whether the breakdown was due to an inherent defect or the direct result of violating rules, it is important to identify what went wrong.

The Gold Standard

People had been using metallic standards for centuries before the late 1800s, but the era of the classical international gold standard can be said to have begun at that time. Extending to all the major industrial nations as well as smaller agricultural economies, this inclusive approach to monetary relations is widely credited by notable economists with helping to further international trade and improve world economic performance. An interesting feature of the pre-1914 gold standard is that it was not "invented" by any nation or regime—it was not based on any collective founding treaty—but rather arose organically. As noted by American economist Ronald McKinnon, while no one country served as the nominal anchor for the system, "the depth of the London capital market, and the unilateral British commitment to free trade in the late 19th century, were essential to the overall success of the classical gold standard in integrating the world economy."[3] In a 1981 article published by the Reserve Bank of St. Louis, Michael Bordo wrote: "The period from 1880 to 1914, known as the heyday of the gold standard, was a remarkable period in world economic history. It was characterized by rapid economic growth, the free flow of labor and capital across political borders, virtually free trade and, in general, world peace."[4]

These descriptions certainly qualify as laudatory and will help inform the comparative evaluation of the benefits from prior international monetary systems. This section will discuss how the classical gold standard actually functioned as a monetary system as the precursor to a closer analysis of how it provided the stable monetary foundation needed to deliver beneficial economic and financial results. Here the perspective will be international, though it's clear no nation would impose on itself a monetary system not perceived as primarily serving its own domestic interests. Indeed, the whole purpose of a "system" for reconciling the currencies of trading nations is to enhance the benefits to all participants. A wholly autarkic nation, having no need or desire to import products or services or to receive financial capital from outside its borders, would have nothing to gain from an international monetary system. But for most nations, interacting with trade partners enables them to move forward with development plans and achieve economic aspirations.

Let's begin by explaining how a gold standard operates as a monetary system. Under a true gold standard, the monetary unit is defined as a specific weight of gold alloy of specific purity. Prices are expressed in terms of that unit or some fractional quantity consistent with the official gold weight. If the government holds a monopoly over coinage, it stands ready to convert gold bullion into gold coins on demand in accordance with the standard monetary unit, or multiples or fractions of it, in unlimited amounts. Money units are created as the public demands to convert bullion into coins under the supervision of the government mint.[5] It could be argued that the quantity of coins is even more surely determined by public demand when minting is not a government monopoly, although the imprimatur of a government's certification may be important to clients.

Paper money can certainly be part of the total money supply, but it must be readily convertible into the standard money unit. "Contrary to popular belief, people generally did not conduct commerce with gold coins," according to Nathan Lewis, author of *Gold: The Once and Future Money*. "Yes, gold coins existed, but people mostly used paper banknotes and bank transfers, just as they do today. In 1910, gold coins comprised $591 million out of total currency (base money) of $3,149 million in the United States, or 18.7%."[6]

Although some gold standard purists argue that every paper claim must be fully backed by gold holdings, Lewis argues that a gold standard can function on a sustained basis with fractional reserves: "Also contrary to popular belief, there was no "100% bullion reserve" system, in which each banknote is "backed" by an equivalent amount of gold bullion in a vault. In the United States in 1910, gold bullion reserve coverage was 42% of banknotes in circulation."[7] The central banks of other major nations likewise maintained gold backing, in the form of not only gold bullion but also foreign bonds denominated in gold-linked currencies, at reserve ratios considerably less than 100 percent of circulating banknotes. In 1910, the level of gold reserve backing was 46 percent for Britain, 54 percent for Germany, 60 percent for France, 41 percent for Belgium, 73 percent for the Netherlands, 68 percent for Denmark, 80 percent for Finland, 75 percent for Norway, 75 percent for Switzerland, 55 percent for Russia, and 62 percent for Austro-Hungary.[8]

The fact that so many countries chose to be part of the classical international gold standard testifies to the universality of its appeal as a way to improve economic performance and enhance financial opportunity. And although we describe the gold standard as an international monetary *system*, it might better be termed an international monetary *order*, because it came into being spontaneously. The need to exchange currencies arises organically when people wish to conduct trade; it becomes necessary to specify value on both sides of the transaction. The rules for participating in accordance with the gold standard were not determined as part of a deliberate design, nor were they the result of an international conference or set of agreements.

As explained by economist Barry W. Ickes, the gold standard is seen as a natural system, as opposed to one that derives from government behavior. Nevertheless, it involves commitment and qualifies as a rules-based system once the government does get involved. The essential features of a gold standard are that participants abide by the following:

- Fix a gold price (parity) and convert gold freely between domestic money and gold at that price.
- Impose no restrictions on the export of gold by private citizens or on the movement of capital across countries.
- Back national banknotes and coinage with gold reserves, and condition long-run money growth on gold reserves.[9]

It should be noted, though, that banknotes don't need to be national; traditionally, they were private. And coinage doesn't need gold reserves behind it because its intrinsic value satisfies that requirement. Determining the money stock means including checking deposits as well as banknotes—all of which need to be backed with gold reserves. In this way, money growth is naturally conditioned on growth in the stock of monetary gold.

Additional aspects may come into play under a gold standard to ensure its viability in times of crisis. Central banks may be required to extend funds at a high interest rate to meet a short-run liquidity issue resulting from a gold outflow. If gold cannot be freely converted due to war or another exigency, the commitment to restore convertibility at the old parity as soon as possible needs to be maintained. Finally, the worldwide price level must be allowed to be endogenously determined by world demand and the supply of gold.[10]

It is worth restating that a gold standard can still be considered genuine without requiring full gold reserve backing of redeemable paper money. Noted currency expert George Selgin clarifies:

> Substantial "backing" of paper money by gold is also both unnecessary and insufficient to make such paper "as good as gold." For that, what's usually required is unrestricted convertibility of paper money into gold coin, for which fractional gold reserves not only may suffice, but in practice usually have sufficed.
>
> … The standard is genuine despite the presence of paper money (or spendable bank deposits) backed by assets apart from

gold itself. The emergence of redeemable substitutes for gold coin, backed only by fractional gold reserves and consisting either of circulating notes or transferable deposit credits, appears to have been both an inevitable occurrence as well as one that, despite setting the stage for occasional crises, has also contributed greatly to economic prosperity.[11]

If the virtues of a gold standard are meant to inform how a new international monetary system might function, a seemingly casual reference to "occasional crises" would seem a cause for worry. It's those financial crises that periodically erupt with devastating results—including the 2008 global financial crisis—that we are trying to avoid in contemplating a new international monetary regime. If the classical gold standard provided no bulwark against financial meltdowns, can it still be deemed worthy of emulating in any way as monetary reformists seek a more promising approach?

On this important question, it is edifying to consider the words of Alan Greenspan speaking on the globalization of finance at the Cato Institute's annual monetary conference in 1997. The key to the success of the gold standard in expediting trade and capital flows, according to the chairman of the Federal Reserve, was its automaticity:

> In the last comparable period of open international trade a century ago the gold standard prevailed. The roles of central banks, where they existed (remember the United States did not have one), were then quite different from today. International stabilization was implemented by more or less automatic gold flows from those financial markets where conditions were lax, to those where liquidity was in short supply. To some, myself included, the system appears to have worked rather well.[12]

The following year, Greenspan would reiterate his conviction that the automatic discipline inherent in the gold standard helped to maintain balance and stability by efficiently calibrating money and credit:

> A key conclusion stemming from our most recent crises is that economies cannot enjoy the advantages of a sophisticated international financial system without the internal discipline that enables such economies to adjust without crisis to changing cir-

cumstances. Between our Civil War and World War I when international capital flows were, as they are today, largely uninhibited, that discipline was more or less automatic. Where gold standard rules were tight and liquidity constrained, adverse flows were quickly reflected in rapid increases in interest rates and the cost of capital generally. This tended to delimit the misuse of capital and its consequences. Imbalances were generally aborted before they got out of hand.[13]

The automaticity of the gold standard exacted monetary discipline both domestically and internationally. Participating nations were individually responsible for maintaining the functional integrity of gold convertibility for their own currency. As Selgin observes, this arrangement exerted a healthy impact on trade and investment:

> In truth the world's most successful international monetary arrangement appears to have worked automatically, with deliberate planning playing an even more minor part in its operation than it had played in its emergence. The institutional setup consisted, first of all, of nothing other than the sum of national gold standard arrangements: there was nothing in it akin to the International Monetary Fund or Special Drawing Rights or other such centralized and bureaucratic facilities. ... The most notable achievements of the classical gold standard—including its tendency to keep international exchange rates from fluctuating beyond very narrow bounds, and thereby encourage the growth of international trade and investment—appear to have required nothing more, in other words, than a resolve on the part of the involved countries to keep their own gold standards in good working order.[14]

As an international monetary standard after 1880, the key rule of the classical gold standard was maintenance of gold convertibility at the established par value; the maintenance of a fixed price of gold by participating nations in turn ensured fixed exchange rates. Each country had to ensure that its commitment to gold convertibility of the national currency remained credible. As mentioned earlier, this was accomplished by fixing an official gold price, or "mint parity," at which rate domestic money and gold were freely convertible. Further, the participating country could not restrict the export or import of gold by private citizens. National banknotes and coinage had to be backed with earmarked gold reserves, and long-run growth in deposit money was conditioned on the availability of gold reserves. In addition to these rules of the game, which are generally cited in describing how the international gold standard functioned, there were also important implicit rules. As McKinnon notes, the role of the national central bank as lender of last resort, along with the obligation to restore the mint parity following a temporary suspension of gold convertibility due to an unforeseen crisis, were important features from an empirical point of view.[15] Known as Bagehot's Rule, the lender-of-last-resort function required the central bank to lend freely to domestic banks at higher interest rates in response to short-run liquidity crises from an international gold drain. The obligation to restore the mint parity for gold convertibility as soon as possible was to be fulfilled even at the cost of deflating the domestic economy.

Although the parameters for maintaining the gold standard as described by McKinnon and others suggest a role for national central banks in managing the system at the national level, the common price level that was attained internationally under such arrangements was achieved autonomously because of the common anchor. Periodic liquidity squeezes and price volatility did occur under the classical international gold standard, but these disturbances tended to resolve fairly quickly, with conditions reverting to the norm rather than escalating into further chaos. The overall feature of the system was to provide a level monetary playing field with permanently fixed exchange rates and purchasing power parity across national currencies.

If people had perceived that an excessive expansion of paper money had occurred within a particular country, leading to higher price levels, they would have begun importing goods from abroad to be sold at a higher domestic price. In purchasing goods from other countries, where they were cheaper, they would use their own gold-backed currency; this would cause gold to flow to the exporting country as sellers redeemed the foreign currency in gold and exchanged it for their own currency. The net effect of the gold drain would be to contract the money supply in the country that had experienced an expansion while increasing the money supply of the exporting country. Equilibrium was achieved when gold was redistributed through exchanges to pay for international trade; when the ratio of gold to the money supply was roughly the same across participating countries, those countries had the same general price levels.

The role of government in such an arrangement is to not disrupt the self-correcting mechanism of the gold standard through central bank intervention. Indeed, as Greenspan noted, a central bank isn't necessary for a gold standard; a central bank could even be seen as detrimental, to the extent that it undermined the self-correcting characteristics of a gold standard. Economists Donald McCloskey and Richard Zecher make the persuasive case that no rules or parameters are necessary to ensure that price levels converge across all nations under a gold standard. Using a monetary approach to the balance of payments, they conclude that international arbitrage resolves deviations between price levels in different countries.[16] The big advantage of a gold standard, according to this interpretation, is that monetary authorities cannot affect the domestic price level, even if they wish to do so, through open market operations—that is, the purchase or sale of government debt securities. As long as the currency unit is defined as a particular amount of gold, central banks cannot "cheat" by not following rules.

Under a gold standard, the money supply is determined by individuals operating in the private sector; reliable price signals permit them to interpret demand-and-supply opportunities, and they respond accordingly to optimize economic prospects. So long as people are comfortable with the amount of paper claims outstanding relative to gold, there is little motivation to exercise convertibility. It is only when people sense that prices have gotten too high or that too much credit has been issued that individuals at the margin might choose to exchange paper claims for gold. This option—which is under the control of currency holders, not central bankers—is what defines the inherent discipline of the classical gold standard.

In general, people choose to utilize paper money to conduct daily transactions or make financial investments because of its simple convenience. The costs for storing and safeguarding gold are high, and it can be awkward to physically carry. But people become strongly motivated to exchange paper currency for gold when they suspect that the paper money has been overissued; at that point, gold is deemed far superior to what is perceived as a debased currency. Trusting in the redeemability of paper claims for actual gold is key to the viability of such a system. Whether the rate of convertibility is established by the government with guaranteed adherence by the central bank or upheld through privately issued notes under conditions of competitive banking, the self-correcting feature is effective only if users are free to act on their own volition in deciding whether to hold paper money or gold.

What would cause people to think the currency was being debased? Government debt issuance becomes a serious concern when persistent fiscal deficits require financing at the expense of monetary integrity. Government debt securities are claims on future tax revenues derived from wealth yet to be created and incomes yet to be earned. The accumulated debt represents an IOU note that reflects annual federal budget deficits. When a nation's central bank purchases government debt securities as part of its monetary policy, it expands the money supply; by crediting the reserve account of the seller with a simple keystroke, the central bank infuses unwarranted cash into the system. As a result, the ratio of gold reserves relative to the amount of money issued has been reduced.

Under an international gold standard, this process of monetizing government debt by any single nation need not endanger the entire monetary system. To the extent that other nations follow more prudent fiscal policies—by maintaining balanced budgets and refraining from overissuing their own currencies through the monetization of government debt—the gold standard would continue to function. Among the community of trading nations willing to commit to a level monetary playing field, members in good standing would voluntarily accept the discipline of gold to uphold the value of their currencies. Even if a core nation began to debase its currency, other participating member nations would not have to suffer negative economic or financial consequences. Under a gold standard, the offending nation is automatically punished as holders of its currency exercise the option to convert into gold. The existence of a gold standard quietly resolves the matter. As people turn in the debased currency for gold, the money supply of the issuing country shrinks until equilibrium is once again achieved.

The driving mechanism of an international gold standard ensures that each individual nation is held responsible for its own fiscal and monetary actions. Qualifying nations gain the right to take part in an international marketplace served by a coherent monetary system based on a common benchmark to measure value. Nations that do not behave responsibly incur the consequences directly and automatically; they can blame only themselves. Meanwhile, individual citizens are protected from the monetary misdeeds of government because they have the option of switching currency into gold at a fixed rate of convertibility.

In short, under an international gold standard, the governments of participating nations are constrained from printing money to cover spending in excess of revenue. This has a stabilizing effect on the purchasing power of money. As economist Lawrence H. White states, "it does not prevent a government from borrowing in the international financial market, provided that it credibly commits to repay, which means that it credibly commits to balancing its budget in present-value terms."[17] Under a gold standard, the money supply is determined through market forces—in stark contrast to monetary policy conducted on the basis of discretionary decisions by central banking officials. Accommodative monetary policy that involves large-scale purchases of government debt may be presented as an action aimed at stimulating economic growth when it actually serves instead to bail out fiscal laxity. The money supply should be insulated from such corruption.

A gold standard is, however, ultimately vulnerable to the tragedy of war. When nations go to war, the top government priority is to win that war. This may require government spending in excess of receipts to acquire needed materials; this has happened throughout history. The inevitable result is postwar inflation as the paper claims issued by the government under the urgency of raising funds to conduct the war increase purchasing power at a time of limited economic supply. The problem is exacerbated if the nation goes back on a gold standard at the old rate of convertibility, because the excess money issuance has raised the general price level.[18]

Reflecting on the last century's monetary mistakes and their fateful consequences in his 1999 Nobel Prize lecture, Robert Mundell offered his own stark assessment:

> The twentieth century began with a highly efficient international monetary system that was destroyed in World War I, and its bungled recreation in the interwar period brought on the Great Depression, Hitler and World War II. The new arrangements that succeeded it depended more on the dollar policies of the Federal Reserve System than on the discipline of gold itself. When

the link to gold was finally severed, the Federal Reserve System was implicated in the greatest inflation the United States has yet known, at least since the days of the Revolutionary War. Even so, as the century ends, a relearning process has created an entirely new framework for capturing some of the advantages of the system with which the century began.[19]

The Bretton Woods System

As mentioned earlier, there were two major differences between the way the classical international gold standard worked and the way the Bretton Woods system worked. Under the gold standard, every nation was required to maintain convertibility of its national currency into gold at a fixed rate. The system was self-enforcing because countries had the incentive to maintain convertibility. Adherence to gold convertibility at a fixed rate served as "a good housekeeping seal of approval," as described by economists Michael Bordo and Hugh Rockoff, because it provided a signal of financial rectitude.[20] Under the Bretton Woods system, only the United States was required to convert its currency into gold on demand at the established rate—a major contrast from the gold standard. Moreover, whereas the convertibility privilege was available to all holders of a currency under the classical gold standard, it was restricted under the Bretton Woods system. Only the central banks of participating nations had the right to redeem U.S. dollars for gold at the established fixed rate of $35 per ounce of gold.

The Bretton Woods international monetary system is thus more accurately described as a gold exchange standard rather than a gold standard. The presumed advantage of having just one nation adhere to actual gold convertibility—with other nations obliged to maintain a fixed exchange rate between their own currency and the gold-convertible currency—is that it is more efficient. John Maynard Keynes concluded as much when, after leaving Cambridge, he began working as a civil service clerk for the India Office in London. He began analyzing how India's developing monetary and financial system was evolving toward a traditional gold standard. Keynes noted that a hybrid system had come into use wherein paper claims on gold were redeemed for export purposes but were not part of the nation's internal currency mechanism. He decided that this gold exchange standard was better than a full-fledged gold standard because it permitted India to link its paper currency to sterling without having to engage in "the needless accumulation of the precious metals."[21]

Keynes thought that paper money was not only more efficient than gold coins but also more flexible, allowing the volume of currency to be temporarily expanded to accommodate seasonal demands of trade. Rather than having every nation maintain reserves in gold to back its currency, Keynes believed it made more sense for India and other countries to guarantee convertibility of their money into sterling, which functioned as an international currency, and keep reserves in London in the form of sterling balances on which they were paid interest. Keynes advocated the use of "a cheap local currency artificially maintained at par with the international currency or standard of value (whatever that may ultimately turn out to be)" as an attractive alternative to the gold standard and "the ideal currency of the future."[22]

When Keynes was asked decades later to take up the challenge of designing a postwar monetary and financial system, he remembered his earlier conclusions. Besides his conviction that a gold exchange standard was more efficient than a classical gold standard, Keynes believed that sweeping multilateral initiatives and extensive financial cooperation among nations were necessary to assist crippled economies and promote political stability. He had drawn this lesson after having been present at the peace conference in Versailles following World War I, where he observed that the economic devastation of a nation (Germany) would end up having negative repercussions for its neighbors. Keynes thought Allied leaders should try to restore Germany's economy rather than seek punitive reparations; he lost that argument but wrote a best-selling book on the topic called *The Economic Consequences of the Peace*. Keynes had also come to believe that governments should act as counterweights within their domestic economies by spending money when private demand failed to meet aggregate output—a notion that would find its way into his masterwork *The General Theory of Employment, Interest and Money*.

These concepts all came into play in 1941 when Keynes was asked by Britain's ambassador to Washington, Lord Halifax, to start thinking about how to build a new world economic order that would foster international trade. Keynes relished the intellectual challenge of designing a "truly international plan" for financial cooperation.[23] Keynes had been working on an arrangement that would provide Britain with defense aid from the United States but had already decided that bilateral agreements were not the answer to the larger question of how to channel capital from net supplier countries to net demander countries.

Building on his earlier idea for setting up an ideal currency, Keynes expanded the concept into the idea of a supranational bank—a central bank for central banks. In Keynes's imagined system, the central banks of nations around the world would maintain accounts at this ultimate central bank, or International Clearing Union (as he came to call it), in the same way that commercial banks maintain accounts with their nation's own central bank. Nations would settle their exchange balances with one another at predetermined par values of an international currency; after first wanting to call the currency "grammor," Keynes settled on "bancor" (derived from the French words for bank and gold). Exchange rates would be fixed in terms of bancor—and bancor itself would be valued in terms of gold.

Keynes believed that international monetary stability was vital. At the same time, he had been advocating expansionary domestic monetary policies as a way to stimulate economic growth. These were inherently conflicting propositions—the notion that stable exchange rates could be achieved while leaving individual central banks free to expand or contract domestic supplies by manipulating interest rates. "There should be the least possible interference with internal national policies," Keynes wrote in the preface to his April 1943 draft proposal.[24] Still, it was clear that some degree of national monetary sovereignty would have to be sacrificed if the plan were to work. The basic objective in setting up an International Clearing Union, after all, was to avoid the chaos of exchange rate manipulations that had characterized the interwar period.

Even as Keynes was trying to reconcile using monetary policy to pursue domestic economic objectives while still maintaining fixed exchange rates, his counterpart in the United States was figuring out his own approach to constructing a stable postwar monetary system. Harry Dexter White, who was senior assistant to U.S. Treasury Secretary Henry Morgenthau, had been tasked on December 14, 1941—one week after the attack on Pearl Harbor—with creating a stabilization fund to help provide monetary assistance to the Allies.

Ideally, the fund would serve as the basis for a future international monetary system that might evolve into some kind of "international currency."[25]

White submitted a report some two weeks later entitled "Suggested Program for Inter-Allied Monetary and Bank Action." It had become apparent to White that stabilizing the international monetary system and supplying cheap loans to Allied countries were two different tasks. He therefore advised that two separate institutions would be required: (1) an Inter-Allied Bank and (2) an Inter-Allied Stabilization Fund. The former would become the International Bank for Reconstruction and Development (and then the World Bank), while the latter would become the International Monetary Fund. In White's assessment, monetary stabilization was a highly specialized function, "calling for a special structure, special personnel, and special organization."[26] White emphasized that a primary purpose of the Fund was to stabilize foreign exchange rates among the nations opposing the Axis powers (Germany, Italy, and Japan), believing that stabilization would encourage the flow of productive capital to the Allied nations. A monetary stabilization fund would also help promote sound note-issuing and credit practices among the Allied nations, White suggested, and would help reduce barriers to foreign trade.

In short, White saw great advantages in pursuing the objective of international monetary stability. In a passage that still rings with clarity and logic, White argued that it was particularly important to stabilize exchange rates among currencies:

> The advantages of obtaining stable exchange rates are patent. The maintenance of stable exchange rates means the elimination of exchange risk in international economic and financial transactions. The cost of conducting foreign trade is thereby reduced, and capital flows much more easily to the country where it yields the greatest return because both short-term and long-term investments are greatly hampered by the probability of loss from exchange depreciation. As the expectation of continued stability in foreign exchange rates is strengthened there is also more chance of avoiding the disrupting effects of flights of capital and of inflation.[27]

White had tremendous technical expertise and analytical skills, but he was also driven by a very human yearning for a more compassionate international economic system. Like Keynes, he believed that formalized international cooperation was the key to preserving peace and saving humankind. He was concerned that, in the absence of cooperation aimed at preserving the benefits of international trade and finance, the world would revert to the sort of economic warfare of trade tariffs and currency devaluations that had taken place in the 1930s—which, in turn, could serve as "the prelude and instigator of military warfare on an even vaster scale."[28] White was convinced that the Allied nations needed to be persuaded that the war was worth winning, that a victory would not mean "a mere return to the pre-war pattern of every-country-for-itself, or inevitable depression, of possible wide-spread economic chaos with the weaker nations succumbing first under the law-of-the-jungle that characterized international economic practices of the pre-war decade." It was in the United States' own interest to help warworn and impoverished nations in the long and arduous task of economic reconstruction, White argued. America should give assurances that something new, powerful, and comprehensive would be done to prevent the "economic uneasiness, bickering, ferment, and disruption" the world had known in the prior decade—in "recognition of the truth that prosperity, like peace, is indivisible."[29]

With his vision of global cooperation and his skepticism that unregulated commerce could be wholly relied on to distribute economic resources in an equitable and orderly manner, White might seem to have been the consummate social liberal. Yet he also embraced certain notions of fiscal and monetary prudence more in keeping with conservative economic principles. As a condition for membership in the proposed Fund, White stipulated that a country must agree "not to adopt any monetary or general price measure or policy" that would bring about "sooner or later a serious disequilibrium in the balance of payments."[30] Unlike Keynes, who embraced his own theories for government stimulation of the economy through fiscal and monetary actions, White maintained that domestic fiscal and monetary policies had to be reconciled with the goal of stable exchange rates among nations.

White also decreed that nations should not be eligible for Fund membership unless they agreed to reduce trade barriers such as import duties, import quotas, tariffs, administrative stratagems, and other obstacles to trade. He also exhorted member nations to agree "not to subsidize—directly or indirectly—the exportation of any commodity or services to member countries."

Members should not permit defaults on the foreign obligations of governments, White affirmed, and he suggested that half of the initial cash payment made by countries to join the Fund should consist of gold.[31]

While Keynes emphasized the importance of "flexibility" in managing exchange rates—as opposed to White's own preference for a constancy of currency values with respect to gold—both men accepted that the viability of their proposed gold exchange system would not rely on rules so much as the discretion of Fund officials. Participating nations would be expected to intervene as necessary in foreign exchange markets to keep their currencies at parity—within plus or minus 1 percent of the agreed exchange rate with the reserve currency, the dollar—but it was understood that the Fund would have final authority to decide what was permitted. If a member nation's economy suffered from "fundamental disequilibrium" in terms of its balance of payments—that is, the difference in total value between payments into and out of the country during a specified period—the Fund might decide to let the exchange rate be adjusted for that particular nation's currency. Typically, this meant the currency of the suffering nation could potentially be officially devalued against the dollar.

In the end, following exhausting deliberations among the representatives from forty-four countries who met over a three-week period in July 1944 at the Mount Washington Hotel in Bretton Woods, New Hampshire, the final charter for establishing the International Monetary Fund would enshrine a seeming contradiction in terms. White would later explain that the compromise that had been achieved would provide a stable, though not rigid, system of exchange rates. It could be compared to the sway of the Empire State Building, with a certain amount of flexibility deliberately built into the design to prevent its destruction. In the short run, exchange rates would be fixed, but there would be tolerance for adjusting rates in the future if needed.

Was the Bretton Woods system doomed from the start? Could an altered gold standard "managed" by a newly created international financial institution prove successful in delivering international monetary stability over the long run—or would the notion of fixed-yet-flexible exchange rates turn out to be a crippling internal flaw? Keynes put his faith in the wisdom and reasonableness of human beings as superior to unbending standards. "If rule prevails, the scheme can be made more water-tight theoretically," Keynes observed. "But if discretion prevails, it may work better in practice."[32] One might argue just the opposite, of course—that faith is better placed in the rule of law than in the discretionary inclinations of technocrat authorities.

Certainly, the declared objectives for the International Monetary Fund reflected the grandiose aspirations held by its two main architects. The establishment of the IMF was meant to usher in a new world economic order based on international monetary equilibrium. As a supranational institution, the IMF would be run by officials deemed to have the economic vision and political savvy to preserve the new global order for the benefit of humankind. This notion was in keeping with an observation by Keynes in a 1938 essay that "civilization was a thin and precarious crust, erected by the personality and the will of a very few, and only maintained by rules and conventions skillfully put across and guilefully preserved."[33] White believed that it was vital to harness the necessary resources and power to ensure that the IMF could stabilize international monetary relations to provide a "stepping stone from shortsighted disastrous economic nationalism to intelligent international collaboration."[34] Both Keynes and White viewed themselves as among those illustrious few whose judgments and insights—not to mention guile—could lead to better outcomes than would be obtained under a self-disciplining mechanism or through the rigid application of rules.

The International Monetary Fund officially commenced operations on March 1, 1947. But even as its number of employees swelled, its impact was minimal. Although Keynes had predicted that hiring 15 highly qualified monetary experts would be sufficient, the staff of the IMF stood at 403 people by April 30, 1948, causing the Fund to rent extra office space adjoining its Washington headquarters at 1818 H Street. Still, neither politicians nor the press seemed to appreciate what the IMF was supposed to accomplish; it was seen as a financial branch of the U.S. government rather than a separate organization. Then, too, the romanticized mission of the Fund was supplanted in the immediate postwar years by the more dramatic Marshall Plan.

U.S. Secretary of State George Marshall was behind the push to supply a generous $13 billion in financial capital to help rebuild warworn Western Europe. This occurred at the same time as the IMF was lecturing member countries that drawings from the Fund could be used only to settle temporary balance-of-payments deficits. The universal brotherhood ideology that had been promulgated at Bretton Woods had given way to perceived stinginess. However, the IMF began to function more responsively by the time the Marshall Plan ended in 1951. Fund officials continued to lecture member nations about laxity in monetary matters and sternly urged them to exercise financial restraint. At the same time, the underlying set of principles for governing international monetary stability inherent in White's original blueprint slowly began to influence international trade.

At the heart of the Bretton Woods agreement, beneath the aspirations to promote high levels of employment and real income growth, was the solid reality that the U.S. dollar was technically worth a specified amount of gold for signatory nations. As the result of a January 1934 proclamation by President Roosevelt, a dollar was equal to 1/35 ounce of gold; thirty-five dollars was equal to one ounce of gold. The U.S. government was obligated to maintain a stable relationship between gold and the value of its currency, at least for international purposes. Private citizens had been ordered in April 1933 to deliver their monetary gold holdings to the Federal Reserve, so they had no such right of convertibility. But the U.S. government agreed to freely convert dollars into gold, or gold into dollars, at the established rate when so requested by the foreign central bank of any member nation in the Bretton Woods system.

Because the Bretton Woods agreement permitted member countries to declare the par value of their currencies in either gold or dollars, there could be no distinction between these two forms of international money. So long as the U.S. dollar was "as good as gold" because of the convertibility privilege, other countries did not need to hoard gold to serve as reserve backing for their own currencies. It was sufficient to maintain a fixed exchange rate with the dollar to ensure the integrity of their own money. Whether the promise to keep the U.S. dollar as good as gold would be guaranteed—or even aligned with the fiscal and monetary incentives of the nation providing the anchor currency—was not addressed.

The discipline of the classical gold standard of the pre-1914 period had been reinstated in some respects—but with key refinements aimed at making it more efficient and less vulnerable to the disrupting effects of temporary imbalances. Dollars functioned as paper claims on gold that could be redeemed by foreign central banks for settling international payments among trading partners. Keynes's earliest proposals for setting up a gold exchange standard on a global basis, based on his analysis of India's currency system, had thus been implemented. At the same time, the domestic monetary policy of the United States was not specifically constrained, which ultimately may have proved irrational as budgetary imbalances and fiscal pressures developed. Edward Bernstein, who helped negotiate the Bretton Woods agreement in 1944 as a Treasury official, offered useful insights some forty years later on the very concept of a system of fixed-but-adjustable exchange rates minus the rigidity of the gold standard:

> In spite of the Gold Reserve Act of 1934, the United States was not really on a gold standard. The essence of the gold standard is that the money supply must be limited by the gold reserve. The last time that the Federal Reserve tightened monetary policy because the gold reserve ratio fell close to the legal minimum was in March 1933. Since then, whenever the gold reserve neared the legal minimum, the required reserve ratio was reduced and finally eliminated entirely. A country that loses more than half of its gold reserve, as the United States did in 1958–71 without reducing the money supply, is not on the gold standard. What happened in August 1971 was the abandonment of the anomaly of dollar convertibility into gold when the United States was not on a gold standard.[35]

The link between the dollar and gold that underpinned the international monetary system of stable exchange rates would turn out to be a key factor in promoting global economic growth, despite Keynes's implicit desire to insulate domestic economies from the fiscal and monetary restraint necessary to maintain fixed exchange rates. The stabilizing influence of the Bretton Woods system would finally kick in, but for reasons more aligned with White's emphasis on the importance of stable exchange rates than with Keynesian stimulus policies. The connection between the dollar and gold provided a solid monetary foundation for increased international trade as producers around the world realized their profits would not fall victim to competitive currency devaluations—at least, to the extent that the Bretton Woods system focused more on "fixed" than "flexible" with regard to maintaining the par value of currencies in terms of gold as a common denominator. The U.S. dollar was anchored to gold, and other countries' currencies were pegged to the dollar at fixed exchange rates; those provisions made for a stable monetary foundation for international trade.

The fact that par values could be adjusted, ostensibly to enable countries to manage temporary downturns, was a feature of the Bretton Woods system that weakened the imputed discipline of fixed rates based on a common denominator. Member nations facing a "fundamental disequilibrium" in their balance of payments were allowed to alter their exchange rate parity under such dire circumstances—but only with the approval of a majority of all voting Fund members. If a member made an unauthorized change in its exchange rate, it could be expelled from the Fund. An example of a fundamental disequilibrium would be a chronic shortfall in a country's balance of payments, with money outflows exceeding money inflows. Devaluations were expected to be rare under the rules of the Bretton Woods agreement, but they were not ruled out, further undermining the system's viability. Despite these failings, the dramatic reduction of currency risk provided a tremendous boon to international trade and economic growth around the world in the 1950s and 1960s.

In short, the fixed exchange rate system that came into being as the result of the arrangements worked out at Bretton Woods set the stage for a golden age of robust commerce and unprecedented global prosperity. The widespread adoption of the Bretton Woods agreement fostered the emergence of a postwar economic order marked by stable monetary relations, impressive productivity gains, and increasingly free competition in the international marketplace.

Economic Performance: Comparing Results

Now comes the task of comparing economic performance under the international gold standard with economic performance under the Bretton Woods agreement. The world was certainly different during the gold standard era of the late 1800s and early 1900s than the world that emerged in the aftermath of World War II, but it is possible to make statistical comparisons on such metrics as financial stability and productive economic growth. Then we can proceed to evaluate the impact of having a rules-based international monetary system in place as compared to what occurred during the floating rate era following the end of the Bretton Woods system in the early 1970s—and to assess the current regime for international monetary relations and its impact on economic performance.

This section will mainly refer to the Bank of England's Financial Stability Paper No. 13, "Reform of the International Monetary and Financial System."[36] I will also cite the *Economic Report of the President* from 2015[37] and make brief reference to Thomas Piketty's *Capital in the Twenty-First Century*.[38] Obviously, it will be difficult to directly correlate observations from these diverse sources. But the goal is to compare as closely as possible how the world's economy performed when a functioning international monetary system was in place—and how broadly the benefits were shared.

The Bank of England paper is useful because it analyzes the performance of the world's economy in the pre–gold standard era, from 1820 to 1869; under the gold standard, from 1870 to 1913; during the "interwar period" from 1925 to 1939; under the Bretton Woods system, from 1948 to 1972; and under the "current system," defined as the system in place from 1973 to 2008. Comparisons of these five different international monetary sets of conditions were made by measuring world economic performance in terms of gross domestic product per capita, levels of inflation, and financial volatility. In describing a "well-functioning" international monetary and financial system (IMFS), the Bank of England report specifically lays out three objectives:

- Internal balance: The IMFS should enable countries to use macro-economic policies to achieve noninflationary growth.
- Allocative efficiency: The IMFS should facilitate the efficient allocation of capital by allowing flows to respond to relative price signals.
- Financial stability: The IMFS should help to minimize the risks to financial stability.

In short, the Bank of England study defines international monetary and financial systems as "the set of arrangements and institutions that facilitate international trade and the allocation of investment capital across nations" and describes the attributes that should ensue:

> A well-functioning system should promote economic growth by channeling resources in an efficient manner across countries, over time, and in different states of the world. It should do this by creating the right conditions for international financial markets

to operate in a smooth and sustainable fashion, discouraging the build-up of balance of payments problems, and facilitating access to finance in the face of disruptive shocks.[39]

Looking at the five different monetary regimes, going back more than two centuries, the Bank of England comes to the rather startling conclusion that it might make sense to consider "whether a more fundamental overhaul of the IMFS—in particular, a move towards an explicit rules-based framework—could be beneficial." Acknowledging that pursuing an initiative to reduce external stresses would certainly represent one of the more radical policy options, "it nevertheless warrants serious consideration given the very large potential costs of inaction."[40] Focusing on the merits of the Bretton Woods system as compared to "today's IMFS," the authors summarize their findings: "Overall, the evidence is that today's IMFS performed poorly against each of its three objectives, at least compared with the Bretton Woods system, with the key failure being the system's inability to maintain financial stability and minimize the incidence of disruptive sudden changes in global capital flows."[41]

Comparing the gold standard to the Bretton Woods system, the quantitative measures used in the Bank of England study show that the era of the Bretton Woods system coincided with superior growth and financial stability, although inflation was higher during that time period. In terms of world GDP growth per capita, the gold standard annual average was 1.3 percent, whereas the comparable figure was 2.8 percent during the Bretton Woods era. Based on a nominal GDP-weighted average of twelve countries, world inflation averaged 0.6 percent under the gold standard and 3.3 percent under the Bretton Woods system.[42] On other measures, the Bretton Woods system outperformed the gold standard; negative world economic growth occurred 7 percent of the time period during which the gold standard was in effect, whereas negative economic growth *never* occurred during the Bretton Woods era.[43] Another comparison made by the Bank of England analysis relates to the number of banking crises per year; under the gold standard, that number averaged 1.3, whereas the comparable figure under the Bretton Woods system was 0.1.[44]

The gold standard was better at reducing currency crises—with only 0.6 per year as compared to 1.7 per year under Bretton Woods[45]—but overall performed slightly less well than the Bretton Woods gold exchange standard using the parameters defined in the Bank of England study. Notably, both of these gold-dependent international monetary systems scored very high on the specific criteria comparing the strength and solidity of economic growth against the risk of financial volatility. Specifically, with regard to allocative efficiency and financial stability, the gold standard performed quite well, with large net capital flows responding appropriately to relative price signals around the world.

Concerning one objective, however—"internal balance," which refers to the ability of countries (that is, governments) to use macroeconomic policies to "stimulate" growth—the gold standard was deemed not as helpful; it did not make it easy for central banks "to help minimize unemployment or to pursue other potentially conflicting domestic objectives" through activist monetary policy. Indeed, central banks were under little pressure to do so, given the automaticity of the gold standard's operational features. Depending on one's view, this might well constitute a major strong point in favor of the gold standard.

In any case, the Bank of England report seems to favor the Bretton Woods system (BWS), after noting how well it performed against the metrics laid out at the outset of the comparison study: "The BWS performed well against a number of metrics. The period stands out as coinciding with remarkable financial stability and sustained high growth at the global level. Moreover, the solid growth outcomes were not simply the result of post-war reconstruction efforts—growth in real per capita GDP was slightly stronger in the 1960s than it was in the 1950s."[46] The only disclaimer the report's authors offer, after pointing out that the world enjoyed high economic growth and low financial volatility under the Bretton Woods fixed exchange rate system, is that causality should not be assumed; that is, "it is difficult to be definitive about whether the BWS was successful in *delivering* growth and stability, or whether it was successful *because* it operated during a period of growth and stability" (italics in the original).[47] The authors note that the period during which the Bretton Woods system existed was relatively short—about twenty-four years—compared with 1973–2008, the period defined as governed by "today's system." One could argue, too, that the post-1973 period cannot be characterized as a purely floating exchange rate regime, given the efforts of governments to intervene in exchange markets.

The authors' hesitation to attribute the impressive economic performance to the fact that a gold-linked monetary system for stabilizing exchange rates was in place may reflect the reluctance of central bank economists to agree with the logical conclusion: we need to initiate serious reforms aimed at recapturing the economic benefits that were earlier achieved—whether that means restoring some of the rules that permitted the Bretton Woods system to function for more than two decades or exploring new proposals for an updated gold standard.

The considerable evidence provided by these statistics certainly suggests that present global arrangements come up short when compared with prior international monetary systems. The current system, as defined in the study, averaged lower world growth (1.8 percent annual average) than under the Bretton Woods system, higher world inflation (4.8 percent) than under either the gold standard or the Bretton Woods system, and more banking crises per year (2.6) than under either of the prior two systems. Perhaps the most powerful indictment against current monetary arrangements as opposed to the earlier Bretton Woods system goes to the claim made by floating rate advocates—notably, Milton Friedman—that abandoning the rules-based approach in favor of allowing the "free market" to determine the relative value of currencies would eliminate currency crises. It most assuredly has not. According to the Bank of England report, the number of currency crises in the post–Bretton Woods period was 3.7 per year versus 1.7 per year during the Bretton Woods period.[48]

Summing up the Bank of England report for *Forbes*, economic commentator Charles Kadlec made the following observation:

> These results demonstrate beyond a reasonable doubt that the experiment with floating paper currencies has been a disaster for the people of the world. Had the trends under Bretton Woods continued, the average person's real income would be nearly 50% higher, the increase in prices would be nearly 50% lower, trade imbalances would be nearly one-third smaller and the world economy over the past four decades would have suffered through 4 instead of 104 banking crises.[49]

It should not be seen as radical to reconsider the benefits—higher economic growth and lower financial instability—that were obtained under gold-linked monetary systems. Given how much has been lost in terms of real income and purchasing power, it is hard to understand the entrenched intellectual resistance to envisioning a new version of the international gold standard or an improved Bretton Woods–type system of monetary rules. The main force working against serious reform of international monetary arrangements would seem to be the entrenchment of central banks as powerful government institutions. Under the influence of Keynesian notions about needing to apply government "stimulus" to compensate for perceived shortfalls in aggregate demand, central bankers have come to zealously guard their discretionary powers for managing the money supply by manipulating interest rates. Even if the model used to justify myriad rounds of quantitative easing has not delivered as promised, the resistance to a rules-based approach remains strong.

The *Economic Report of the President* transmitted to the U.S. Congress in February 2015 underscores the assessment that economic performance was decidedly more impressive under the Bretton Woods fixed exchange rate system than under current monetary practices. In a special section entitled "A Brief History of Middle-Class Incomes in the Postwar Period," this report testifies to high economic growth from 1948 to 1973, which correlates with the period during which the Bretton Woods system operated. On the three measures deemed most important in the president's economic report—described as (1) productivity growth, (2) income distribution, and (3) participation in the labor force—the period from 1948 to 1973 achieves the best results. These three factors are together seen as particularly significant for those in the middle-income category; effects on people in this category are defined as "the ultimate test of an economy's performance."[50]

The report goes on to compare economic performance during the Bretton Woods era with subsequent results for the 1973–1995 period and the 1995–2013 period. In both of these periods subsequent to Bretton Woods, the decline in middle-class income growth was dramatic, with average household income for the bottom 90 percent going from 2.8 percent growth under Bretton Woods to negative growth for the entire post-1973 period through 2013. No wonder the 1948–1973 period—described as "The Age of Shared Growth"—is exalted in the report:

All three factors—productivity growth, distribution, and participation—aligned to benefit the middle class from 1948 to 1973.
The United States enjoyed rapid labor productivity growth, averaging 2.8 percent annually. Income inequality fell, with the
share of income going to the top 1 percent falling by nearly one-
third, while the share of income going to the bottom 90 percent
rose slightly. Household income growth was also fueled by the
increased participation of women in the workforce. Prime-age (25
to 54) female labor force participation escalated from one-third
in 1948 to one-half by 1973. The combination of these three factors increased the average income for the bottom 90 percent of
households by 2.8 percent a year over this period. This measure
functions as a decent proxy for the median household's income
growth because it ignores the large, asymmetric changes in income for the top 10 percent of households. At this rate, incomes
double every 25 years, or about once every generation.[51]

Without quite bringing itself to state the obvious—that the period from
1948 to 1973 that coincided with the existence of the Bretton Woods system
represented economic and social nirvana—the report closes out its brief history of middle-class incomes in the postwar period with a wistful lament:
"Finally, if all three factors had aligned—if productivity had grown at its Age
of Shared Growth rate, inequality had not increased, and participation had
continued to rise—then these effects would have been compounded and the
typical household would have seen a 98 percent increase in its income by 2013.
That is an additional $51,000 a year."[52]

If a final observation is needed to point out the correlation between
broadly shared economic growth and the existence of a rules-based international monetary system, we can close this chapter by referring to French
economist Thomas Piketty's tome *Capital in the Twenty-First Century*. Commenting on the economic advances of France and its neighbors starting in
the late 1940s, Piketty writes: "Western Europe experienced a golden age of
growth between 1950 and 1970, only to see its growth rate diminish to one-
half or even one-third of its peak level during the decades that followed."
Piketty observes that nostalgia exists for this era of rapid economic gains.
"People still do not understand what evil spirit condemned them to such a

low rate of growth beginning in the late 1970s," he notes. "Even today, many people believe that the last thirty (soon to be thirty-five or forty) 'pitiful years' will soon come to an end, like a bad dream, and things will once again be as they were before."[53]

Nostalgia? Piketty's comment suggests merely a wistful longing for the era of rapid economic gains that he unselfconsciously labels "a golden age of growth between 1950 and 1970." He avoids considering the possibility that the abandonment of an orderly international monetary system—rather than any evil spirit—influenced the subsequent low growth rates experienced in the post–Bretton Woods era. This underscores the importance of looking objectively at the economic results obtained under prior monetary systems anchored by gold. Intellectual blindness should not preclude evaluating the impact of gold-linked currencies on individual well-being, on trade and capital flows, and on the wealth of whole nations.

5

Golden Link to the Future

THIS CHAPTER ADVANCES the driving force of the entire book by answering the question, How do we unleash the power of sound money? How do we begin to restore honest money as a fundamental economic objective for the United States—and then extend those principles toward establishing an orderly international monetary system? The objective is to put forward a specific initiative that would build on the lessons of the past to provide a stable monetary foundation that utilizes free-market mechanisms to attain optimal economic outcomes. An irrational fear of pursuing stable money by linking its value to gold characterizes many discussions on how to improve the functioning of the economy; this chapter embraces that goal as an imperative. The task then becomes to provide a feasible plan based on solid steps toward achieving that goal.

The world enjoyed far greater increases in prosperity through productive growth annually when a link existed between currencies and gold; moreover, those economic benefits were widely shared across entire populations. The dollar served as the anchor for the Bretton Woods system, perhaps imposing too heavy a burden on the United States even as it was considered a privilege. If having to endure a dwindling gold supply as foreign central banks exchanged overvalued dollars for gold is deemed a burden, it was largely self-inflicted by U.S. fiscal and monetary irresponsibility and exacerbated by a burgeoning balance-of-payments deficit. Although the Bretton Woods approach worked quite well for many years, it could not survive the "guns and butter" policies that caused the United States to issue increasing amounts of government debt.

Since the end of the Bretton Woods system in 1971, the United States has continued to increase the amount of federal debt it has accumulated—most dramatically in the relatively recent years following the 2008 global financial crisis and at breathtaking speed since the COVID-19 pandemic in 2020. It is mind-boggling to consider that total U.S. federal debt stood at roughly 400 billion in August 1971 but began rising at an alarming pace during the 1980s and 1990s. Spurred on by increased social spending, the accumulated debt had reached more than $10 trillion by October 2008. Between that time and March 2020, a dozen years, the federal debt climbed to $23 trillion and then skyrocketed with the onset of COVID and its aftermath to reach more than $34 trillion by the end of 2023.[1]

There are obvious lessons here for our nation today. Overspending puts a burden of its own on a country's future—one that is growing heavier by the day as U.S. policymakers refuse to come to grips with the enormous amount of debt that has been issued by the U.S. government and the soaring costs of servicing it. In July 2021, the Congressional Budget Office (CBO) projected that the ten-year cost of servicing U.S. government debt for the years 2022 to 2031 would be $5.4 trillion. Less than two years later, in May 2023, the CBO's projected ten-year cost of servicing U.S. government debt from 2024 to 2033 had increased to $10.6 trillion—nearly double the original estimate.[2] The current outlook for fiscal discipline indeed looks bleak, with budget numbers showing that projected government spending growth will outpace revenue growth for the next thirty years, even though both are already above historical averages as a percentage of gross domestic product.[3]

This is no time to give in to despair, however. We need to find solutions. The continued viability of the United States depends on putting our own financial house in order, with an emphasis on curbing government spending while encouraging productive economic growth. This is the moment to find a way to utilize what has been learned about the restraining impact of gold convertibility. Instead of writing off lessons from the past, why not seek to replicate the strong economic performance that can be attained when a monetary system linked to gold promotes both fiscal discipline and stable exchange rates? To be sure, it is vital to address the vulnerabilities of prior international monetary systems even as we seek to harness the benefits. But those who disparage any role for gold in fostering more responsible fiscal and monetary policies from government officials are needlessly overlooking a unique strength held by the United States as the world's largest official holder of gold reserves. Moreover, the U.S. stockpile sets up our nation to exercise leadership in pushing for more stable international monetary arrangements. Why gold? Given that nearly one-fifth of all the gold ever mined is held by central banks—with U.S. holdings far exceeding those of the next three largest gold-holding nations combined—gold provides a logical choice to serve as the reserve asset that provides a benchmark for rational currency relations.[4]

The reference point for a common monetary unit of account doesn't have to be specified in terms of gold—but then again, why *not* utilize gold? Global central banks hold more than 36,000 metric tons of gold in their reserves and have been net buyers for more than a decade since commencing a buying spree in 2010. The financial crisis of 2008 had driven down the value of the dollar against other currencies in 2009, and increasing debt levels for European countries began pushing the euro to four-year lows in 2010. Foreign central banks began flocking to gold as a better safe-haven asset than either the dollar or euro, with the central bank of Russia leading the way.[5] Timing is always a major factor when it comes to bringing an idea to fruition as a valid policy initiative; the fact that gold buying by central banks in 2022 reached its highest level in fifty-five years[6] testifies to good prospects for serious consideration of a new proposal, even as some prominent economists are quick to dismiss a role for gold in stabilizing currencies.

We start with a logical question: Why do central banks wish to hold gold as an important part of their reserves? At a time when government expenditures are outpacing revenues, with pressure on national budgets around the world, one would expect that central banks would divest themselves of a seemingly irrelevant asset such as gold. Yet they have chosen not only to maintain but to augment their gold holdings for two main reasons: (1) gold performs well during times of crisis, and (2) gold is recognized as a long-term store of value. As the World Gold Council observed in January 2023, "It's hardly surprising then that in a year scarred by geopolitical uncertainty and rampant inflation, central banks opted to continue adding gold to their coffers and at an accelerated pace."[7]

An accord was first set up in 1999 among twenty-one European central banks—and renewed three times, in 2004, 2009, and 2014—setting quotas on how much gold they could sell; many were selling legacy gold stocks accumulated during the Bretton Woods era. The agreement came to an end, however, in 2019, when the Bank of England and the European Central Bank chose not to renew their participation. The large gold holdings of central banks had given them considerable pricing power in gold markets, and the goal of earlier agreements was to limit collective sales in any one year that might destabilize the market value of reserves. But the mood had changed by the end of 2018, with central banks holding around 33,200 metric tons of gold; they had long since stopped selling off their holdings, preferring to keep gold as an important part of their official global monetary reserves for reasons of asset diversification. Moreover, since 1999, the price of gold had increased around fivefold.[8] "There has been a sea change in central banks' attitude toward gold since the financial crisis," observed a managing director at the World Gold Council in the *Financial Times.* "Europe is itself now a net buyer of gold—no one needs a sales agreement anymore."[9]

The United States holds more than 8,100 metric tons of gold, making the U.S. government the largest holder of gold reserves in the world. U.S. official reserve assets include (1) monetary gold, (2) Special Drawing Rights holdings, (3) the net U.S. reserve position in the International Monetary Fund, and (4) official foreign currency holdings. The Department of the Treasury records the value of the gold based on a book value of just over $42 per troy ounce, established by law going back to 1973—which means the 261 million ounces of gold owned by the U.S. government are carried as an asset worth slightly more than $11 billion.[10] If the gold were valued at $2,400 an ounce, say—a price much closer to its market value ($2,391 on April 19, 2024)—U.S. gold holdings would be shown as an asset worth over $620 billion dollars.

This chapter advances a serious-minded response to the challenge of sound money, urging the United States to undertake a specific initiative to link the dollar to gold through an innovative Treasury bond offering. The objective would be to signal a new commitment to fiscal and monetary accountability by offering an official debt instrument backed by the U.S. government that reaffirms gold convertibility for the first time since the Bretton Woods system was dismantled. The immediate benefit would be to establish a beachhead for confronting the damage wrought by excessive government spending and to move toward building a solid platform for productive growth. Spurred by the powerful example of U.S. leadership, the initiative may ultimately provide the needed catalyst for moving to a new international monetary system.

The first section will focus on the mechanics of the Treasury instrument itself—how it would be presented to the public and how it would work. The second section will examine how the existence of a gold-linked Treasury instrument could serve as a reference point for measuring the extent to which the currencies of nations that trade with the United States have depreciated relative to a common benchmark: gold. By focusing on the performance of the U.S. dollar relative to gold and then comparing the performance of other currencies relative to gold, we gain a straightforward way to evaluate whether currency devaluation has granted an unfair advantage to trade partners at the expense of U.S. producers. Other nations might be required to offer their own sovereign debt instruments convertible into gold at a specific rate of exchange as a condition for favorable trade relations with the United States. The final section will explore the contours of an international trading community whose participating nations voluntarily abide by rules that identify to what extent currency depreciation has impacted the terms of trade. The goal is to construct a level monetary playing field through a stable exchange rate system anchored by gold-convertible sovereign debt instruments.

Making the Transition: Gold-Linked Bonds

The fundamental dissonance in the implicit monetary contract that exists today between the U.S. government and those who hold dollars is this: there is no guarantee that the value of the money will be upheld. No government-certified mechanism is provided through which U.S. dollars can be redeemed in an asset of recognized worth at a fixed price by mutual consent. So every dollar-denominated contract to buy or sell goods, to lend money or seek funds from investors, bears the risk that the terms of the agreement may be significantly altered by factors beyond the control of the participating parties. In other words, those dollars may be worth considerably less in the future than their current value. How can the contractual obligations of any financial agreement be meaningfully enforced if the monetary unit of account is subject to unpredictable changes in its value?

My plan for establishing a marker for sound money is achieved through the introduction of U.S. government debt securities redeemable in gold at maturity to be designated Treasury Trust Bonds. This limited issuance of gold-linked debt obligations would begin to hold the U.S. government responsible for fiscal and monetary policies that debase the value of the dollar. Some might argue that gold is too narrow a focus: Why not use a basket of commodities against which the stability of dollar-purchasing power might be held accountable? Proposals for using a basket of commodities rather than gold have been put forward in the past as a way to improve the international monetary system. In the 1930s, Benjamin Graham suggested that the dollar be defined in terms of a fixed-weight basket of twenty-three commodities—including coal and wood pulp—with the Federal Reserve issuing notes against warehouse receipts for the basket of commodities thus defined.[11] Modern-day proponents of using a basket of commodities as the anchor for monetary stability include Vivek Ramaswamy, a presidential candidate in 2024, who has suggested tying the dollar to gold, silver, nickel, and agricultural commodities.[12]

The main idea is to link the national currency to the real economy in a way that helps to anchor the price level. Gold has intrinsic worth—its value derives from its utility and rarity—and it is accepted as a currency worldwide. In contrast, storable commodities are subject to deterioration and shifting industrial practices. Moreover, changes in the composition of the basket to reflect updated usage trends would complicate its utility as a reliable measure and store of value. Gold is far preferable because of its simplicity and universal recognition. It is already well established as an important element of monetary reserves held by central banks around the world. The designation of a basket containing specific commodities, various metals, or some combination of these is subject to being redefined and may have variations across different countries; but gold has a quality of permanence and provides an easily observable price in terms of various currencies. In short, gold provides a straightforward and collectively acknowledged measure that instantly resonates as a historical proxy for money.

Given that any proposal to transition to a stable currency system based on sound money must be initiated by the United States—the issuer of the dominant global reserve currency—the fact that gold dovetails with U.S. monetary history is also important. It is evident that the definition of a dollar has drifted far from the doctrine of America's earlier monetary concepts when the chairman of the Federal Reserve states that the dollar is defined by "what it can buy"—as Ben Bernanke did, testifying before Congress in March 2011.[13] The dollar had been defined in terms of a precise weight of gold or silver ever since the Coinage Act of 1792; under the Bretton Woods system, it was officially convertible into gold at the rate of thirty-five dollars per ounce of gold. The reasons were both pragmatic and moral, reflecting American founding principles. Roger Sherman, a statesman who served as a delegate to the 1787 Philadelphia Convention, which produced the U.S. Constitution, was adamant that money should serve as a reliable standard of value. As cited in Chapter 1, Sherman wrote a monograph inveighing against the negative consequences of a fluctuating medium of exchange, labeling it as "evil" and the violation of a promise from government.[14]

The guarantee of U.S. monetary integrity could begin with the launching of Treasury Trust Bonds. It would represent an opening salvo in a broader citizen campaign demanding sound money and sound finances from the government. The issuance of gold-convertible debt securities by the U.S. Treasury would essentially test the proposition that future fiscal and monetary policies could be brought into alignment through the discipline of a balanced budget; lower government borrowing would mean a less intrusive central bank presence in financial markets. It's a fundamental question that goes to the heart of accountability: Would the U.S. government be willing to redeem a special class of Treasury obligations in *either* dollars or gold at maturity? Would the government stand ready to honor an agreement to repay holders of Treasury Trust Bonds the promised amount of principal at maturity, expressed as a nominal dollar amount *or* a specific weight of gold?

Potential interest in such an instrument would reflect the concerns of those who accept that all Treasury debt obligations are backed by the full faith and credit of the U.S. government. While lenders may generally believe that the borrower will perform honorably in repaying the amount borrowed, having the option to be paid in gold by contractual agreement in advance provides a solid guarantee of value. Having this trust-yet-verify provision as part of the integral structure of a special U.S. Treasury instrument would be a way for the United States to issue a dollar-denominated financial instrument that is, literally, as good as gold. To assure full confidence, Treasury Trust Bonds would need to be explicitly protected from any future acts by a presidential administration or Congress to void gold clauses that allow creditors to demand payment in gold, such as occurred under President Roosevelt during the 1930s.

Here's how the bonds would work: Restoring the integrity of U.S. money begins with a limited issuance of Treasury obligations denominated in dollars, yet redeemable at maturity at either the face value of the bond in dollars or the prespecified equivalent in gold. Treasury Trust Bonds would incorporate similarities with traditional government debt securities while offering something new through the convertibility option; the bonds could prove attractive to investors looking for diversification. Imagine you have the opportunity today to purchase a long-term debt instrument from the Treasury with a principal amount of $2,400 and the option to receive either $2,400 or one troy ounce of gold at maturity. How much would you be willing to pay for that instrument? The answer to this question will not only interest potential creditors but will also matter to the U.S. government as a borrower.

Investors who think the dollar price of gold will be considerably higher than that amount on the day the bond matures (the term for the bonds could be set at 20 or 30 years, or perhaps even 50 years)—because they suspect too many dollars will be created during the interim—will likely pay a substantial premium for Treasury Trust Bonds redeemable in gold. These investors would effectively be purchasing a U.S. government obligation priced in the same way conventional Treasury bills are priced: the inherent rate of interest is determined by the difference between the purchase price and the face amount received at maturity.[15] But these investors would also be purchasing a call option on gold, so if the dollar price for a troy ounce of gold at maturity is higher than $2,400, they could instead choose to exercise the option of receiving payment in the form of physical gold (one troy ounce, for example) at that time.

Treasury Trust Bonds could be presented as comparable to Treasury Inflation-Protected Securities (TIPS), which the U.S. government has made available to investors since January 1997. The incentive for offering an inflation-linked bond at that time was to provide investors with specific protection against inflation to ensure a real rate of return over the investment period. A normal or "nominal" Treasury bond pays a fixed interest rate annually on the principal amount, which is repaid at maturity; inflation is a major risk to a nominal bondholder, because increasing inflation means reduced purchasing power as the general price level rises. With the creation of TIPS, those willing to lend money to the U.S. government were able to ensure for the first time that no loss of purchasing power in dollar terms would diminish the value of the investment over its duration. As of December 2023, Treasury Inflation-Protected Securities held by the public amounted to just over $2 trillion, representing 7.6 percent of marketable Treasury debt totaling $26.3 trillion.[16]

In a manner that parallels the rationale for TIPS, the introduction of Treasury Trust Bonds would protect holders of U.S. government debt against loss of purchasing power as defined relative to gold. Whereas TIPS reimburse the bondholder for the impact of inflation as measured by the Consumer Price Index (CPI), Treasury Trust Bonds would reimburse the bondholder for the impact of inflation as measured by the dollar price of gold. Interest in such an instrument could prove surprisingly robust, if the decision of retail giant Costco to begin selling one-ounce gold bars to its members provides a harbinger of marketability.[17]

Here it is important to clarify that the term "inflation" as commonly used measures changes in the price level of consumer goods and services typically purchased by households. Yet the excessive issuance of money can also result in financial asset bubbles—which can suddenly burst. Perpetual low-grade inflation over a long period of time may seem benign, but distorted price signals lead to misallocations of capital. The sort of financial panics that prove most debilitating to whole economies are usually the result of some unanticipated meltdown in financial markets related to a specific type of credit instrument or derivative. Gold is widely perceived as a surrogate for an array of commodities traded worldwide; changes in the dollar price of gold can thus provide early warning that overly expansionary U.S. monetary policy is fueling asset bubbles. As Robert Mundell noted in an October 2010 interview in the *Wall Street Journal*, "The price of gold is an index of inflation expectations. The rising price of gold shows that people see huge amounts of debt being accumulated and they expect more money to be pumped out."[18]

Whether an investor chooses Treasury Inflation-Protected Securities or Treasury Trust Bonds (TTBs), protection from the consequences of monetary policy malfeasance is an important feature for investors wary of losing purchasing power. The availability of a Treasury instrument that includes inflation protection—either because it provides additional dollars as compensation (TIPS) or because it is redeemable for a specific amount of gold (TTB)—empowers investors and thus makes them more willing to hold U.S. government debt.

In marketing TIPS, the website of the U.S. Treasury Department explains that these bonds are sold for a term of 5, 10, or 30 years. "As the name implies," the website explains, "TIPS are set up to protect you against inflation."[19] The way the inflation protection works is by adjusting the principal amount of the bond in accordance with changes in the price level due to inflation or deflation—which is measured by the Consumer Price Index for All Urban Consumers (CPI-U) as determined by the U.S. Bureau of Labor Statistics. In explaining how TIPS protect the holder against inflation, the Treasury website explains: "The principal (called par value or face value) of a TIPS goes up with inflation and down with deflation. When a TIPS matures, you get either the increased (inflation-adjusted) price or the original principal, whichever is greater. You never get less than the original principal."[20]

Treasury Trust Bonds could likewise be offered to potential investors as a way to protect against unexpected inflation as contrasted with conventional Treasury bonds. Unlike a regular Treasury bond—with expected inflation built into the yield—the real value of a TIPS bond holds steady in terms of purchasing power and thus provides a real yield. TTB securities would maintain steady purchasing power for investors interested in gold as a store of value. TIPS bondholders are assured that they will never receive less than the amount invested: they are guaranteed the original amount even if the principal is lower than the original amount at maturity. Holders of TTB obligations would be assured that they will never receive less than the amount of gold linked to the original purchase of the security, even if the dollar price of gold has decreased over the life of the bond; if the dollar price of gold has increased over the life of the bond, bondholders have achieved a higher return than expected measured in dollars.

Considerations for issuing the first series of gold-backed U.S debt obligations should include the following:

- A decision could be made to initially restrict the purchase of these instruments in the same way that Series EE savings bonds are currently restricted; they are subject to a maximum purchase of $10,000 per calendar year per entity. To own U.S. savings bonds, you must have been issued a Social Security number. According to the U.S. Department of the Treasury website, "Series EE savings bonds are a low-risk way to save money. They earn interest regularly for 30 years (or until you cash them if you do that before 30 years). For EE bonds you buy now, **we guarantee that the bond will double in value in 20 years**, even if we have to add money at 20 years to make that happen."[21]

- Treasury Trust Bonds could be created either through legislation or as an initiative by the Department of the Treasury in consultation with the Federal Reserve. Recommended legislation would specifically authorize the issuance of five-year Treasury securities—or Treasury bonds of longer duration, up to fifty years—that pay no interest over the life of the bond but provide for payment of principal at maturity in either ounces of gold or the face value of the security. The instrument is an obligation of the U.S. government to be redeemed in terms of the precise weight of gold stipulated in advance or the dollar amount (face value) established in advance as the monetary equivalent at the time of redemption.

- A portion of U.S. official gold holdings currently carried as Treasury assets and pledged to the Federal Reserve as "gold certificates" on its balance sheet should be set aside as collateral to provide adequate cover for outstanding redemption obligations engendered by the issuance of Treasury Trust Bonds. If an initial offering encumbered 12 million ounces of gold that could potentially be called, that amount would represent less than 4.6 percent of the U.S. official gold reserves of 261.5 million ounces (8,133.5 metric tons). Subsequent offerings over the next three years, each maturing in five years, could likewise allocate 12 million ounces of gold each time, for a total commitment of 48 million ounces for TTBs issued annually as part of a four-year test program. The total exposure of potential gold redemption would equal 18.4 percent of U.S. government holdings; both the Treasury and the Fed carry these official gold reserves at a value of $42.22 per ounce versus current market value.[22] The option to pledge the entire gold holdings of the United States as collateral backing for TTBs maturing in fifty years presents an opportunity to stake U.S. official gold reserves—currently underutilized and undervalued—on our nation's firm resolve to demonstrate fiscal and monetary rectitude.

- Auction bidding for initial and subsequent annual issuances of gold-backed Treasury Trust Bonds would reveal the level of public confidence in fiat dollar obligations versus confidence in gold. Yield spreads would clearly reflect aggregate expectations of their comparative values. If market expectations anticipate dollar inflation—that is, a decline in the future purchasing power of the dollar—the bonds would sell at a premium over their face value. The prospect of receiving a fixed amount of gold in the future versus receiving the principal amount denominated in an eroding dollar would appeal to those concerned about losing purchasing power in terms of gold, which has intrinsic value and can be seen as a surrogate for real goods in general. The downside of holding gold is that no interest is paid on gold, as compared to dollar-denominated debt, and storing gold has a carrying cost. But if cash loses purchasing power because the principal amount at maturity expressed in nominal dollars is worth less due to inflation, the gold alternative gains more appeal as a store of value.

- If inflationary concerns over the life of the bond are sufficiently addressed through fiscal adjustments to reduce budget deficits, thus mitigating fears of monetary accommodation through expansionary policies, holders of Treasury Trust Bonds may have little incentive to redeem in gold. It is possible that the price of gold may decrease over the bond—particularly if the U.S. government outperforms investors' expectations in taking actions consistent with disciplined monetary and fiscal practices. If real interest rates on Treasury debt are positive and predicted to remain so, investing cash that earns interest income is attractive. If the dollar is expected to remain stable against the value of gold, and real interest rates are positive, TTBs could be expected to sell at par value—signaling a victory for Congress in meeting the challenge of sound money and sound finances.

- The Treasury and the Federal Reserve should broadly publish and internally utilize the information inherent in the yields of Treasury Trust Bonds to evaluate investor expectations about future inflation.

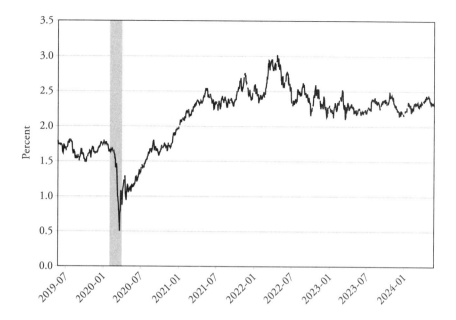

Source: Federal Reserve Bank of St. Louis, FRED, n.d., accessed June 12, 2024, https://fred.stlouisfed.org/series/T10YIE.

Figure 5.1. Ten-Year Breakeven Inflation Rate

It would be highly useful for Fed officials to observe the comparative yields on gold-backed U.S. government obligations with conventional Treasury bonds of the same maturity. The Fed looks closely at the ten-year "breakeven" inflation rate, which reflects what market participants are estimating inflation to be in the next ten years, on average, as a way to gauge investors' expectations. The chart in Figure 5.1 is based on comparing the TIPS yield to the nominal yield on conventional Treasury securities for the same maturity; the line shows the rate of inflation at which both types of securities will yield the same return. For example, investors were pricing TIPS to yield a breakeven rate of inflation compensation equal to 2.35 percent in early May 2024; if future inflation exceeds that rate, TIPS will end up having a higher return than nominal Treasury securities, and vice versa.

Just as inflation-indexed bonds (TIPS) provide an indication of aggregate inflation expectations as measured by the CPI, gold-backed

Treasury Trust Bonds would provide Fed policymakers with useful feedback regarding investors' estimates of the dollar's future value relative to gold—in its capacity as a monetary surrogate for purchasing power.

In summary, Treasury Trust Bonds would provide security to investors who are willing to hold U.S. debt obligations but do not wish to have the value of their investment reduced through debasement of the monetary unit of account in which its contractual terms are denominated. An instrument that embodies a commitment to maintain the value of the dollar in terms of the purchasing power inherent in a specified weight of gold will function as a barometer of the credibility of the Federal Reserve's competence in fulfilling its goal of stable prices. This will also be seen as a way to constrain government deficit spending as debtholders require assurances in the form of TTBs that fiscal irresponsibility will not be accommodated through inflationary monetary policies. Market expectations will reflect aggregate assumptions about the likely future performance of policymakers—with the bid price for TTBs adjusted accordingly. The success of issuing TTBs will be measured not only by whether they are embraced by investors as an appealing option for holding U.S. government debt, but also by the power of the signal they convey to the public regarding the prospects for balancing the federal budget and safeguarding the soundness of the dollar.

Investors may well be interested in an alternative Treasury debt instrument that is specifically structured to provide a store of value. The prospect of receiving an asset with intrinsic value in the future will hold greater appeal than worrying that the purchasing power of dollars to be received at maturity has decreased over the duration of the bond. Although it is certainly true that the dollar price of gold might be lower at maturity than at the time the bond was purchased, the bondholder will have the option to choose the form of repayment. The objective is to have U.S. fiscal and monetary policies prove to be more responsible than bondholders collectively anticipated, so that payment in future dollars is deemed literally "as good as gold."

Defining Currency Manipulation

The possibility of applying tariffs to punish trade partners that have indulged in currency depreciation to gain an unfair price advantage rose to the top of the political news in January 2016. Republican presidential candidate Donald Trump reportedly informed the editorial board of the *New York Times* that he would favor a 45 percent tariff on Chinese exports to the United States.[23] During a televised debate the following week, Trump proceeded to explain that the amount of the proposed tariff was directly related to the amount of devaluation that he attributed to China's currency against the dollar. Trump suggested that a 45 percent tariff, or tax, on Chinese exports to the United States would be equivalent to the impact of the devalued yuan relative to the dollar.[24]

Equating the amount of a tariff with the amount of competitive depreciation carried out through currency manipulation by a trade partner does seem fair. After all, changing the terms of trade by deliberately devaluing one currency against another is not legitimate competition; it is not the same as delivering a product at a legitimately lower price. The currency aspect is strictly a matter of altering relative price signals by changing the unit of account for measuring comparative value. But why 45 percent? Over what time period can it be said that the yuan was devalued against the dollar by 45 percent? Moreover, to what degree can the government of China be held responsible for intentionally depreciating the value of that nation's money?

Defining a nation as a "currency manipulator," based on current practices for making that official determination, is not a straightforward task. For example, under the criteria applied by the International Monetary Fund, China's currency might not be considered undervalued. As David Lipton, the IMF's first deputy managing director, explained in May 2015: "While undervaluation of the renminbi was a major factor causing large imbalances in the past, our assessment is that the substantial real effective appreciation over the past year has brought the exchange rate to a level that is no longer undervalued."[25]

The announcement was not welcomed by the U.S. Treasury, which maintained the view that China's currency was "significantly undervalued" in its *Semi-Annual Report to Congress on International Economic and Exchange Rate*

Policies released a month earlier.[26] The IMF's pronouncement was likely seen as a betrayal by certain powerful members of Congress, such as Representative Sander Levin (D-MI), ranking member of the House Ways and Means Committee. Levin had published a blog post in February 2015 focusing on the Trans-Pacific Partnership trade agreement, arguing that strong and enforceable discipline against currency manipulation needed to be included in the trade agreement to prevent foreign governments from engaging in unfair tactics.[27] According to Levin, the economic damage imposed through currency manipulation was significant and had to be addressed:

> Over the past decade, currency manipulation by foreign governments has resulted in an increase in unfairly traded imports into the United States and has made it more difficult for U.S. exports to compete in foreign markets. The practice has cost U.S. workers between one million and five million jobs—and is responsible for as much as half of excess unemployment in the United States. It has contributed to stagnant wages and to inequality in the United States. And it contributed to the global financial crisis.[28]

Such a powerful indictment against currency manipulation as a root cause for excessive unemployment, stagnant wages, and income equality in the United States can hardly be ignored. Moreover, Levin also suggests that currency manipulation was a contributing factor to the 2008 global financial crisis. Yet the blog post goes on to cite "existing IMF guidelines" as the basis for establishing an enforcement mechanism through the Trans-Pacific Partnership trade agreement—the same guidelines that presumably informed the IMF assessment a few months later that China's currency was no longer undervalued. The World Trade Organization (WTO) pursues the problem of currency manipulation indirectly through its antidumping investigations. According to an online tutorial on currency manipulation sponsored by the American Automotive Policy Council, however,

> manipulating currency to gain an unfair competitive advantage is already prohibited for members of the IMF and WTO, but the prohibitions lack teeth. The solution is simple: strong and enforceable currency rules must be included in all future trade agreements. If these rules are included, any country found to be in violation would lose the benefits of the trade agreement. This

will strongly discourage currency cheating and protect free trade and free market principles.[29]

So we have a dilemma if the objective is to meaningfully identify a government that is guilty of using currency manipulation to gain a trade advantage for its exports. The Omnibus Trade and Competitive Act of 1988 requires the secretary of the treasury to provide semiannual reports on the international economic and exchange rate policies of the major trading partners of the United States (as explained in the opening section of the Treasury's report). Under section 3004 of the act, the report must consider "whether countries manipulate the rate of exchange between their currency and the United States dollar for purposes of preventing effective balance of payments adjustment or gaining unfair competitive advantage in international trade."[30]

One could also point out that we have a dilemma in identifying currency manipulation when it is practiced by a central bank. The task becomes particularly difficult when we seek to distinguish whether currency devaluation is done with intent or whether it occurs as a secondary effect as the result of monetary policy. Is there a difference, if the impact on relative price signals is the same? Does it matter whether the central bank of a nation or group of nations is deliberately trying to gain a trade advantage for exported goods or services in the global marketplace? Is it conceivable that central bankers are unaware of the "secondary" effects that are transmitted through monetary policy decisions?

Instead of delving into the motivation behind the actions of a government or central bank that cause a currency to weaken relative to the currencies of its trade partners, it makes more sense to focus on the degree to which the changed valuation of currencies, as reflected in the exchange rate between them, brought about a change in the terms of trade as a direct result of currency movements. It would be more straightforward, more transparent, to document the extent to which one currency depreciated against another as measured in terms of a neutral monetary standard of value. Intentional or not, what matters to those impacted—unemployed workers, failing manufacturers, victims of the 2008 global recession—is that the economic prospects of one group or another were damaged by an exchange rate shift unrelated to the underlying value of the product or service brought to the global marketplace.

One way to document comparative depreciation would be to utilize gold as the neutral measure for calculating the differential paths of currencies against one another. Gold could provide a benchmark for establishing whether one currency depreciated or appreciated against the common denominator: If two currencies at the beginning of a specified time period have a certain exchange rate value relative to gold, to what extent does that exchange rate between them change over time? Gold would serve as the baseline measure of value so that deviations in one currency compared to another are tracked in terms of the price of gold in either currency over time. Charts are available that indicate the movements of currencies relative to gold over different periods leading to the present; one can observe gold spot prices in various currencies and see divergences in their paths over time. The World Gold Council, for example, provides charts displaying the price of gold over a range of time frames going back to 1978 in thirteen major currencies: the U.S. dollar, British pound, euro, Australian dollar, Canadian dollar, Swiss franc, Japanese yen, South African rand, Indian rupee, Chinese yuan, Hong Kong dollar, Mexican peso, and Singapore dollar.[31]

In the chart in Figure 5.2, the dollar price of gold over the ten years from May 7, 2014, to May 3, 2024, increased from $1,296 per ounce of gold to $2,294.5. This signifies a 77 percent increase in the number of dollars (USD) required to purchase an ounce of gold over the course of the decade.

Next, we will look at how the currencies of the top five U.S. trading partners in 2023—based on their share of goods imported by the United States—performed over the same period in terms of their gold price. Through the first half of 2023, the largest supplier of U.S. imports was the European Union, accounting for 18.6 percent of total imports to the United States; Mexico was the second largest, supplying 15.2 percent of total U.S. imports; Canada was third largest with 13.5 percent; China was fourth with 13.2 percent; and Japan was fifth with 4.6 percent of U.S. imports.[32] In the five charts that follow (Figures 5.3 through 5.7), we can see how the price of gold increased over the same ten-year period shown earlier in Figure 5.2 for the dollar price of gold, in each of the following currencies: the euro (EUR), the Mexican peso (MXN), the Canadian dollar (CAD), the Chinese yuan (CNY), and the Japanese yen (JPY).

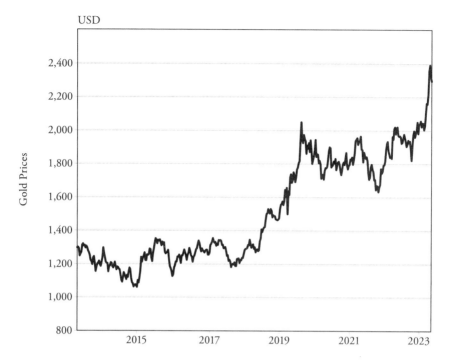

USD

Gold Prices

Source: FastMarkets, ICE Benchmark Administration, Thomson Reuters, World Gold Council, https://www.gold.org/goldhub/data/gold-prices.

Figure 5.2. Gold Prices in U.S. Dollars, May 2014–May 2024

Figure 5.3 shows that the price of gold in euros increased from 931.2 euros per ounce of gold at the beginning date of the same ten-year period (May 7, 2014) to 2131.9 euros at the ending date (May 3, 2024), which means that the price of gold in euros increased 129 percent during that time. This compares to the 77 percent increase in the U.S. dollar price of gold. Thus, the euro depreciated significantly more against gold than did the U.S. dollar.

The following four charts (Figures 5.4 through 5.7) illustrate the depreciation in the value of the other four top trading partners with the United States in terms of total U.S. imports from abroad. We can see that the price of gold in Mexican pesos increased from 16,864.2 pesos per ounce at the beginning date to 38,959.7 at the ending date, meaning that the price of gold in Mexican pesos increased 131 percent over the ten-year period. For Canada, the price

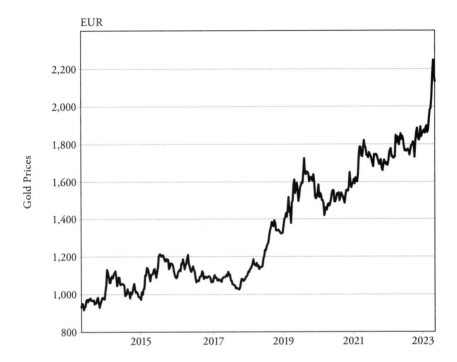

EUR

Source: FastMarkets, ICE Benchmark Administration, Thomson Reuters, World Gold Council, https://www.gold.org/goldhub/data/gold-prices.

Figure 5.3. Gold Prices in Euros, May 2014–May 2024

of gold in Canadian dollars increased from 1,412.5 to 3,135.6, representing a 122 percent increase. For China, the number of Chinese yuan required to purchase an ounce of gold was 8,080.2 at the beginning date and 16,595.5 at the ending date, an increase of 105 percent. For Japan, the number of Japanese yen required to purchase an ounce of gold went from 132,043 yen at the beginning of the ten-year period to 350,411 yen at the end, an increase of 165 percent.

It is thus a straightforward calculation to assess whether a particular nation's currency—or in the case of the euro, a regional currency—has devalued relative to the dollar by comparing the price path of both currencies against the benchmark. By using a measuring standard defined by the price per ounce of gold, which is recognized worldwide, it becomes possible to avoid more direct national tensions. If one currency has depreciated more than the other

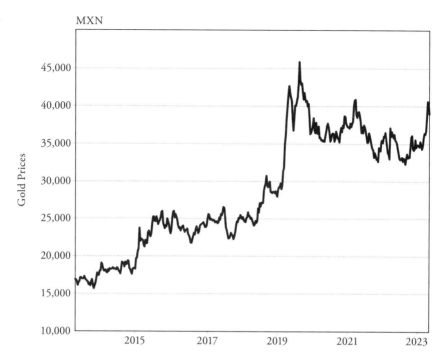

Source: FastMarkets, ICE Benchmark Administration, Thomson Reuters,
World Gold Council, https://www.gold.org/goldhub/data/gold-prices.

Figure 5.4. Gold Prices in Mexican Pesos, May 2014–May 2024

relative to its price in gold at the beginning of the period being examined, as measured by the increase in the number of units of that currency required to purchase gold at the end of the period, the issue of manipulation becomes a factor in the trade relationship. To determine the extent of the impact as an unfair trade practice requires comparing the paths of the two currencies—one of them being the dollar—to identify the amount of devaluation. Whether the devaluation was intentional or not, it becomes possible to assess an appropriate tariff to apply as compensation for the impact of currency devaluation on the terms of trade between nations. This approach helps to avoid the pejorative of "currency manipulator" while also acknowledging the damage imposed through currency movements. The tariff can serve to both discourage deliberate currency manipulation and also to compensate those injured by unfair terms of trade due to divergent currency paths.

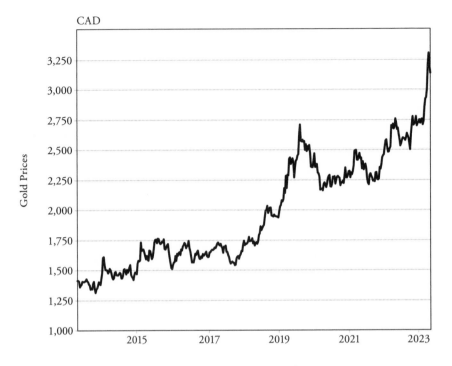

CAD

Source: FastMarkets, ICE Benchmark Administration, Thomson Reuters,
World Gold Council, https://www.gold.org/goldhub/data/gold-prices.

Figure 5.5. Gold Prices in Canadian Dollars, May 2014–May 2024

The objective is not to prevent consumers from having access to cheaper goods or to reduce jobs created in import industries. Instead, the goal is to acknowledge that currency movements can influence trade relations in ways that supersede the qualities of the traded goods or services themselves. Governments and central banks violate the principles of free trade when they intervene in currency markets, effectively subsidizing their exports by distorting the natural mechanism of supply and demand. It is not fair for workers to be forced to compete in an open global marketplace that allows such abuses to proceed unaddressed.

China has often been cited as an offending nation in this regard, using currency devaluation as a tactical advantage in its trade relations with the United States. The latest U.S. Treasury report on the foreign exchange policies of major trading partners concludes that "no major U.S. trading partner

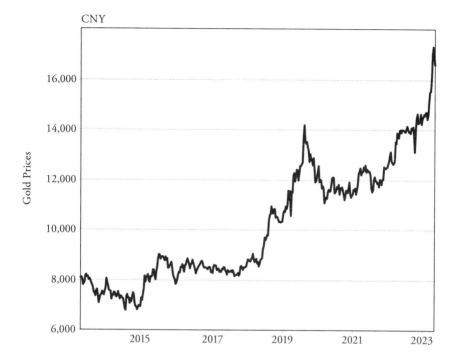

CNY

Gold Prices

16,000

14,000

12,000

10,000

8,000

6,000

2015   2017   2019   2021   2023

Source: FastMarkets, ICE Benchmark Administration, Thomson Reuters,
World Gold Council, https://www.gold.org/goldhub/data/gold-prices.

Figure 5.6. Gold Prices in Chinese Yuan, May 2014–May 2024

manipulated the rate of exchange between its currency and the U.S. dollar for
purposes of preventing effective balance of payments adjustments or gaining
unfair competitive advantage in international trade during the four quarters
through June 2022."[33] However, the report also notes that seven economies are
on the Treasury's "monitoring list" of major trading partners that merit close
attention to their currency practices and macroeconomic policies: China,
Japan, Korea, Germany, Malaysia, Singapore, and Taiwan.[34]

In conformance with the Trade Facilitation and Trade Enforcement Act
of 2015, the Treasury reviews the twenty largest U.S. trade partners on the
basis of three criteria defined by specific numerical thresholds:

1. A significant bilateral trade surplus with the United States is a goods
   and services trade surplus that is at least $15 billion.

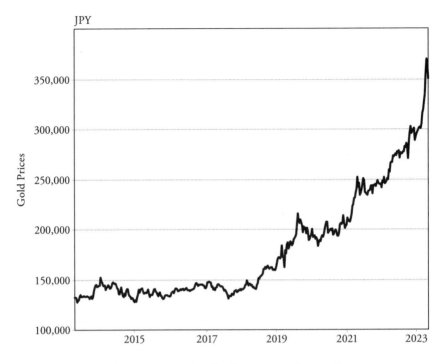

JPY

Source: FastMarkets, ICE Benchmark Administration, Thomson Reuters,
World Gold Council, https://www.gold.org/goldhub/data/gold-prices.

Figure 5.7. Gold Prices in Japanese Yen, May 2014–May 2024

2. A material current account surplus is one that is at least 3% of GDP, or a surplus for which Treasury estimates there is a material current account "gap" using Treasury's Global Exchange Rate Assessment Framework.
3. Persistent, one-sided intervention occurs when net purchases of foreign currency are conducted repeatedly in at least 8 out of 12 months, and these net purchases total at least 2% of an economy's GDP over a 12-month period.[35]

The problem with the Treasury response to assessing currency manipulation is that key criteria are defined by data not readily available and subject to revision. Moreover, a lack of transparency in other nations' currency practices requires the Treasury to estimate net purchases of foreign currency as a proxy for intervention. China is specifically cited for its failure to publish statistics on its foreign exchange intervention and its broader lack of transparency concerning key features of its exchange rate mechanism. In August 2019, for the first time since 1994, China was designated as a currency manipulator by Treasury Secretary Steven Mnuchin "under the auspices of President Trump," according to a U.S. Treasury press release. Noting that China had a "long history of facilitating an undervalued currency through protracted, large-scale intervention in the foreign exchange market," the statement further asserted: "In recent days, China has taken concrete steps to devalue its currency, while maintaining substantial foreign exchange reserves despite active use of such tools in the past. The context of these actions and the implausibility of China's market stability rationale confirm that the purpose of China's currency devaluation is to gain an unfair competitive advantage in international trade."[36]

The decision by the United States to brand China a currency manipulator was reversed in January 2020 as the two nations sought to de-escalate a tit-for-tat tariff war. "China has made enforceable commitments to refrain from competitive devaluation, while promoting transparency and accountability," stated Mnuchin.[37]

The advantage of using a straightforward measure such as the spot price of gold to determine whether an accusation of currency manipulation can be meaningfully lodged against a nation is that it avoids politicization while meaningfully drawing attention to the problem. In addition, its application is not limited to retroactive examination. Instead of looking at what happened in the past, which can become a matter of selecting an operative time frame, utilizing a neutral gold monetary benchmark in real time can serve to move the trade relationship forward. Establishing a gold reference point provides a way to measure the behavior of currencies from an agreed beginning point to ensure that devaluation tactics are not utilized *after* a trade agreement is signed.

If the currency of one signatory nation to an agreement is deliberately devalued by that nation's government to attain a trade advantage, the amount of the retaliatory tariff would be ascertained in correlation with the degree of the devaluation. For example, if China were to devalue the yuan over a one-year period following the signing of a trade agreement with the United States—as measured by the difference between the change in the value of the yuan against gold compared to the change in the value of the dollar against gold—the amount of that difference would be an appropriate starting point for assessing the amount of the tariff to be applied. Indeed, the simplest remedy would be to stipulate an automatic tariff that is equal to the difference in the devaluation against gold of the currencies of trade partner countries. At the same time, it would be important to prevent special interests from capturing the retaliatory tariff mechanism for their own benefit; having a neutral reference point that is also a commodity traded worldwide mitigates this risk. There is also the matter of reciprocity: the United States would have to reconcile the impact of its own domestic monetary policy on the value of the dollar relative to gold.

Utilizing gold as the benchmark monetary standard of value helps to downplay the issue of whether the offending nation's central bank is deliberately devaluing its currency or if the devaluation is incidental to monetary policy conducted for purposes of achieving domestic economic objectives. It can become an awkward and politically sensitive exercise to distinguish "criminal intent" on the part of monetary authorities. The better path is to secure the important benefit of subjecting the performance of currencies to an objective gold monetary standard, thereby quantifying the impact of devaluation. After all, a monetary policy aimed at tightening rather than loosening the money supply of a nation (or group of nations) could have the effect of making a currency *stronger* relative to other currencies—which could be viewed as predatory by nations competing for global financial capital. The seeming trade advantage for nations that deliberately manipulate downward the exchange rate value of their currency to enhance their exports might well be dwarfed by the capital flight that often accompanies the weakening of a nation's currency.

Advancing Sound Money with Gold-Linked Currencies

One lesson from monetary history is that it is very difficult to maintain sound money in isolation. Attempts to instill monetary discipline through gold convertibility will run into problems if they fail to weigh the impact on trade with nations that do not practice similar restraint. As Argentina learned after committing to a currency board regime in 1991 that made its currency interchangeable at a fixed rate with the dollar, the system can be undermined by neighboring countries. Argentina and Brazil are members of the same trade group, Mercosur, which provides a common space for business and investment opportunities by integrating national economies. But when Brazil allowed its currency to depreciate, it became virtually impossible for Argentina to remain economically viable as the exchange rate value of its currency strengthened relative to the Brazilian real, seriously hurting Argentine exports. The currency board arrangement in Argentina collapsed in late 2001.

What would be the impact of a U.S. decision to issue government debt with a gold-convertibility feature? Domestically, we can look to an assessment of the introduction of TIPS bonds for some guidance—at the same time recognizing that a security issued by the U.S. Treasury that linked the dollar to gold, like the Treasury Trust Bond, would likely generate press coverage far beyond the typical analyses of credit market analysts. Certainly, the issuance of such a security would be a historic event that would bring up the subject of past monetary systems anchored by gold, perhaps raising public interest in whether the use of those systems was accompanied by financial stability and prosperity. But even TIPS have been deemed useful in helping to improve both the conduct of monetary policy and fiscal policy. A study published by the Federal Reserve Bank of New York in July 2009 states:

> The existence of TIPS helps to improve the conduct of monetary policy in a number of ways. Foremost, the program provides up-to-date information about the evolution of inflation expectations and real ex ante interest rates, which are important inputs to monetary policy decisions. Because increases in inflation expectations are often difficult to predict and to reverse, up-to-date information from TIPS about expectations may be important in helping monetary policymakers keep inflation expectations in check.[38]

The same Fed study further states:

> TIPS may also offer incentives for improved fiscal policy. They provide an explicit incentive for the fiscal (as well as monetary) authorities to conduct policy with an eye toward the consequences for inflation. Recognition by the public that the government is accountable for high inflation in the form of higher inflation payments to TIPS holders may help hold down inflation expectations and cause inflation expectations to be more firmly anchored, that

is, less responsive to inflation shocks. Moreover, TIPS can help improve the management of the national debt. Because payments on TIPS are tied to realized inflation, the receipts and expenditures of the Treasury Department are (all else equal) likely to be better matched—since tax receipts are also nominal and likely to rise and fall with shifts in the underlying inflation rate. Thus TIPS issuance may help reduce the overall volatility of the Treasury's financing needs.[39]

Beyond these important considerations for improving fiscal and monetary policy in the United States through gold-linked Treasury bonds, which might have an even greater impact on both fronts, there is the international aspect to consider. How would other nations react to the issuance of Treasury Trust Bonds by the United States? This is a critical question because the challenge today is not only to define the dollar in a way that will help establish the necessary foundation for real economic growth domestically; we also need to facilitate meaningful international monetary reform as a way to bring back the productive economic gains associated with earlier times when there existed a functioning international monetary system.

The conclusion from the preceding analyses is the key premise of this book: international monetary reform requires getting to gold. To the unsophisticated, gold may seem like a throwback. But we are compelled by recent financial and monetary turmoil to seek vital lessons from the past. The restoration of gold as a universally acknowledged store of value has long drawn the attention of modern financial experts with a global perspective. Robert Zoellick, a former Treasury official who also presided over the World Bank, suggested a potential role for gold in a new international monetary system dedicated to economic growth and free trade. In an opinion piece for the *Financial Times* in 2010, Zoellick stated that a new international monetary system "should also consider employing gold as an international reference point of market expectations about inflation, deflation and future currency values." The essay would elicit plenty of criticism, but Zoellick was bold in presenting his argument: "Although textbooks may view gold as the old money, markets are using gold as an alternative monetary asset today."[40]

The benefit of offering Treasury Trust Bonds as the leading edge toward the creation of a gold-anchored approach to exchange rate stability is that making the dollar officially convertible into gold could be achieved as an initiative by the U.S. Treasury—albeit on a limited basis. If demand for TTBs exceeded the limited issuance authorized by legislation or enacted under the directive of a Treasury secretary, one would expect private market firms to replicate the same financial instrument. They could combine gold futures contracts with conventional Treasury bonds to effectively provide the same investment instrument with the same provisions for payment at maturity. Although the active participation of the U.S. government in designing and administering a program for issuing TTBs would establish the intent of the United States to make the dollar as good as gold as official policy, it would not preclude the involvement of private financial firms. Indeed, by harnessing the vast investment resources of financial firms in the private sector, the transition toward a new gold-anchored monetary system would be accomplished with greater market depth and rapidity. Whether the existing gold stock would be sufficient to support redeemability more broadly is a matter of speculation—but one that has garnered recent attention from monetary scholars.[41]

Public demand for Treasury Trust Bonds would provide a signal to other nations that the United States had established a beachhead for building a gold-based international monetary system. Countries with large holdings of gold reserves—Germany, Italy, France—might well decide to demonstrate their own allegiance to monetary stability through the issuance of long-term sovereign bonds convertible into gold. Pooling gold collateral among eurozone nations wishing to participate in euro-denominated bond offerings could ultimately lead to the joint issuance of gold-linked financial instruments. With successively larger issuances among a broader group of countries, a convergence toward monetary stability centered on gold would lead to fixed exchange rates—effectively providing a universal monetary unit of account, defined as a precise weight of gold, that would function as a common currency.

The key test for other nations in deciding whether to participate in offering gold-linked debt securities is their willingness to abide by market assessments of the future value of their national currencies relative to a neutral monetary unit of account. This requires national or regional monetary officials to be prepared to subject their monetary policy decisions to the scrutiny of consumers—and to permit the gold-convertibility option on sovereign debt instruments to reveal such assessments. How far into the future would participating nations be willing to provide for the convertibility of their currencies into gold at a fixed rate? What repercussions would be in place for nations that ultimately reneged on their obligation to honor the convertibility privilege? Given the vulnerability of the Bretton Woods system to the suspension of gold convertibility by the United States, it would be important to stipulate the establishment of specific legal protections to strengthen the validity of the promise to redeem on demand; it might be necessary to assign gold used as collateral for backing the debt instruments to an independent government entity or private agency.

The benefit of requiring each participating nation to uphold its obligation to honor the terms of a gold-convertibility sovereign debt instrument is that doing so would enhance that nation's ability to attract capital, thus providing a strong incentive for an individual country to abide by the rules. This alignment of interests would provide a self-enforcing mechanism that would sustain the system as a whole. Countries that failed to adhere to their monetary commitment could expect to be punished with higher borrowing costs and reduced capital flows from foreign suppliers.

The introduction by the United States of a gold-linked Treasury obligation would constitute a specific monetary challenge to nations, such as China and Russia, that seek to dethrone the U.S. dollar from its position as the leading reserve currency. It would be a strong response to developing nations that have complained about the economic damage imposed by a gyrating dollar. Instead of lamenting the lack of a reliable global reserve currency or whining about the dollar's unpredictable impact on trade and financial capital flows, other nations' central banks and regional monetary authorities would likewise need to step up to the problem of restoring monetary integrity.

The basic template for structuring the bonds should be the same for every issuer, with the instrument representing a government obligation to pay at maturity either in gold—with the precise weight stipulated in advance—or by paying the nominal amount of currency fixed at the outset as the monetary equivalent. The rate of convertibility would remain permanent throughout the life of the bond, serving to define the gold value of the currency in which the instrument was denominated.

One interesting question is whether individual governments would be willing to pledge their proprietary gold reserves on a national basis versus pooling them. Would the twenty countries that are members of the eurozone turn over physical gold to the European Central Bank to hold as collateral? Would they designate some portion of ECB official holdings now held as common reserves to serve as collateral for a gold-linked instrument? According to the World Gold Council, as of April 2024 the ECB held 506.5 metric tons of gold on behalf of member countries, an amount equal to 36.9 percent of its total reserves.[42] Might the ECB itself issue a debt security in keeping with the parameters for gold convertibility on behalf of all eurozone members—or a subset of borrowers? In a sense, ECB officials would be lashing their own member nations to the masthead of fiscal discipline to avoid being tempest-tossed on broader seas of monetary turmoil. An ECB offering or a joint issuance of gold-linked financial instruments by Europe's leading nations in response to a U.S. initiative could provide the catalyst needed to build confidence in a stable global monetary order.

The same might be said about a joint issuance among Asian nations using pooled gold holdings as collateral. It would also make sense for emerging market nations to boost confidence in their fiscal intentions by jointly issuing gold-linked bonds; willingness to offer the gold-convertibility option to prospective bondholders would signal the nation's interest in participating in any new international monetary system based on honoring such a requirement. Issuing bonds with the prescribed gold-convertibility parameters might even become a condition for joining a union of trade partners devoted to maintaining a level monetary playing field.

An important feature of this entire proposal is that other nations would make a voluntary decision whether to join a new gold-anchored international monetary system initiated by the United States; the system would not be imposed on them. Any nation willing to comply with the rules might choose to become a participating member. The more nations opt to join, the more attractive membership becomes for others. The objective, individually and collectively, is a stable monetary platform for conducting mutually beneficial trade and financial transactions.

It is necessary to think in terms of a monetary system that transcends borders because goods and services are made available through the global marketplace, and financial capital travels instantly around the world. The only closed economy is the global economy, as Robert Mundell observed. But that doesn't mean we should have a global central bank—indeed, just the opposite. What's needed is to return to a rules-based currency system wherein participating nations abide by those rules. The most concise and most transparent rule is to require trade partners to maintain a link between gold and the value of their currencies by issuing gold-backed bonds. Exchange rates among different currencies would reflect the fact that all of them are essentially anchored by the same benchmark for monetary value; though each contractual instrument is denominated in a specific currency, they all represent a claim on gold in the future.

The market-determined exchange rate among various currencies would be transparent at all times—and the stability of that rate would become more fixed as maturity dates converged. Whether an investor held a Treasury Trust Bond issued by the U.S. government or a parallel obligation jointly issued by member countries of the eurozone, or an analogous debt instrument issued by China, the investor would be entitled to a specified quantity of gold on the date of maturity. Therefore, an imputed rate of exchange would exist among all the currencies because they would all translate into the same common asset—just as during the period of the classical international gold standard.

The only differentiating factor would pertain to the validity of the promise from the issuing government or central bank. Will holders of gold-linked sovereign debt instruments have confidence in the belief that their contractual rights will be upheld? The basic premise for initiating this new type of instrument is to uphold the monetary integrity of currencies—to ensure that they represent a dependable store of value—so that distortions to trade and financial markets are not conveyed through beggar-thy-neighbor policies. The United States would be the logical nation to launch gold-linked government bonds, both for historical reasons and as a reflection of its continued global monetary dominance. Why is the gold-convertibility feature such a vital aspect of this innovative borrowing instrument? It essentially captures the wisdom exercised by President Reagan in his dealings with the former Soviet Union on nuclear arms treaties: trust, but verify. Governments can be presumed to be dealing honorably when they issue money that is meant to provide a stable unit of account, but there must be safeguards to ensure that the original terms are fulfilled.

Indeed, it was during the Reagan administration that the question of tying the value of the dollar to gold was seriously taken up by a bipartisan commission of seventeen preeminent individuals appointed by Treasury Secretary Donald Regan. In submitting a report of the commission's findings in March 1982, Regan stated: "We hope that this report on the role of gold in the domestic and international monetary systems will be of help to the Congress and the public in evaluating the spectrum of proposals advanced with the objective of restoring greater monetary and economic stability in the United States, an objective we strongly support."[43]

Among the proposals being put forward at the time was an idea by Alan Greenspan, who had served as chairman of the Council of Economic Advisers under President Ford and also headed a commission on Social Security reform under President Reagan. In September 1981, Greenspan, in a *Wall Street Journal* opinion article, observed that "growing disillusionment with politically controlled monetary policies has produced an increasing number of advocates for a return to the gold standard—including at times President Reagan."[44] Expanding on the widening interest in bold proposals for monetary reform, Greenspan noted:

> In years past a desire to return to a monetary system based on gold was perceived as nostalgia for an era when times were simpler, problems less complex and the world not threatened with nuclear annihilation. But after a decade of destabilizing inflation and economic stagnation, the restoration of a gold standard has become an issue that is clearly rising on the economic policy agenda.[45]

Greenspan suggested that the feasibility of returning to a gold standard might be tested through the issuance of five-year Treasury notes payable in gold. "The degree of success of restoring long-term fiscal confidence will show up clearly in the yield spreads between gold and fiat dollar obligations of the same maturities," he explained. "Full convertibility would require that the yield spread for all maturities virtually disappear."[46] Though it would be six years before Greenspan would be appointed chairman of the Federal Reserve, he clearly recognized that the discipline imposed by gold convertibility of the dollar would lead to more rational budgeting decisions and growing fiscal confidence. Greenspan expressed his concern that the immediate problem of restoring a gold standard was deciding where to fix the gold price. If the offering price by the Treasury were too low, heavy demand could quickly deplete the total U.S. government stock of gold. If the gold price were set too high, the Treasury would be inundated with gold; as the Fed paid accordingly by crediting commercial bank reserves by drawing on the Treasury's account, Greenspan noted, it would expand the money supply and potentially unleash inflation.[47]

> The only seeming solution is for the U.S. to create a fiscal and monetary environment which in effect makes the dollar as good as gold, i.e., stabilizes the general price level and by inference the dollar price of gold bullion itself. Then a modest reserve of bullion could reduce the narrow gold price fluctuations effectively to zero, allowing any changes in gold supply and demand to be absorbed in fluctuations in the Treasury's inventory.[48]

As a preparatory action for making the dollar as good as gold, Greenspan laid out in fairly explicit terms his suggestion for introducing a limited issue of dollars convertible into gold, effectively creating a dual currency. "Initially they could be deferred claims to gold, for example, five-year Treasury Notes with interest and principal payable in grams or ounces of gold."[49] Greenspan elaborated that successive issuances of these gold-linked dollars would provide the barometer on whether the fiscal and monetary environment required for stability had been achieved—and further asserted that issuing such bonds "would have positive short-term anti-inflation benefits and little cost if they fail."[50] Greenspan posited that gold-convertible bonds would likely carry lower interest rates than conventional Treasury debt obligations, thus reducing current budget deficits. But he also acknowledged the potential exchange risk of Treasury gold notes, noting that prior Treasury obligations denominated in foreign currencies had resulted in both gains and losses in terms of dollars as exchange rates fluctuated.

Greenspan's innovative concept has yet to become reality, although the former Fed chief has continued to champion the virtues of gold convertibility since stepping down as chairman of the Federal Reserve in January 2006.

In an interview published by the World Gold Council in February 2017, Greenspan observed:

> The gold standard was operating at its peak in the late 19th and early 20th centuries, a period of extraordinary global prosperity, characterized by firming productivity growth and very little inflation. But today, there is a widespread view that the 19th century gold standard didn't work. I think that's like wearing the wrong size shoes and saying the shoes are uncomfortable! It wasn't the gold standard that failed; it was politics. ...
>
> We are already in danger of seeing the ratio of federal debt to GDP edging toward triple digits. We would never have reached this position of extreme indebtedness were we on the gold standard, because the gold standard is a way of ensuring that fiscal policy never gets out of line.[51]

Link to American Principles

The proposal for Treasury Trust Bonds presented in this chapter clearly finds its antecedents in Greenspan's 1981 recommendation. But it goes back much further, proclaiming its most profound legacy in the commitment of the early architects of America to an unchanging monetary standard. To establish a money unit for the United States worthy of universal recognition was to abide by unwavering principles consistent with America's vision for self-government based on equal rights and the rule of law. A trustworthy dollar was testimony to the honest ambitions and remarkable capabilities of a striving people dedicated to freedom. It paid tribute to their unprecedented success, inspiring even greater performance in the future.

The U.S. dollar can still do so. We should not underestimate the potential impact of a unilateral initiative by the United States to promote a stable dollar. As a contribution to global monetary stability, it would be a powerful signal and would likely motivate other nations to follow suit, perhaps in rapid succession. If the nation that issues the world's most commonly used currency moved toward stabilizing its money with reference to gold through a sovereign debt instrument offering the option of convertibility to bondholders, it would set a powerful example by showing confidence in America's fiscal future.

The issuance of Treasury Trust Bonds would establish a commitment by the U.S. government to restore the integrity of the dollar as a dependable standard of value. This would constitute a groundbreaking approach to monetary policy both at home and abroad. It would change the very terms for discussing the role of money as a meaningful unit of account and as an essential tool for supporting free-enterprise capitalism. Instead of deferring to central banks on whether economic activity should be stimulated or restricted—manipulating the cost of capital as the primary tool—the main objective would be to maintain the money unit as a consistent and reliable measure. The pseudoscience of managing the economy through central bank intervention in credit markets should give way to reaffirming the importance of a stable monetary foundation to enhance domestic opportunities and increase prosperity—and to maximize the benefits of international trade and investment.

Linking U.S. money to gold through Treasury Trust Bonds would resonate both at the domestic level in the United States and as a global initiative. Gold has functioned historically not only as a monetary unit of measure; gold is also recognized by central banks and international financial institutions as an important reserve asset. The International Monetary Fund is one of the world's official holders of gold, holding some 90.5 million ounces (or 2,814.1 metric tons) of gold at designated depositories.[52] Established in 1944 as part of the Bretton Woods agreement, the IMF has as its primary purpose "to ensure the stability of the international monetary system—the system of exchange rates and international payments that enables countries and their citizens to buy goods and services from each other."[53]

The IMF today has largely spurned its heritage of ensuring a stable international monetary system based on fixed exchange rates anchored by gold. But using the price of gold as a way to help steer monetary policy was still on the economic agenda for the Reagan administration—even if the Gold Commission had officially rejected going on a gold standard. In September 1987, in a speech to the 151 countries represented at the annual meetings of the IMF and the World Bank, U.S. Treasury Secretary James Baker told participants that the Reagan administration would consider including gold as part of a price index of various commodities and other indicators to provide an early warning sign of price trends among currencies:

We have agreed that we should be concerned about the predictability and stability of exchange rates. Our coordination process takes this into consideration. It is equally important that the policies resulting from the coordination process not be inflationary. It would be unfortunate if our efforts to foster exchange rate stability among currencies led to stable currency relationships—but in a context of inflationary economic policies that reduced the real value of all currencies.

Accordingly, the United States is prepared to consider utilizing, as an additional indicator in the coordination process, the relationship among our currencies and a basket of commodities, including gold. This could be helpful as an early warning signal of potential price trends.[54]

Although the Baker proposal was met with uncertainty and anxiety by those favoring a floating international exchange rate system, it was strongly supported by those who were worried about fiscal and monetary policies leading to inflation. "This is very far from a gold standard," commented economist Robert Mundell. "But it is a step in that direction."[55] Lawrence Kudlow, at the time chief economist at Bear, Stearns & Co., stated approvingly: "The proposal to link currency values to a gold-commodity price index provides a reentry for the discipline of gold into the world monetary system."[56] Kudlow would later be appointed director of the National Economic Council by President Donald Trump, serving from 2018 to 2021.

It is intriguing to speculate how economic and financial developments might have turned out differently had the U.S. adopted Baker's suggestion to grant gold a role to help stabilize currency relationships. It is notable that former vice president Mike Pence suggested in a speech before the Detroit Economic Club in November 2010 that a debate was starting anew over an anchor for the global monetary system. Massive government borrowing and spending, compounded by central bank purchases of government debt, had made it necessary to reevaluate the international currency system, Pence asserted—including the role of gold: "The time has come to have a debate over gold and the proper role it should play in our nation's monetary affairs."[57]

When an idea has merit and holds out the potential to help restore the principles and values that can underpin economic renewal, it is never too

186 | *Good as Gold*

late to put that idea into action. The idea put forward in Greenspan's 1981 proposal for gold-backed Treasury bonds would be broached three decades later, in March 2011, during a congressional hearing with then–Fed chairman Ben Bernanke. Citing Greenspan's *Wall Street Journal* article in the context of finding a way to create boundaries for monetary policy, Senator Jim DeMint of South Carolina asked, "Have you given any thought to the idea of issuing bonds payable in gold that would begin to create some standard for our currency?" Bernanke responded by stating that "the Federal Reserve is not debasing the currency" and by asserting that inflation was low. Dismissing concerns over the dollar's value as "overstated," Bernanke said that moving to a gold standard would not provide a "panacea" for current economic ills. But he also acknowledged that a gold standard "did deliver price stability over very long periods of time."[58]

Price stability over very long periods of time seems a worthy goal—especially in the aftermath of the inflation that emerged as a significant economic problem following the COVID-19 pandemic. It is no coincidence that new legislative efforts have been launched to restore sound money and sound finances by relinking the value of the U.S. dollar to a fixed weight of gold. In March 2023, Representative Alex Mooney (R-WV) introduced the Gold Standard Restoration Act to make Federal Reserve notes "redeemable for and exchangeable with gold" at a fixed price to be determined by the closing market price of gold on a designated date following enactment of the legislation. The bill cites a more than 40 percent loss of dollar-purchasing power since 2000 and criticizes the Federal Reserve for creating inflation rates that pushed the cost of living for many Americans to "untenable levels." The bill seeks to discourage excessive deficit spending and encourage balanced federal budgets by relinquishing control of the money supply to the market instead of the Federal Reserve. "The American economy needs a stable dollar, fixed exchange rates, and money supply controlled by the market," the bill proclaims, "not the government."[59]

The legislative initiative received praise from sound money advocacy groups such as the Foundation for Economic Education. "Government cannot continue to spend and print on a massive scale without producing existential threats to the currency and our economy," commented Lawrence Reed, president emeritus of the organization. "The gold standard never failed America, bad ideas and bad politicians did. If we do nothing, disaster awaits us just as it drowned earlier civilizations that spent and inflated their way to ruin."[60]

Sentiments of this sort indicate a deep-seated desire to restore founding values by linking the dollar's value to gold. Convertibility provides the ultimate simple rule for regulating the money supply in accordance with individual rights and free-market principles.

6

The Leadership Imperative

THE DEMAND FOR sound finances and sound money is reaching a crescendo as the consequences of irresponsible fiscal and monetary policies take their toll in both economic and political terms. In May 2023, the prospect of a first-ever debt default was causing deep divisions among American voters, with 45 percent of respondents to a *Wall Street Journal* poll saying they did not favor Congress lifting the debt ceiling, while 44 percent did want to see it lifted.[1] The dilemma was captured by a sixty-three-year-old Republican who told a reporter, "I want them to stop printing money. Should the country default? No."

In a separate Gallup poll, results showed that Americans had declining confidence in economic leaders, including Federal Reserve Chairman Jerome Powell and President Joe Biden, as well as both Democratic and Republican leaders in Congress.[2] The rating for Powell was the lowest Gallup rating for any prior Fed chair, with only 36 percent expressing confidence that he would do or recommend the right thing for the economy.

What do such negative assessments say about granting increased powers to government officials to manage the economy? Congress is authorized by the U.S. Constitution to coin money and regulate its value—yet it would seem that Congress has outsourced this function to the Federal Reserve. When citizens express angst over the ability of government authorities to "print money out of thin air" in tandem with their desire to avoid default, they are properly acknowledging the connection between government overspending and accommodative monetary policy. But it has become increasingly clear that U.S. voters have little faith in the government to competently address its most basic tasks: (1) to balance the federal budget and (2) to ensure stable money.

This gaping hole in the American fabric of self-government now threatens the values that underpin a society based on equal rights, private property, the rule of law, and individual liberty. The damage can be mended only through bold leadership to restore the U.S. dollar as a dependable and constant standard of value in keeping with American founding principles. Just as government should function as a servant to the people, and not vice versa, money was supposed to function as a useful measuring tool for free people engaged in free enterprise. Money was not intended to serve as just another policy instrument to be wielded by the government.

Leaders have long recognized that the presence of a threat can also bring opportunity—indeed, it sharpens focus on the goal. The goal is clear: we must rise to the challenge of sound money. If the collective "we" seems to clearly reference U.S. citizens, the reason is that the United States is the issuer of the world's most utilized currency for foreign exchange transactions. The U.S. dollar is the dominant global reserve currency—accounting for 58 percent of total allocated currency reserves held by central banks at the end of 2023, according to the International Monetary Fund.[3] The other official reserve asset held by central banks is gold. The solution to providing sound money at home and abroad is to link the value of the dollar once again to gold. Not all at once and not overnight—but we need to begin the effort, with clarity of purpose, to restore faith in our currency as an honest measure and a dependable store of value and to reinforce the integrity of the U.S. dollar as the most trustworthy currency in the world.

The launching of Treasury Trust Bonds would serve as the opening salvo in a campaign aimed at moving toward sound money and away from economic management through central bank intervention. The dollar is made as good as gold by pledging gold convertibility of a Treasury bond at maturity with a nominal face value defined in dollars. This initiative, straightforward and honest as it is, could simultaneously be dismissed by detractors as trivial while being hailed by supporters as monumental. For the first time since President Nixon ended the Bretton Woods system on August 13, 1971, the dollar would be officially convertible into gold at a fixed rate. Not all U.S. dollars would be convertible; it would not be feasible to guarantee the $2.3 trillion in

Federal Reserve notes currently in circulation using the 261 million ounces in gold owned by the U.S. government as collateral. Nor would the convertibility privilege be granted to foreign central banks as it was under the Bretton Woods system as a condition for pegging their currencies to the U.S. dollar.

The issuance of Treasury Trust Bonds would link the dollar to gold for those investors willing to lend money to the U.S. government on a long-term basis—perhaps as long as fifty years—but who want the security of knowing their investment will be paid off at maturity either in dollars or the promised amount of gold. Reflected in the price they are willing to pay for the bond is its imputed yield; if the bond sells for a premium relative to comparable Treasury borrowing instruments, it will indicate the additional value investors attach to having the gold option. This is an important feature, as investors might well pay a premium for reasons that transcend sheer financial calculation.

Restoring Confidence in Government

The U.S. president under whose leadership this initiative would be launched as a pilot program would become a historic figure for restoring metallic backing for U.S. dollars paid at maturity in gold at the option of those willing to place their faith in Treasury Trust Bonds. The genesis for moving forward with such an agenda could be the appointment of a commission "to investigate possible ways to set a fixed value for the dollar," as called for in the 2012 Republican Party Platform.[4] The concept was put forward again four years later with further elaboration in the 2016 Republican Party Platform:

> Determined to crush the double-digit inflation that was part of the Carter Administration's economic legacy, President Reagan, shortly after his inauguration, established a commission to consider the feasibility of a metallic basis for U.S. currency. In 2012, facing the task of cleaning up the wreckage of the current Administration's policies, we proposed a similar commission to investigate ways to set a fixed value for the dollar.
>
> With Republican leadership, the House of Representatives has passed legislation to set up just such a commission. We recommend its enactment by the full Congress and the commis-

sion's careful consideration of ways to secure the integrity of our currency.[5]

The legislation referenced in this statement was approved in November 2015. Championed by Representative Kevin Brady of Texas, who served as chairman of the House Ways and Means Committee, the bill sought "to establish a commission to examine the United States monetary policy, evaluate alternative monetary regimes, and recommend a course for monetary policy going forward."[6] Its companion bill in the Senate, sponsored by Senator John Cornyn of Texas, was S.1786, the Centennial Monetary Commission Act of 2015.[7] Both pieces of legislation would assign to a commission the task of evaluating various operational regimes under which the Board of Governors of the Federal Reserve System may conduct monetary policy to achieve the maximum sustainable level of output and employment and price stability over the long term—including using (1) discretion in determining monetary policy without an operational regime, (2) price level targeting, (3) inflation rate targeting, (4) nominal GDP targeting, (5) monetary policy rules, and (6) the gold standard.

Although the Senate bill did not pass, it had powerful cosponsors in Senator Rand Paul of Kentucky and Senator Ted Cruz of Texas; the House version had twenty cosponsors and passed 241–85 by recorded vote.[8] The prospect that a new attempt to secure the integrity of U.S. currency by setting a fixed value for the dollar would find strong political support appears likely. Given that the performance of the Federal Reserve in delivering price stability has been found wanting in the aftermath of the COVID-19 pandemic—with inflation hitting forty-year record highs in 2022—it seems that a candidate for the U.S. presidency who emphasized the need for sound money could attract significant numbers of voters. It could become a signature act for a sitting president to direct the secretary of the treasury to issue gold-linked Treasury Trust Bonds early in a new administration. It would be a sign of resolve and commitment toward restoring a sound dollar—and the first installment of a program for achieving fiscal rectitude.

Over the life of the bond, which would extend for decades, the resale market for Treasury Trust Bonds would serve as a testimonial about budgetary discipline at the federal level. If the relative yields on TTBs and conventional

Treasury debt instruments did not radically diverge, it would mean that investors in the aggregate were correct in assessing how prudently Congress would address its excess spending tendencies. On the other hand, if TTBs became much more highly valued than comparable Treasury instruments offering no gold-convertibility option at maturity, it would be clear that the value of U.S. dollars had decreased considerably over the life of the bond—likely because of budgetary malfeasance. Notwithstanding the immediate windfall gain from issuing a Treasury security that sells at a premium to investors and thus reduces the cost of financing debt, the Treasury will have gained in issuing TTBs if Congress performs better than investors expect in balancing the budget. So long as deficit spending and accommodative monetary policy do not result in more dollar debasement relative to the price of gold over the duration of the bond than investors generally anticipate, investors will not choose to exercise gold convertibility of the principal at maturity.

If a monetary commission were established under an incoming administration to examine the impact of the Federal Reserve on the economic performance of the United States and to investigate ways to set a fixed value for the dollar, the introduction of Treasury Trust Bonds could be the logical follow-up action to exploring alternative approaches and recommending a course for monetary policy going forward. Certainly, issuing Treasury securities denominated in U.S. dollars with the future principal amount payable in gold would fulfill the 2016 Republican platform recommendation that such a monetary commission, once enacted, would give "careful consideration of ways to secure the integrity of our currency."

Does the problem of having a dollar that is progressively debased as a matter of official monetary policy resonate with the average American voter beyond the frustration of having to pay higher prices every year? The Federal Reserve's definition of its mandate to promote "stable prices" does not mean that the dollar should maintain its purchasing power through time or provide a dependable store of value. "The Federal Open Market Committee (FOMC) judges that an inflation rate of 2 percent over the longer run, as measured by the annual change in the price index for personal consumption expenditures, is most consistent with the Federal Reserve's mandate."[9]

Inflation has certainly exceeded the Federal Reserve's 2 percent target since 2021, both in terms of the consumer price index (CPI) and the Fed's preferred personal consumption expenditures (PCE) index. The cumulative increase in U.S. inflation from January 2021 to May 2024 for all items was 20.1 percent, according to the U.S. Bureau of Labor Statistics—a yearly average of roughly 6 percent.[10] And the Fed's favorite measure of inflation, the core PCE index (which strips out food and energy prices), rose at an annual rate of 3.7 percent in the first quarter of 2024, again exceeding the Fed's 2 percent inflation target rate. Even 2 percent annual inflation, however, diminishes the dollar as a reliable measure of value over time and a valid monetary standard. If inflation increases perpetually at 2 percent per year, the price level will double in thirty-five years; over a lifetime, that constitutes a considerable difference. Savings kept in the form of cash will steadily deteriorate in terms of purchasing power—amounting to an expropriation of wealth by the government without due process. Deliberate efforts by Federal Reserve authorities to reduce the value of the dollar by 2 percent annually through inflation targeting would seem to violate the private property rights of U.S. citizens.

How was the 2 percent inflation rate target chosen by the Fed as the appropriate metric for delivering on its mandated objective of achieving stable prices? The 2 percent target was made official in 2012 under Fed chairman Ben Bernanke and has been sustained by his successors, Janet Yellen and Jerome Powell, as described in the "Statement on Longer-Run Goals and Monetary Policy Strategy" adopted by the Federal Open Market Committee in January 2012 and reaffirmed in January 2024.[11] The genesis of selecting a definition of price stability that amounts to the programmed diminution of the dollar traces back to the boardroom of the Federal Reserve in July 1996, when Alan Greenspan was chairman and Janet Yellen was a Fed governor. The transcript of that meeting makes for remarkable reading given today's concern about inflation as a risk to productive economic growth.[12] Greenspan opened the discussion by asking, "When we talk about price stability as a goal, setting aside the measurement problem, are we talking about price stability or are we talking about zero inflation?" Yellen responded by making a case for 2 percent inflation as the preferable target based on what she described as a "greasing-the-wheels" argument. Citing an academic paper coauthored by her husband, well-known economist (and future Nobel laureate) George Akerlof, Yellen said that "a little inflation lowers unemployment by facilitating adjustments in relative pay in a world where individuals deeply dislike nominal pay cuts."[13]

The theory behind this assertion is that workers resist—and firms are hesitant to impose—nominal pay cuts even when firms are experiencing losses. The logic aligns with Keynesian notions about "sticky wages" that do not come down, even during an economic downturn. Under such conditions, inflation can ostensibly provide cover for achieving real wage cuts without imposing the psychological blow of reducing nominal pay. Inflation allows firms to increase the amount they pay workers while still achieving a wage cut, so long as the wage increase is lower than the impact of higher inflation. If there were no inflation, firms would have to actually reduce pay to achieve a real reduction in wages. In her discussion with Greenspan, Yellen emphasized the importance of assuaging human emotion even when real wages were being decreased. "I think we are dealing here with a very deep-rooted property of the human psyche," she noted.[14]

According to the transcript, Yellen told her colleagues around the table about a survey posed to a random sample of Americans by Yale economist Robert Shiller to measure their aversion to inflation. The survey asked respondents whether they agreed with the statement: "I think that if my pay went up, I would feel more satisfaction in my job, more sense of fulfillment, even if prices went up just as much." Yellen reported that 28 percent fully agreed, and another 21 percent partially agreed. "Only 27 percent completely disagreed," she observed, "although I think it will comfort you to learn that in a special subsample of economists, not one single economist Shiller polled fully agreed and 78 percent completely disagreed." The transcript notes parenthetically that this last comment prompted laughter in the Fed boardroom.[15]

An initiative by a bold political leader to counter such government-knows-best thinking is sorely needed. It is time to challenge the presumptuous attitude so prevalent among Keynesian-influenced economists that ignorant workers can be tricked into believing their wages are rising through the inflation ruse. Indeed, it was time to challenge such thinking even back in 1996, when Yellen carried the debate over a suitable inflation target. The efforts of another monetary authority at the table that day bear testimony to the need for intellectual diversity among discussants at FOMC meetings to ensure that alternative views receive a fair hearing. Jerry Jordan, president of the Federal Reserve Bank of Cleveland, took the position that businesses and households make their best decisions about the future when they expect the purchasing power of the dollar to remain constant, whether those decisions involve personal investments or business. "If I could be persuaded that permanently eroding or conceivably increasing the purchasing power of the currency, changing the standard of value over time, somehow improves resource allocation and standards of living, I would be very interested," Jordan stated. "But I am not persuaded."[16]

Jordan suggested a different scenario: "If we can create a situation in which people say that the dollar will purchase the same in the future as it does today and they proceed to base their decisions on that expectation as the most probable outcome, we then would get standards of living that rise at their maximum potential."[17] He asserted that such conditions would further bring about maximum employment and other developments that foster economic well-being. In direct contrast to the survey results cited by Yellen in her arguments promoting low-level inflation as a deliberate policy objective, Jordan proposed asking a different question:

> If I were going to do surveys about wage cuts or increases of the sort that Janet reported on, one of the surveys I would want to conduct is to ask people as we approach the end of this century to choose between two things. If the central bank had an objective of reducing the purchasing power of the dollar to 13 cents or 7 cents over the next century, which would you prefer? I would expect the majority of the responses to be, why are you going to reduce it at all? Explain to me why the dollar is not going to purchase the same at the end of the next century as it does today. The difference between 13 cents and 7 cents is the difference between a 2 percent rate of inflation and a 3 percent rate of inflation over 100 years. I think most people would view that as a silly alternative. They would say, why not zero inflation.[18]

When impeccable logic trumps scholarly bunkum, it doesn't mean it will become official policy, especially when one is dealing with government agencies as powerful as the Federal Reserve. But it does mean that the logic of maintaining a constant monetary standard of value over time becomes even more compelling in the aftermath of debilitating episodes of financial instability and forty-year record-high levels of inflation. Why not zero inflation? Why not a stable dollar that provides a reliable measurement tool for making decisions about the future? A skilled political leader will comprehend the powerful appeal of putting forth the question that is treated with belittlement by central bankers while strongly registering with people who must contend daily with the real economy: Why not sound money?

Taking on the Federal Reserve is no easy task, and an aspirant to the presidency of the United States needs to make the case that Americans deserve money they can trust. America's next leader should publicly embrace the conviction that money is a moral contract between the government and its citizens. Doing so is the first step toward restoring confidence in the basic competence of officials in Washington, D.C., to fix what has broken—in terms of both monetary and fiscal policy.

Securing Dollar Dominance

America has a leading position in global financial and economic matters. Though Americans constitute less than 5 percent of the world's population, they generate more than 20 percent of the world's total income. America is the world's largest national economy and leading global trader.[19] It was the United States that instigated the creation of a new international monetary system even as World War II was still raging, to provide a stable foundation on which devastated nations could rebuild their economies and attain new levels of prosperity. The dollar still retains its anchor position among the world's major currencies long after the central tenet of the Bretton Woods agreement, its gold convertibility, was unilaterally suspended. According to a comprehensive study from the Atlantic Council, "Dollar Dominance Monitor," the dollar currently represents 58 percent of the value of foreign reserve holdings worldwide, while the next most-used currency, the euro, constitutes 21 percent of foreign reserve holdings.[20] Dollar usage is reinforced by its widespread acceptance in trade and financial markets; these network effects further support dollar dominance.

Yet there are increasing efforts by rival nations to find ways to diversify away from the dollar. Russia is working particularly hard to remove the U.S. dollar as the primary currency for conducting trade and financial transactions among the BRICS nations—the five leading emerging economies of Brazil, Russia, India, China, and South Africa. Alexander Babakov, deputy chairman of Russia's State Duma, called for the creation of a "fundamentally new currency" at the Saint Petersburg International Economic Forum gathering held in New Delhi, India, in March 2023.[21] Babakov said that work on the proposed currency was already underway and would be formally introduced at a future summit of BRICS leaders.

Meanwhile, BRICS countries are showing a new willingness to carry out cross-border transactions using the Chinese yuan for settlement purposes. Russian president Vladimir Putin held talks with Chinese leader Xi Jinping in March 2023, resulting in fourteen economic agreements, and followed up their meeting by announcing, "We are in favor of using the Chinese yuan for settlements between Russia and the countries of Asia, Africa, and Latin America. I am confident that these forms of settlement in yuan will develop between Russian partners and their counterparts in third countries."[22] Shortly thereafter, in April 2023, Brazil's president Luiz Inacio Lula da Silva echoed the call for developing countries to work toward replacing the U.S. dollar by using their own currencies for trade or by creating an alternative common currency. "Every night I ask myself why all countries have to base their trade on the dollar," Lula stated at a speech in Shanghai, according to the *Financial Times*. "Why can't we do trade based on our own currencies? Who was it that decided that the dollar was the currency after the disappearance of the gold standard?"[23]

For its part, China has been pushing to use its own currency to buy Russian commodities—switching to yuan to pay for some $88 billion in commodities such as oil, coal, and metals from Russia since the Ukraine war began in 2022.[24] The decision by Russia to accommodate China by accepting a payment role for the yuan is no doubt prompted by the economic pressure of Western resistance to Russian military aggression, but China clearly welcomes the opportunity to further its long-standing ambition to internationalize the yuan. Economic necessity is also a factor for Argentina, which imports many products from China; with U.S. dollar reserves in short supply, Argentina's government announced in April 2023 that it would pay for $1 billion worth of Chinese imports with yuan rather than dollars.[25]

But the potential threat to the dollar's global dominance takes on more serious implications now that oil-rich Saudi Arabia has said it will consider trading in currencies other than the U.S. dollar. China is Saudi Arabia's largest trade partner and the chief destination for Saudi oil exports; although U.S. dollars have been used to denominate payments for oil from Saudi Arabia and other member nations of the Organization of Petroleum Exporting Countries (OPEC) since 1974, the Saudi minister of finance stated in January 2023 that trade arrangements could be settled in other currencies besides the dollar.[26] When oil trades involve dollars, central banks around the world have a greater need to keep dollar reserves to pay for energy imports. Moreover, profits earned in dollars through Saudi sales are often used to purchase U.S. Treasury debt, helping to lower interest rates.

So much is at stake if the dollar becomes vulnerable to displacement as the world's reserve currency. Given the small role currently occupied by China's yuan—it accounted for 3.2 percent of global payments in January 2022—there would seem to be no immediate need to worry. But China is determined to keep making progress on this front by continuing to procure high-profile bilateral trade deals that include the adoption of yuan-clearing arrangements, such as a March 2023 agreement between China and Brazil. Insult was added to injury when French energy giant TotalEnergies completed a transaction for the sale of liquefied natural gas denominated in yuan in March 2023. This was followed in April 2023 by an announcement by French bank BNP Paribas that it would collaborate with the Bank of China to facilitate the use of China's central bank digital currency by its corporate clients.[27]

The United States can take the attitude that these are meaningless developments not worthy of diverting attention from other economic priorities or national security objectives. But it would be a mistake to forget the lessons that motivated the architects of the Bretton Woods system, who recognized the need to prevent currency wars from becoming real wars. The stirrings among developing nations to align their economic and financial future with China by utilizing the yuan to denominate the value of goods and services traded across borders—and to make payments—should not be ignored. Indeed, such challenges bolster the case for acting now to solidify both the dollar itself and its dominant position among currencies. World disorder is not helped by the lack of a coherent and dependable international monetary system. The absence of American leadership on this vital issue leaves a dangerous vacuum.

Can a new American president signal to the world that the monetary integrity of the U.S. dollar is high on the agenda of an incoming administration?

Can the link between genuinely fair trade and a level international monetary playing field be asserted with vigor and conviction? One cannot advocate for free trade while allowing currency manipulation to make a mockery of free-market competition. The need for stable exchange rates has become a political imperative as much as an economic one. Americans have traditionally had a positive view of free trade, but those opinions began to change after 2014 as sliding currencies imposed distortions that hurt entire classes of people, mostly in manufacturing. According to a Pew Research Center survey taken in March 2016, support for free-trade deals had dropped since its peak in 2014, when 59 percent of Americans had a favorable view; by 2016 only 51 percent of Americans viewed free-trade agreements positively, with 39 percent believing they had been a bad thing for the United States.[28] Criticism of trade deals was particularly strong among Republican and Republican-leaning supporters of Donald Trump, who would win the U.S. presidential election that year. A more recent poll conducted by Gallup showed that independents had likewise cooled on the benefits of trade, with 30 percent in 2021 viewing foreign trade as a threat to the U.S. economy.[29]

The messaging task is to link the need for an honest dollar that can be trusted—both at home and abroad—with individual economic liberty and the future of free-market capitalism. When currency movements alter the terms of trade to the detriment of Americans engaged in manufacturing products or providing services that must contend with underpriced foreign competition, the notion that free-trade agreements are beneficial garners skepticism. Citizens are governed by legal-tender laws; they conduct their daily transactions, collect their paychecks, and pay their taxes using the national currency as the monetary unit of account. There is no recourse for an individual who is negatively impacted by the actions of another nation to deliberately enhance the appeal of its exports on world markets through currency manipulation—even though the personal prosperity of the individual in the targeted country is reduced. Clearly, using a common currency would eliminate this threat, but the idea of a global central bank is antithetical to monetary accountability. Instead of granting yet more powers to government officials, the goal should be to empower individuals by providing broad access to sound money.

American leadership should be at the helm of steering toward that goal. Mere rhetoric and empty bromides from a new U.S. president about getting

America's fiscal house in order will not suffice. Words must be supported by concrete actions to have real impact: When the U.S. Treasury issues a long-term bond redeemable in either dollars or gold at the option of the holder, the entire world will take notice. The move would signal that a new sheriff is in town, so to speak; it would convey America's serious commitment to balancing its budget so that budget deficits do not further add to outstanding debt. The action would put federal officials on notice that monetizing government borrowing is no longer an option—and that would affect the conduct of monetary policy.

The connection between fiscal irresponsibility and monetary accommodation should not be ignored. Nor should it be diminished by the claims of a Fed chairman who regularly intones, "Price stability is the responsibility of the Federal Reserve."[30] While it may seem convenient, even noble, to claim exclusive responsibility for maintaining a stable dollar, it is highly inappropriate to absolve the occupant of the White House and members of Congress of causing inflation through deficit spending—which is the classic Keynesian prescription for fiscal stimulus that comes with the associated risk of inflation. Sound finances and sound money must be pursued simultaneously to achieve a stable foundation that allows free enterprise to flourish to the benefit of all. Higher productivity and higher output increase individual prosperity and raise the standard of living for an entire society of citizens.

Certainly, as became very clear during the anxious period surrounding negotiations to raise the debt ceiling in May 2023, foreign governments saw a direct link between the possibility of U.S. default and the high standing of the dollar. "Rich and poor nations alike fear a possible U.S. default, which would torpedo the financial markets and deal a massive blow to the dollar," according to a *Washington Post* article.[31] Treasury Secretary Janet Yellen told reporters before attending a Group of Seven meeting in Japan that default "would spark a global downturn" and "would also risk undermining U.S. global economic leadership and raise questions about our ability to defend our national security interests."[32] President Biden warned that if the United States defaulted on its debt, the entire world would be in trouble. "Our economy would fall into recession and our international reputation would be damaged in the extreme."[33]

The question is whether U.S. global economic leadership turns on getting the latest extension on borrowing to finance unending revenue shortfalls in the federal budget, or whether it's more important that the world's superpower nation does not go bankrupt. If the standing of the dollar in the global arena depends on the ability to temporarily delay having to realistically address non-sustainable spending trends, then its future reduced status is just a matter of time. A better approach is to lay out a marker of fiscal rectitude and monetary integrity by issuing Treasury Trust Bonds that bind the nation to fulfilling its intention to achieve sound finances as the means to certifying a sound dollar—literally requiring the government to put its money where its mouth is.

Trade partners fully understand the logic for a level monetary playing field, even if they try to avoid commitments to currency stability that would have any enforcement provisions. As explained by economist Robert Mundell—and exemplified through the adoption of the euro by twenty-seven countries representing 341 million people—using the same monetary unit increases trade and maximizes economic efficiency. "The benefits of the common currency are immediately obvious to anyone traveling abroad or shopping online on websites based in another EU country," states an official website for the European Union.[34] But just as former World Bank president Robert Zoellick's suggestion in November 2010 to consider using gold as an international reference point in constructing a new currency system was dismissed as overly restrictive, policymakers today can likewise be expected to balk at proposals that impose monetary and fiscal discipline. The ability to issue government debt and sell it to central banks has temporarily solved many budgetary exigencies; arguments for "flexibility" can easily win the day. Still, Zoellick pointed out that the increasing use of gold as a monetary asset was an "elephant in the room" being ignored by policymakers wrestling with global trade and fiscal imbalances.[35]

A bold proposal from a new U.S. president to establish a trade alliance among nations that embrace the same set of economic principles—notably, genuine competition based on clear price signals facilitated through the shared use of a common monetary reference point—could be the catalyst for inspiring a new economic partnership among like-minded nations affirming a renewed dedication to free-market capitalism. Stable exchange rates are the starting point for authentic free trade based on valid price signals. The goal is to have a unified money system while ruling out a central banking authority with the power to manipulate the cost of capital to stimulate or restrict economic activity. The money supply should not be controlled by a small committee of appointed officials but rather determined by all the individuals operating in the real economy—expanding and contracting in accordance with their aggregate expectations about profitable opportunities worthy of financial investment.

An appeal to trade partners to prove their allegiance to honest competition and a level monetary playing field would put many countries on the spot. Canada and Mexico are two of the top three U.S. trading partners; in 2021, trade flows in North America reached $1.3 trillion. After the North American Free Trade Agreement (NAFTA) was renegotiated, the replacement United States–Mexico–Canada Agreement (USMCA) was implemented in 2020 to support "mutually beneficial trade leading to freer markets, fairer trade, and robust economic growth in North America."[36] A significant change from the prior agreement is the addition of a chapter that addresses unfair currency practices and requires commitments to refrain from competitive devaluations and targeting exchange rates; this part of the agreement also makes provisions for increased transparency and accountability. As noted on the fact sheet for the agreement provided by the Office of the U.S. Trade Representative, "this approach is unprecedented in the context of a trade agreement, and will help reinforce macroeconomic and exchange rate stability."[37] Most important, by focusing on the impact of exchange rate movements as a key factor in determining whether trade among nations is both free and fair, the revised agreement established a model for negotiating future trade agreements—especially in cases where currency manipulation has been an issue.

China is the other major trade partner of the United States, with two-way trade in goods between the two nations in 2023 amounting to $575 billion; the United States exported $148 billion worth of goods to China while importing $427 billion worth of goods from China.[38] Given that China was formally cited as a currency manipulator under the Trump administration in August 2019 (though this action was rescinded in February 2020), it is not surprising that the subject of currency manipulation was specifically addressed in the "Phase One" trade agreement between the United States and China concluded in January 2020. Under a section on exchange rate practices, the agreement stipulates: "The Parties shall refrain from competitive devaluations and not target exchange rates for competitive purposes, including through large-scale, persistent, one-sided intervention in exchange markets."[39] Yet the exchange rate of seven yuan for a dollar that triggered the official charge of currency manipulation against the Chinese government in 2019 was broached again some two years later as the yuan slid against the dollar. China's top central bank official, Yi Gang, stated in an April 2023 speech that his government had largely ended regular foreign exchange intervention, while also maintaining that Chinese monetary authorities still "reserve the right" to intervene in the market.[40]

It is clear that the criteria for evaluating the impact of currency movements on trade and financial flows—as well as enforcement mechanisms and transparency violations—have rendered efforts to address this serious infraction against free and fair trade mostly useless for practical purposes. Whether governments pursue currency manipulation through central bank decisions or other policies, the nation victimized by such abuses is left to decipher self-reported statistics furnished by the offending governments themselves. Worse, the trade agreements that have linked sliding exchange rates with trade fairness—certainly a sign of progress—nevertheless rely on the International Monetary Fund to serve as arbiter. The irony is that the IMF, though created specifically to prevent member countries from manipulating their exchange rates to gain an unfair trade advantage, has never in its eight-decade history publicly determined a member to be manipulating its currency.[41]

New leadership coming from the nation that issues the dominant reserve currency and steers interest rate policy for the world's major central banks is a potential game changer. Today it is still common to hear references to the supposed rules-based global trading system adopted in 1944 as if it somehow still existed. In a speech before the World Economic Forum at Davos in January 2017, British prime minister Theresa May praised liberalism, free trade, and globalization as "the forces that underpin the rules-based international system that is key to our global prosperity and security."[42] Paradoxically, Chinese president Xi Jinping likewise extolled the virtues of a rules-based economic order at Davos, winning widespread praise for defending free trade and globalization.[43] Some two years later, the IMF would dispute President Trump's assertion that China was manipulating its currency for an unfair trade advantage—four days after U.S. Treasury Secretary Steven Mnuchin announced he had formally made that designation after China's central bank allowed the managed exchange rate to depreciate beyond seven yuan to the dollar for the first time in eleven years.[44]

One way to draw world attention toward the need for international monetary reform would be for the United States to question the IMF's disregard for its founding responsibility to safeguard exchange rate stability and suggest that the organization has outlived its original purpose—indeed, that it works against leveling the international monetary playing field. If the IMF were true to the mission espoused by its architects to bring about financial disarmament by preventing beggar-thy-neighbor currency depreciation from undermining trade, it would facilitate a move toward a new international monetary order based on gold convertibility for a class of long-term government debt instruments issued by participating nations using their own currencies. But it seems doubtful that the IMF would seriously entertain any such proposal; despite being charged with exercising firm surveillance over its members' exchange rate policies, the IMF refrains from disparaging currency manipulators. Meanwhile, the organization holds more than ninety million ounces of gold; noting on its website that "gold remains an important reserve asset," the IMF refers to itself as "one of the world's largest official holders of gold."[45]

Today's international financial institutions seem incapable of confronting disorderly currency movements. But that failure heightens the imperative of leadership. Just as it did when the United States rose to the challenge of inspiring desperate nations with a promise to establish stable and trustworthy monetary rules to undergird international commerce in compliance with free-trade principles, the needed initiative falls once again to America. And just as then, the advantages of a sound money approach to ensure a level playing field that maximizes the rewards from true competition will serve our own best interests.

When a U.S. president announces that a level monetary playing field is the key to ensuring that gains from international trade serve to strengthen economies rather than hollow them out, the announcement will be a particularly poignant reminder that America is still the world's leading nation. It was President Nixon, after all, who ended the Bretton Woods system by suspending the right to convert U.S. dollars into gold. The Bretton Woods system was based on fixed exchange rates precisely to bring order to international trade and investment so that currency depreciation could not be used by cheating nations to skew financial outcomes to their own advantage. The system had been enormously successful in enriching its participants and had greatly enhanced the position of the United States in the world, both economically and politically. On August 15, 1971, the day that Nixon announced in a televised address to the nation that he had directed his Treasury secretary to "suspend temporarily the convertibility of the dollar," he emphasized that the United States had always been a forward-looking and trustworthy trading partner. Nixon vowed that "we will press for the necessary reforms to set up an urgently needed new international monetary system."[46]

It has been more than half a century since the United States government has maintained an official link between the dollar and gold through convertibility at a fixed rate. If a new American president restored gold convertibility through the issuance of a fifty-year Treasury bond, it would truly be a historic achievement. President Reagan expressed his own desire to link the dollar to gold: in a 1980 campaign commercial, he expressed his belief that government causes inflation—not business, not labor. "We'll never regain price stability until we restore some form of gold backing to the dollar. As President, my first priority will be to make the dollar the most trusted currency in the world."[47] However, to his disappointment, Reagan was not able to make the change happen; according to former congressman Ron Paul, the president once told him in secret that "no nation has abandoned gold and remained great."[48]

A bold new American president could establish an official link between the U.S. dollar and gold that would serve as a beachhead for fixing what broke under the Bretton Woods system—that is, by championing the importance of a level monetary playing field for international trade. Guaranteeing future gold convertibility for a U.S. government debt instrument would demonstrate a commitment to sound finances and sound money. It would restore faith in the viability of American founding principles of self-government through responsible elected officials. It would repair the damage represented by the collapse of Bretton Woods under Nixon and fulfill the promise of pressing for the necessary reforms to set up a new international monetary system, even as it would quell the fears and honor the aspirations of Reagan. Issuing a gold-linked Treasury bond on July 4, 2026, that would be slated to mature fifty years later on July 4, 2076—the three-hundred-year anniversary of America's independence—would be a glorious way to celebrate the history and principles of the United States. It would provide a signal to the world that the United States had an optimistic and confident view of the future and that freedom works.

Forging New Ties

On the international front, an intriguing avenue for exploring new paths to sound money has recently arisen as the result of the election of Javier Milei as the new leader of Argentina. A self-described "anarcho-capitalist," Milei has pledged to abolish Argentina's central bank and slash government spending. He canceled public projects and announced cuts to energy and transportation subsidies shortly after being inaugurated in December 2023. In addition, Milei eliminated or merged numerous federal ministries as part of his effort to significantly downsize the size and scope of government. A proponent of small government, individual liberty, and economic and social freedom, Argentina's president seeks to reverse decades of bloated bureaucracy and government intervention in the economy. "The challenge we have in front of us is titanic, but the true strength of a people can be measured in how it confronts the challenges when they present themselves," Milei declared upon taking the presidential oath.[49]

The titanic challenge centers on a failing currency that has confounded the functioning of Argentina's economy and stymied its access to financial capital. The value of the nation's money, the peso, has all but collapsed; inflation in Argentina was officially measured at 211.4 percent year-on-year for 2023, the highest rate since the early 1990s.[50] The monetary breakdown is the result of an explosion in the money supply—which in turn is the consequence of printing money to fund vast budget deficits annually, due to chronic government overspending. The size of the state has doubled as a share of the economy since 2010; between 2011 and 2022, according to the Institute on Argentine and Latin American Reality, public-sector employment increased 34 percent while private-sector job growth was only 3 percent.[51]

It remains a big question whether the sheer determination exhibited by the new leader in Buenos Aires, whose motto is "Long live freedom, damn it!," will prove sufficient to revive free-market capitalism in Argentina—a nation that was once one of the world's richest economies. Measured by income per person, Argentina ranked among the ten richest countries in the world in 1914; today, 40 percent of Argentineans live in poverty.[52] (In comparison, the official poverty rate in the United States was 11.5 percent in 2022, based on U.S. Census Bureau statistics.)[53] Plans to revamp the Argentinean economy initially appeared to center on dumping the peso in favor of adopting the U.S. dollar as the nation's official legal tender and unit of account. But by early February 2024, Milei was forced to push dollarization down the list of economic priorities in order to focus on other reforms. In an interview published on *Cenital*, an Argentine website, he explained that dollarization of the nation's economy would take place after broader financial reforms were achieved, including reducing the balance sheet of the central bank. Milei stressed that he was seeking "free competition of currency" as the solution to the hyperinflated peso, which is not the same as exclusively advocating for U.S. dollars to replace the local currency.[54]

Dollarization is a subject that has come before the U.S. Congress as a matter for discussion. A hearing sponsored by the Subcommittee on Economic Policy and the Subcommittee on International Trade and Finance took place before the Senate Banking Committee in April 1999 to specifically address the question whether the United States should encourage official dollarization for emerging market countries.[55] The subject was deemed sufficiently important to draw both Lawrence H. Summers, who was deputy secretary of the treasury at the time, and Alan Greenspan, who was chairman of the Federal Reserve. Four witnesses (including myself) were asked to testify regarding the potential costs and benefits of dollarization.

Argentina had been using a currency board type of arrangement to regulate its money supply since April 1991. Domingo Cavallo, as minister of the economy during Carlos Menem's presidency, had implemented the measure as a way to stop the hyperinflation that was fueling political and social crises. By setting up a currency board to maintain a fixed exchange rate with an approved reserve asset—a foreign currency, a basket of currencies, or gold—a country's money supply is restricted to issuing one unit of local currency for each unit of the reserve asset held in its vault. The oft-stated drawback of such a system is that the country is no longer able to conduct monetary policy to achieve other domestic objectives; the advantage is that a currency board approach prevents the central bank of the country from printing money to finance the deficit spending of its own government. Although the convertibility mechanism set up in Argentina did not strictly meet all the criteria for an orthodox currency board, it was nevertheless remarkably successful in its early years; the adoption of the "Convertibility Plan" brought inflation down from an annual average of 1,382.4 percent for the period 1986–90 to an annual average of 22.9 percent for the period 1991–95. In 1996, the inflation rate in Argentina was a mere 0.1 percent.[56]

Against this backdrop, the Senate Banking Committee hearing sought to discern whether dollarization would reduce interest rates and inflation in countries that adopted U.S. money as their own currency, while also reducing currency risk for U.S. firms doing business in those countries. At the same time, members of the committee were interested in asking whether the Fed would need to consider the economic conditions of dollarized countries in setting monetary policy.[57] Summers noted the potential significance of an increase in economic links that might result from creating a broader dollar area: "The fact of sharing a currency would reduce the cost of doing business with dollarizing countries, reduce the uncertainty about future exchange rate changes, and might therefore increase the capacity for capital and trade flows." However, he also identified "the opposing risk that at difficult times, the loss of domestic monetary sovereignty would foster resentment and encourage policymakers to deflect blame for problems onto the United States."[58] Greenspan pointed out that a very substantial amount of U.S. currency was already circulating outside U.S. borders. Concerning the resulting effect on the Fed's conduct of monetary policy, he observed, "Our basic monetary policy does take into consideration what is going on in the rest of the world largely because the rest of the world does affect us, but what we do not do is focus on the well-being of the rest of the world as a whole, as distinct from the well-being of the United States."[59]

My own view expressed at the committee hearing was that the United States was compelled to take a position with regard to countries wishing to utilize the U.S. dollar to replace their own domestic money or grant their citizens a choice in currencies: "I believe that a policy stance by U.S. officials which suggests measured ambivalence, or worse, institutionalized indifference, carries with it an opportunity cost of historic proportions."[60] The problem was that, in its attempt to be "balanced" about the costs and benefits of dollarizing, the United States was emphasizing false virtues. It suggested to countries wishing to use our currency that they would be sacrificing the benefit of being able to expand their own money supply through fiscal and monetary laxity—that they might wish to preserve instead the ability to use money illusion to influence the economic behavior of their citizens. The United States was additionally implying that competitive depreciation was a legitimate option to deploy in trade relations that countries should not give up lightly.

> The distressing reality is that when government has the capacity to inflate the money supply and defile the value of the currency used by its citizens, it exercises undue influence—not only over the returns to workers, savers, and investors, but over the very perception of business activity and entrepreneurial endeavor. The successful businessman is made to feel like a greedy member of society, or perhaps the fortunate but altogether passive recipient of economic largess, rather than an innovative risk-taker whose creative actions brought greater wealth and higher economic returns for his fellow citizens.
>
> So it is no wonder that entrepreneurs would seek a better solution to monetary management than the failed policies of their own government. The United States should feel highly complimented that citizens of other nations would look to the dollar to serve as their own monetary unit of account. They trust it. Tired of piling up the phony rewards from inflated domestic prices or the self-defeating gains from export sales achieved through competitive depreciation, they just want money that plays it straight. They are willing to go with the world's best brand.
>
> But if entrepreneurs see an opportunity, governments see a threat. The political response to dollarization is predictable: Defend the status quo and question the patriotism of those who would abandon the national currency in favor of a more reliable form of money. The populist argument in opposition to dollarization is as predictable as it is despicable, misleading people into thinking that switching to the dollar is an act of political submission rather than economic liberation.[61]

There is no question that Argentina's newly elected president cares deeply about preserving individual freedom. Milei, after all, is the man who warned his audience at the 2024 meeting of the World Economic Forum in Davos that the West is in danger "because those who are supposed to defend the values of the West find themselves co-opted by a vision of the world that—inexorably—leads to socialism, and consequently to poverty." Any delays in his administration's sweeping plans for cutting spending and granting the Argentine people access to more reliable money likely reflect a perceived need for pragmatism during the transition. Still, it is worrisome that resistance may accelerate as the pain of making such dramatic changes takes its toll on the population and boosts opportunities for detractors to sabotage reforms that would hurt their vested interests.

Given the fact that Milei is a well-trained economist, with two master's degrees, who embraces the ideas of Friedrich Hayek and Ludwig von Mises of the Austrian School of economics, it seems a strong prospect that he would respond enthusiastically to an initiative by the United States to issue gold-convertible bonds; he would well appreciate that doing so shines a light on government overspending and the hazards of discretionary monetary policy. It seems especially propitious that Milei is an admirer of Murray Rothbard, an American libertarian economist who robustly opposed central banking and fiat money. Rothbard wrote a book, originally published in 1963, entitled *What Has Government Done to Our Money?* A year earlier, Rothbard had published an essay that included a detailed proposal for monetary reform, *The Case for a 100 Percent Gold Dollar.*[62]

Could an incoming president of the United States forge a meaningful tie with Argentina's new leader by orchestrating a synchronized issuance of long-term sovereign bonds convertible into gold as a mutual expression of commitment to monetary integrity? Such a move could be the opening salvo for trade relations conditioned on a level monetary playing field—utilizing the gold-linked instruments to serve as benchmarks for measuring the impact of currency movements that alter the relative value of goods and services across borders. By demonstrating the willingness to use a common reference point to evaluate whether currency depreciation has changed the terms of trade, the United States and Argentina would jointly be taking a strong stand in condemning an unfair trade practice.

Advancing the Digital Frontier

One of the common accusations launched by people who have not studied monetary economics is that any reference to gold as part of any new proposal leading to stable money is a nonstarter. It is easy to dismiss the impact of a gold-convertibility link to a long-term sovereign debt obligation as somehow a throwback to prior monetary systems throughout history, even if such an initiative would herald an innovative approach to achieving stable exchange rates in the future. What about the possibility of capturing the benefits of a gold benchmark for currencies while utilizing twenty-first-century advances in providing monetary payments?

Digital currencies came on the scene in October 2008, when an author using the name Satoshi Nakamoto published a nine-page paper online: "Bitcoin: A Peer-to-Peer Electronic Cash System."[63] The paper notes in its introductory section that Internet commerce requires participants to rely on financial institutions serving as trusted third parties to process electronic payments. "While the system works well enough for most transactions," the paper continues, "it still suffers from the inherent weaknesses of the trust based model."[64] The issue of trust goes beyond merely being able to verify financial transactions; much of the appeal of cryptocurrencies reflects disenchantment with centralized control by the government over the money supply, extending to the actions taken by central banks. It is no coincidence that Bitcoin arose in the wake of the global financial crisis. Its proponents resent the bailout of banks and subsequent monetary policy decisions that occurred in the aftermath of the meltdown. As Nakamoto (whose real identity has yet to be ascertained) observed in a blog post in February 2009, "The root problem with conventional currency is all the trust that's required to make it work. The central bank must be trusted not to debase the currency, but the history of fiat currencies is full of breaches of that trust."[65]

If the democratization of money is an aspirational goal of crypto advocates—finding a way to bypass central bank policymakers and empower individual citizens—the fact that central banks around the world are now actively exploring ways to launch their own digital currencies would seem to thwart such libertarian leanings. Central bank digital currency (CBDC) is a virtual form of money issued and backed by a central bank; its rapid development shows that central banks have taken notice of cryptocurrencies and made the decision to offer their own digital alternative to paper currency. According to the Central Bank Digital Currency Tracker monitored by the Atlantic Council, 134 countries and currency unions representing 98 percent of global GDP were exploring a CBDC in May 2024—with 68 countries in an advanced phase involving development, a pilot program, or full launch. China's pilot project for a digital yuan was the largest program, reaching 260 million wallets across twenty-five cities.[66]

Given the privacy concerns that have surfaced in the wake of China's lead in developing CBDCs, Americans have demonstrated strong resistance to the idea that the U.S. central bank might likewise proceed to issue a digital currency. Skeptical of government overreach and leery of surveillance abuse, large numbers of American citizens have contacted their representatives in Washington, D.C., to register concern—prompting bipartisan legislation in May 2023 to prohibit the Federal Reserve from issuing a central bank digital currency. Introducing the bill, jointly sponsored by Representative French Hill of Arkansas and Representative Jake Auchincloss of Massachusetts, Hill announced: "Americans have a right to financial privacy. That's why I'm proud to stand with the gentleman from Massachusetts to protect civil liberties, the role of the dollar as the global reserve currency, and prevent a surveillance state over everyday Americans."[67]

The Federal Reserve so far has been tentative about pursuing a central bank digital currency, no doubt aware of public concerns that it would make the Fed even more powerful as a government agency, with enhanced capabilities for surveillance and oversight that could be abused. The Fed does offer a payments service called FedNow, which enables financial institutions to send and receive funds in real time, almost instantly, much like Venmo, Cash App, and other money transfer apps. But the FedNow system is not meant to replace the dollar and should not be seen as a digital currency, according to the Federal Reserve's own website, which further explains:

> While the Federal Reserve has made no decisions on whether to pursue or implement a central bank digital currency, or CBDC, we have been exploring the potential benefits and risks of CBDCs from a variety of angles, including through technological research and experimentation. Our key focus is on whether and how a

214 | *Good as Gold*

CBDC could improve on an already safe and efficient U.S. domestic payments system.

CBDC is generally defined as a digital liability of a central bank that is widely available to the general public. Today in the United States, Federal Reserve notes (i.e., physical currency) are the only type of central bank money available to the general public. Like existing forms of money, a CBDC would enable the general public to make digital payments. As a liability of the Federal Reserve, however, a CBDC would be the safest digital asset available to the general public, with no associated credit or liquidity risk.[68]

Despite Fed assurances that the U.S. central bank will not necessarily follow the lead of other central banks—including the European Central Bank, which is moving forward to launch an official central bank digital currency for the twenty-seven countries in the European Union in the next three or four years, subject to legislative approval from the European Commission—the pressure to respond to increasing competition is strong. Initial enthusiasm for CBDCs has waned somewhat; not only privacy concerns but larger questions about the impact of digital currencies on commercial bank deposits have arisen. If people can make payments directly through a central bank, avoiding the need to have a checking account at a bank, what happens to lending and the normal credit services provided by private-sector financial institutions? While the Federal Reserve notes the importance of keeping up with technological advancements involving money and payments, it also acknowledges the potential negative aspects: "A CBDC could pose certain risks and raise a variety of important policy questions including how it might affect financial-sector market structure, the cost and availability of credit, the safety and stability of the financial system, and the efficacy of monetary policy."[69] Still, as China is demonstrating, if a government is intent on pressuring the public to utilize its own central bank–issued currency as part of its social policy, it can force cash to disappear and pay employees who work at state-owned companies and public institutions with electronic money recorded and traceable in the government's digital ledger.

Is there a way to harness innovative technical improvements to increase the efficiency of payments while also providing users with an established and widely accepted monetary unit for carrying out transactions? Private-sector alternatives to money controlled by central banks are clearly at a disadvantage so long as they are not granted legal-tender status; cryptocurrencies cannot escape the taxation trap when they are translated into domestic money issued by governments. In the United States, virtual currency is treated as property for federal tax purposes and therefore subject to capital gains tax. People who hold, trade, or use cryptocurrency create a tax liability if they get more value than they paid when acquiring the cryptocurrency.

But what about stablecoins? Stablecoins are cryptocurrencies that maintain a stable value relative to another asset—which could be the U.S. dollar. They function in the same way as a currency board system, which is an approach to issuing money that is 100 percent backed by reserves. For example, when Argentina adopted a currency board, it required its national currency to be convertible into the U.S. dollar at a fixed exchange rate; by law, the nation's monetary base had to contain gold or foreign exchange reserves equal to the value of currency issued. So long as holdings of the reference asset are sufficient to maintain the peg, stablecoins can deliver the benefits of blockchain technology while also providing a familiar form of money for consumer usage. Stabilization mechanisms—the process by which stablecoins maintain their peg with the real-world asset—include establishing a custodian to safeguard the assets used as collateral for the new currency. The collateral used to maintain a dollar could include dollar-denominated securities, but these should be deemed riskless and readily marketable in anticipation of possible redemptions.

The most promising avenue of combining the appeal of a stablecoin with the notion of gold convertibility starts by looking at existing gold-backed cryptocurrencies. Digital gold currency (DGC) is backed by physical gold reserves held in vaults. So far, gold-backed cryptocurrencies have mostly been issued by private companies, with varying degrees of success. Problems have arisen as government authorities have cited providers of digital currency backed by precious metals for allowing online transfers of funds for transactions involving illegal activity. Some companies offering digital gold currency failed because they did not hold adequate reserves in gold as promised; others were not able to protect their customers against malware that allowed hackers to access the user's account. Still, the market for gold-backed cryptocurrencies has reportedly experienced significant growth in 2024, with at least six gold-backed options to hold gold-linked digital assets being touted by CoinCodex as "top options" for crypto enthusiasts: PAX Gold, Tether Gold, GoldCoin, Kinesis Gold, Meld Gold, and tGOLD.[70] While the combination of digital assets and physical commodities is appealing—combining intrinsic value with blockchain technology—the challenge of guaranteeing that digital tokens are backed up by physical gold reserves remains a major issue. Each token of digital gold currency is meant to represent a specific amount of gold, as measured by weight in ounces or grams. The most widely used DGCs store physical gold in secure vaults and claim full collateralization of tokens, which can be redeemed for real gold. At least one of the providers, Meld Gold, provides a live audit website purporting to list the number of users and transactions and the value of gold being held within its independently audited system.[71] The use of DGCs is still considered risky, however, due to cases of poor oversight and lack of transparency. In short, users are exposed to a largely unregulated developing market; moreover, acceptance of payments using DGCs is not universal.

Government involvement in providing digital currency backed by gold introduces potential new opportunities—depending on the credibility of the program. Zimbabwe's currency was effectively scrapped in favor of the U.S. dollar after hyperinflation reached 5 billion percent in 2008; although the government of Zimbabwe reintroduced a national currency in 2019, it quickly devalued once again. In April 2023, the central bank of Zimbabwe announced that it would introduce a gold-backed digital currency to stabilize its money unit against the dollar. The program stipulates that gold-backed digital tokens can be held in either e-gold wallets or e-gold cards and that they will be used "both as a means of payment and a store of value."[72] The initial reception from economists, as well as Zimbabweans generally, was lukewarm. Although the digital tokens are supposedly 100 percent redeemable into gold, a subsequent announcement in April 2024 by the governor of Zimbabwe's central bank that new national banknotes were about to be launched caused further skepticism. The new "structured" currency—which features a drawing of gold ingots being minted—will reportedly be backed by foreign currencies, gold, and precious minerals. Zimbabweans were given twenty-one days to convert their old cash into new money.[73] According to the nation's former finance minister, Tendai Biti, "the Zimbabwe dollar has failed because of the absence of trust in the regime. The digital currency will suffer the same brutal fate that the local dollar has suffered."[74]

The possibility that Russia or China might issue some kind of gold-backed digital currency has attracted more serious interest. A report published in October 2022 on *Fox Business* suggested that China and Russia might be working in tandem on a gold-backed currency to displace the dollar as the world's primary reserve currency.[75] China's surge in gold purchases, in combination with Russia's desire to avoid dollar transactions due to sanctions imposed after its invasion of Ukraine, have further fueled speculation about the potential introduction of a joint Russo-Sino currency. The diminution of the dollar in the world's financial system tends to be the focus of such stories, but it would not be the first time that the concept was put forward for China to peg its currency to gold as a way to improve its geopolitical standing. Kwasi Kwarteng, who would briefly serve as Britain's chancellor of the exchequer in 2022, wrote an op-ed for the *New York Times* in 2014 that posed challenging questions: "Could China someday peg its currency to gold, as Britain did in 1821? China has the reserves to do this, and it could have the political will, if the dollar proved to be unreliable as a store of value in the future. … With a balanced budget and a gold-backed currency, China's economy could be even more formidable than it is today."[76]

Closer to home for Americans considering the possibility of a gold-linked digital currency, legislation being pursued in Texas would permit people to deposit gold or silver into the state's bullion depository—which was created by law in 2015—and have access to spend it from their account as if they were using a debit or credit card. Bills in both the House and Senate of Texas were advanced in May 2023, with proponents arguing that using the Texas Bullion Depository, which operates under the Texas Comptroller of Public Accounts, would help put Texas at the forefront of developing a state-backed digital currency with the added benefit of using tangible precious metals to reduce uncertainty.[77]

One can imagine utilizing various elements of these developments to roll out a stablecoin backed by Treasury Trust Bonds. Because the U.S. dollar is already the predominant reserve currency, the appeal of a stablecoin offering digital payment capabilities would only be enhanced by the gold-convertibility feature of the assets held as collateral. Indeed, such a stablecoin would provide solid justification for maintaining the stock of gold currently held by the Federal Reserve in conjunction with the U.S. Treasury—putting an end to voices that have called for selling the gold to increase the statutory debt limit.[78] A stablecoin backed by Treasury Trust Bonds (or the equivalent ratio of Treasury securities and gold futures) might be designated as "SolidUS" because it represents a U.S. dollar solidly backed by gold redeemability. The fact that the word "solidus" hearkens back to the most successful currency of the Middle Ages further supports the message of quality and dependability.

Whether such a digital currency might be made available through the U.S. government depends on the extent to which citizen concerns over privacy can be adequately resolved; unless proper safeguards can be constructed, this obstacle might prove insurmountable. If private-sector innovators are permitted to launch stablecoins backed 100 percent by Treasury Trust Bonds, the program has strong potential for success. Implementation will require special warehousing of the physical gold serving as collateral for the U.S. government's debt obligation. Moreover, the offering will need to comply with forthcoming stablecoin regulation from the U.S. Congress.[79]

A guarantee that a stablecoin is backed in full by Treasury Trust Bonds convertible into gold would present an attractive option for users wary of inflation—and would bring attention to the fundamental challenge of restoring the monetary integrity of the dollar. Immediate benefits might include revaluing the 261 million ounces owned by the U.S. government from the statutory book value of $42.2222 per fine troy ounce (the price set by law since 1973) to the current market price; this would magnify the value of Treasury gold from its current book value of $11.04 billion to $626 billion based on a price for gold of $2,400 per troy ounce. From a fiscal point of view, issuing TTBs might furnish a windfall source of revenue for the federal budget from the outset. Moreover, if investor sentiment is favorable, it will be reflected in the willingness of lenders to pay a premium for TTBs—thus providing a low-cost financing option for the U.S. government.

The interesting aspect of the SolidUS concept for launching a stablecoin backed by gold-convertible Treasury Trust Bonds is that it holds out unlimited potential for replication and amplification, both at home and abroad. If the United States were to initiate such an offering, it could light the fire of resistance to socialism everywhere. What started out as a gold anchor against the drift toward government interventionism—shining a light on the perils of fiscal indulgence and monetary activism—could prove to be the salvation of democratic capitalism.

Epilogue
Real Money for the Real Economy

THE FUNDAMENTAL ASSERTION of this book is that money should serve as an honest measure—one that provides a meaningful unit of account and a dependable store of value. Earlier monetary systems that utilized gold convertibility to deliver stable money both domestically and internationally provide a basis for comparison. Contemporary approaches based on government-issued fiat currencies have not proved capable of providing sound money. When monetary policy becomes a more important determinant of future value than the money itself, and "price stability" is defined in terms of an inflation target, the reliability of the money unit is already compromised. In evaluating prior systems as a precursor to laying out a solid plan for unleashing the power of sound money, *Good as Gold* emphasizes the importance of learning best practices. As it turns out, the gold standard of money is the gold standard. To meet the highest standard for monetary integrity, we need to make the U.S. dollar as good as gold.

Instead of manipulating the value of money by controlling interest rates, the government should let free-market mechanisms work through accurate price signals. The logic of embracing free-enterprise capitalism as the best way to achieve optimal economic outcomes rests on the assumption that money can be trusted. When money is reliable, supply and demand find their own levels as individual producers and consumers weigh the relative value of competing products and services. Investment finds its highest and best use in accordance with opportunities that are accurately priced in meaningful units of estimated future value.

Even though the economic benefits of honest money provide more than enough justification for fundamental reform of current arrangements, it is important to also consider the political and social implications of restoring monetary integrity—as these may prove even more compelling. When government has the power to depreciate the currency, democracy is severely weakened. Grover Cleveland, who served as the twenty-second and twenty-fourth president of the United States, cogently expressed this point in an address to Congress in August 1893:

> The people of the United States are entitled to a sound and stable currency and to money recognized as such on every exchange and in every market of the world. Their government has no right to injure them by financial experiments opposed to the policy and practice of other civilized states. Nor is it justified in permitting an exaggerated and unreasonable reliance on our national strength and ability to jeopardize the soundness of the people's money.
>
> This matter rises above the plane of party politics. It vitally concerns every business and calling and enters every household in the land. There is one important aspect of the subject which especially should never be overlooked. At times like the present, when the evils of unsound finance threaten us, the speculator may anticipate a harvest gathered from the misfortune of others, the capitalist may protect himself by hoarding or may even find profit in the fluctuations of values; but the wage earner—the first to be injured by a depreciated currency and the last to receive the benefit of its correction—is practically defenseless. He relies for work upon the ventures of confident and contented capital. This failing him, his condition is without alleviation, for he can neither prey on the misfortunes of others nor hoard his labor.[1]

Class warfare eats away at American founding principles when citizens no longer believe that equality under the law translates into equal opportunity. One of the most damaging aspects of unsound money is precisely its differential impact on the wage earner and the speculator, as President Cleveland noted. People who receive a paycheck are cheated by inflation until they get wise to it and demand higher nominal compensation; they have every right to do so, as the decline in purchasing power caused by inflation is not their fault. The wrongdoing can be blamed on fiscal and monetary policies that do not prioritize the importance of sound finances and sound money. Federal Reserve officials are leery about stating that they do not wish to see wages increase at rates that perpetuate inflation, so they instead refer to the need for sustainable wage growth "consistent with 2 percent inflation."[2] Meanwhile, people who earn money from their portfolio of investment securities learn to pay attention to every nuanced statement from a monetary official to glean possible hints about future interest rates or exchange rate movements and invest accordingly. Speculation replaces careful analysis as profits are found in being nimble at arbitraging fleeting opportunities in unsettled financial markets.

Money should work for every citizen in the same way. When money—that is, monetary policy—seems to favor the government, large corporations, and wealthy investors, it undermines faith in free-market capitalism and prompts accusations that the system is rigged. Income inequality has been exacerbated by interest rate decisions that have rewarded one segment of the population at the expense of another. An analysis performed by the Federal Reserve examining the distribution of U.S. household wealth shows that total wealth from corporate equities and mutual fund shares went from $22.46 trillion in the first quarter of 2020 to $37.16 trillion in the first quarter of 2021—with some 83 percent of the $14.7 trillion gain accruing to those in the top 10 percent by wealth.[3]

When the Fed maintains near-zero interest rates—as it did from December 2008 to December 2015 and again from March 2020 to 2022—the vast majority of households are forced to accept extremely low nominal rates of return on savings kept in bank accounts. These low interest rates amount to a negative real yield if they do not even rise to the level of positive inflation rates. At the same time, those who hold investment portfolios of financial securities enjoy windfall profits. In crafting its monetary strategy to stimulate economic growth, the Fed gives short shrift to the middle-income households that fuel the private sector. If theory worked in practice, with suppressed rates working powerfully to increase economic growth—delivering higher employment at higher wages in the process—people might consider the monetary experiment to be worth the price. But when economic gains seem limited and selective, and where the economic costs include crowding out private-sector lending, it is reasonable to question both monetary theory and practice. The implementation of monetary policies that skew financial rewards to those who have already reached the highest levels of income and wealth is anathema to the founding principles of a nation that prides itself on equality and the consent of the governed.

Heal Thyself

What would it mean for American citizens if the United States were to issue gold-backed Treasury obligations? How would the action affect the federal budget process? Would it have an impact on borrowing and lending activities—and on price levels? These are issues very close to the heart of most Americans as they contemplate the future of their nation. But taking such a bold step toward addressing the current unsustainable financial outlook for the United States would also have repercussions beyond our borders. What kind of message would it send to the world if a link between the U.S. dollar and gold was restored through the issuance of a long-term Treasury bond? Would other nations choose to emulate America's initiative?

If we look first at the federal budget process, one major benefit would be immediate: the very existence of U.S. debt obligations called Treasury Trust Bonds would serve as an observable barometer of fiscal prudence—with the convertibility rate of the dollar into gold providing the lodestar for evaluating whether the promise of "stable prices" so revered by the nation's central bank is being met. Deviations from the yield spreads of conventional Treasury offerings would put pressure on the U.S. government to bring revenues and expenditures into balance; the reason is that the variance from TTB yields would starkly reflect aggregate expectations about future dollar stability. It would surely have a curtailing effect on congressional spendthrifts, who would be held accountable for undermining the integrity of U.S. money by requiring the government to borrow money to finance budget deficits. Citizens understand that excess purchasing power is created when the government obligates itself—rather, U.S. taxpayers—to pay back money to lenders from future wealth yet to be created. When the Federal Reserve purchases that debt by crediting the depository accounts of sellers with a keystroke, it monetizes government borrowing. This process dilutes the value of money because it infuses purchasing power without adding to the productive output of the real economy.

The budget process would be made more transparent as citizens resisted government spending to finance budgetary excesses. Either by exercising the right to redeem the face value of Treasury Trust Bonds in gold at maturity or by merely reselling them in financial markets at any time leading up to the maturity date (with price differentials highlighting the difference from conventional U.S. debt instruments), individuals would be empowered to begin securing monetary integrity despite fiscal profligacy. They would be able to transcend the inflationary consequences of monetizing the debt. The more citizens began exercising their convertibility privilege—opting to accept the preestablished amount of gold at maturity versus the stated face value of the bond in nominal dollars—the greater the reproach to those deemed responsible for fiscal and monetary uprightness. It would be a boon to democracy to make the whole budget process more transparent and to hold its executors more accountable. Citizens should be able to fully understand how their tax money is being spent; accordingly, they may register their approval or disapproval. The sheer magnitude of federal spending provides the key indicator of the government's role both in society and the economy, indicating its size relative to the private sector—and accordingly, its influence. The issuance of TTBs would acknowledge the right of citizens to monitor the spending decisions of their government representatives. Forcing budgetary disputes into the light of public scrutiny is a healthy practice.

The government's ability to borrow money to resolve fiscal imbalances, while at the same time using monetary policy to influence interest rates, is a conflict of interest that needs to be resolved. The intermingling of fiscal and monetary actions creates tremendous distortions for the real economy by setting up incentives for malinvestment and speculative financial behavior. This conflict of interest favors an increasing role for government policymakers, escalating the prominence of the nation's central bank in allocating credit at the expense of productive economic growth. The private sector deserves far better—stable purchasing power at home and stable exchange rates with trade partners—so that free-market forces can work effectively to deliver optimum economic outcomes. The stop-and-go policies of monetary officials, who foment too much spending in the name of stimulus only to create economic mayhem when resulting inflation forces a switch to contractionary policies, throw a wrench into rational economic and financial planning.

If people cannot reasonably count on stable money, it is hard to convince anyone that achieving their personal economic goals is truly a matter of exercising the will and effort to succeed. When interest rates and price levels are controlled by a government agency—even a so-called independent government agency—financial outcomes appear to be capricious or, worse, rigged. The Federal Reserve's ability to move interest rates up or down gives it unique power to determine the success or failure of personal business ventures. Fed decisions aimed at stimulating economic activity can chip away at the moral virtue of saving by making it seem foolish to sacrifice immediate gratification for the sake of future consumption. During periods of high inflation, borrowers are rewarded, while savers are hurt. Meanwhile, the social divisiveness caused by perceived monetary favoritism carries over into social resentments that ultimately find their political voice in demands to make the rich "pay their fair share."

Sound money goes hand in hand with sound finances. Both are needed to restore faith in government and to reinstate the proper functioning of a competitive free-market system consistent with personal economic liberty. Restoring founding principles may seem retrogressive to certain economists, but they miss the profoundly liberating impact of empowering individuals with honest money—which is conducive to achieving greater prosperity by exploiting future economic opportunities made possible through technological advances. The sense of financial security that can be derived from having sound money that provides stable purchasing power and a dependable store of value is especially important during times of rapid technological advances and changing industrial practices. Workers may experience anxiety over the prospect of being replaced through automation or artificial intelligence. Even as technical innovation helps to improve workers' well-being by replacing physically demanding tasks, it can also spur job insecurity—among blue-collar employees in factories as well as highly skilled white-collar employees in offices.[4] Inflation worsens the situation, raising stress levels, because it requires workers to pursue constant-cost-of-living adjustments under the tension of automation anxiety.

The benefit of having sound money that can be trusted not to lose value because of inflation is that it clarifies options for the future and helps individuals make rational job decisions. The goal is not to prevent technological progress but rather to harness it. When people can be confident that the monetary foundation is solid, they are better able to deal with the future. The world will

always need goods and services; having access to sound money enables workers to recognize and embrace new possibilities for providing them through
innovation. As the brilliant futurist George Gilder explains in his 1989 book
Microcosm, the world is dramatically changing because of the technological
revolution in computing capabilities and telecommunications.[5] For Gilder,
technology provides the key to moving away from defining wealth in terms
of material resources and relying instead on utilizing human knowledge to
maximize prosperity. Individual creativity is unleashed by such developments,
which permit people to increase their productive output in accordance with
their personal ambition. Instead of being held back by the physical limitations of material wealth (think of huge manufacturing plants that must have
proximity to iron and coal mines), economic development can now derive
from the brain of a software genius. Whereas national wealth has historically been determined based on physical resources located within territorial
boundaries, the new sources of wealth throughout the world dwell inside the
minds of creative entrepreneurs who find new ways to improve productivity,
devising new services or new methods for manufacturing, or who invent
entirely new products.

If Gilder is right, the balance of power in the world has shifted in favor of
the entrepreneurs who harness technology to achieve greater levels of wealth,
not only for themselves but in terms of benefits that accrue to users of their
products and services. Humankind advances through such innovative break-
throughs, which often defy national boundaries while raising living standards
worldwide and improving the quality of life itself. In his 2016 book *The
Scandal of Money*, Gilder posits that financial innovation in payment systems
and the need for a new global standard of value will lead to the development
of alternative currencies that combine former monetary standards with new
technology:

> New systems based on gold and blockchain innovations can
> evolve into a new world monetary infrastructure. Rooted in
> time, governed by entropy, intrinsically scarce, and always re-
> liable, the money of the future can provide for a true global
> economy of knowledge and learning. Springing from the same
> information theory that is the basis of American enterprise, the

new global money could extend the American Dream of stability
and futurity.[6]

Elaborating on his concept that money needs to evolve to unleash entrepreneurial energy and facilitate expansionary growth in digital commerce,
Gilder cites "what now might be called 'Shelton bonds'"—that is, Treasury
notes payable in gold—as a potential step toward eliminating government
taxation of gold-backed money. "Anyone serious about the reform of money
must start by eliminating government obstruction of actual money," Gilder
states, noting that alternative currencies will always be relegated to niches
unless the differential tax treatment of official legal tender is eliminated.[7]

Indeed—doubling down on both his criticism of current monetary arrangements and his support for Treasury Trust Bonds as a way to restore
monetary integrity to the dollar—in a 2019 monograph, "Three Steps to Save
America from Collapse," Gilder outlined his recommendations to set America
on the right path toward a robust and broadly shared capitalism.[8] The first
step, according to Gilder, would be to abolish capital gains tax on currencies.
The second step would be to remove obstacles to alternative forms of money.
"That brings us to the third step: fixing the dollar," Gilder continues:

> How do we do this? Monetary scholar Judy Shelton already de-
> vised a play. The chief instrument would be the recreation of
> Treasury Trust Bonds—five-year Treasuries redeemable in either
> dollars or gold. They could be enacted either through legislation
> or as a Treasury initiative. Legislation would specifically authorize
> the issuance of five-year Treasury securities that pay no interest,
> but provide for payment of principal at maturity in either ounces
> of gold or the face value of the security, at the option of the holder.
> The instrument would be an obligation of the U.S. government
> to redeem the nominal value ("face value") in terms of a precise
> weight of gold stipulated in advance or the dollar amount es-
> tablished as the monetary equivalent. The rate of convertibility
> (in gold grams) is permanent throughout the life of the bond; it
> defines the gold value of the dollar.[9]

Gilder concludes that his three steps could "restore integrity to the monetary system" and thereby counter the ill effects of a broken monetary system
that has resulted in low growth, a shrinking job force, inequality beyond what

a healthy economy would produce, inefficiency, and the unnatural growth of finance as a portion of the economy. "This is how we can save Main Street from the menace of monopoly money, transcend the dismal science of stagnation and decline, and restore the American mission and dream."[10] It might also be a way to redress the confiscation of private gold holdings in the 1930s under President Roosevelt. Since 1974, after President Ford signed an act of Congress, U.S. citizens have been able to own and deal in gold. Holders of gold-convertible Treasury bonds must feel confident that their right to convert, if they so choose, cannot be abridged through any subsequent executive act or legislation.

The fact that Gilder would specifically endorse what he calls "Shelton bonds" as a way to "fix the dollar" goes a long way toward identifying how to restore the monetary integrity of America's currency. Gilder envisions the issuance of Treasury Trust Bonds as a transformative step toward building a new monetary system that would liberate entrepreneurial initiative around the world. If gold-backed currency instruments could be combined with digital technology in service to the goal of enlarging the array of goods and services available in the global marketplace—with sound money defining both the terms of trade and the terms of payment—it could lead to unprecedented levels of shared wealth for humankind.

The Power of Ideas

It is perhaps no surprise that Gilder's 1981 book *Wealth and Poverty* was embraced by Republican politician and American visionary Jack Kemp for its explanation of capitalism as "the systematic behavior of free individuals making productive investments of their time, energy and resources in acts of faith."[11] Kemp likewise believed that stable money was imperative for upholding the morality of democratic capitalism. He made the connection between the importance of sound money for an individual citizen and the importance of stable exchange rates among nations. Noting that he had "never had any problem explaining this to the average voter," Kemp told a group of monetary specialists and financial officials attending a congressional summit on exchange rates held in Washington in November 1985,

> We have talked at this conference about the importance of mon-
> etary reform for trade among nations. We have talked about its
> importance for debtor nations and creditor nations. Let's not for-
> get that what is true of nations is also true of individual workers,
> savers, investors, businesses, and families.
>
> People are creditors when they save for their children's college
> education or for retirement. They are debtors when they borrow
> to buy a house or start a business. They deal with exchange rates
> when they travel or shop for an automobile—or when the local
> steel plant lays off workers because of imports. They experience
> the high cost of capital when they take out a car loan. They experi-
> ence the depreciation of money when they buy food at the super-
> market. The monetary issue is anything but remote from people's
> experience. In my experience, honest, sound, stable money is a
> popular, blue-collar, bread-and-butter, winning political issue.[12]

If honest, sound, stable money is a winning political issue, it would
seem that now is the time for strong political leadership to put forward a
powerful initiative for achieving monetary reform. The Federal Reserve has
certainly gained prominence in recent years, as its scope of authority and influence has been enlarged. The Fed's performance on inflation following the
COVID-19 pandemic, however, revealed vulnerabilities that brought criticism for misjudging the impact of government stimulus programs and the
rise of inflationary pressures. Under a new U.S. presidential administration,
the issuance of gold-convertible Treasury Trust Bonds could be launched as
an act of good faith that fiscal and monetary transgressions were coming to
an end through competent oversight. Monetary policymakers at the Federal
Reserve may resist the notion that their decisions should be guided by the performance of TTBs relative to nominal Treasury securities over the duration
of the time to maturity, but they will find it difficult to ignore what market
prices and comparative yields are signaling about the credibility of central
bank promises not to diminish the purchasing power of the U.S. money unit.

The authority for launching Treasury Trust Bonds could be assigned to the
incoming Treasury secretary. It could be offered as an innovative borrowing
instrument with appeal for investors concerned about the depreciation of the
dollar—both in terms of domestic purchasing power and with respect to other
currencies. Instead of five-year notes payable in either dollars or gold at matu-

rity, as suggested earlier, my recommendation now would include a provision for issuing a special class of Treasury Trust Bonds with a much longer term to maturity—that is, fifty years. The reason is that linking the dollar to gold for the first time since the end of Bretton Woods constitutes a dramatic break from the status quo for an incoming U.S. president. It will stand as a signal to other nations, both friendly and unfriendly, that the United States is not only stepping up to its fiscal challenges but also expressing its commitment to monetary integrity through responsible government.

The official introduction of Treasury Trust Bonds could be coordinated with the celebration of an important milestone for the United States—the 250-year anniversary of American independence. Launching a 50-year U.S. government bond with a gold-convertibility feature on July 4, 2026, would symbolize the perpetuation of the American Idea from its original founding in 1776 to its 300-year anniversary on July 4, 2076. America's independence and the radical notion of self-government would be jointly commemorated with a newly strengthened commitment to the founding principles expressed by the American Idea. Treasury Trust Bonds would honor the precept that inalienable rights are granted by our creator; they would signify renewed allegiance to ensuring equal treatment under the law. Formally linking the U.S. dollar to gold acknowledges the necessity of sound money to preserve the rewards and responsibilities of American freedom.

Notes

Preface

1. "Nominations of Judy Shelton and Christopher Waller," Hearing Before the Committee on Banking, Housing, and Urban Affairs, U.S. Senate, February 13, 2020, https://www.congress.gov/116/chrg/CHRG-116shrg40240/CHRG-116shrg40240.pdf, 1.

2. Editorial Board, "The War on Judy Shelton," *Wall Street Journal*, February 12, 2020, https://www.wsj.com/articles/the-war-on-judy-shelton-11581525292.

3. Editorial Board, "This Is No Way to Run a Central Bank," *New York Times*, February 11, 2020, https://www.nytimes.com/2020/02/11/opinion/judy-shelton-fed-trump.html.

4. Catherine Rampell, "Yes, Trump's Latest Fed Pick Is That Bad. Here's Why," *Washington Post*, February 10, 2020, https://www.washingtonpost.com/opinions/yes-trumps-latest-fed-pick-is-that-bad-heres-why/2020/02/10/a13fa1ec-4c44-11ea-9b5c-eac5b16dafaa_story.html.

5. "Nominations of Judy Shelton and Christopher Waller," 2.

6. "Nominations of Judy Shelton and Christopher Waller," 4.

7. "White House Stands by Fed Nominee After Contentious Senate Hearing," Reuters, February 13, 2020. https://www.reuters.com/article/us-usa-fed-shelton-whitehouse/white-house-stands-by-fed-nominee-after-contentious-senate-hearing-idUKKBN2072TY#.

8. Jeff Cox, "Doubts Emerge About Trump Fed Nominee Judy Shelton After Tough Questioning," CNBC, February 13, 2020, https://cnbc.com/2020/02/13/trump-fed-nominee-judy-shelton-hammered-by-democrats-in-confirmation-hearing.html.

9. Catherine Rampell, "Judy Shelton Is a Dangerous Pick for the Fed Board," *Washington Post*, July 11, 2019, https://www.washingtonpost.com/opinions/for-all-the-wrong-reasons-judy-shelton-is-a-decidedly-un-trumpian-choice-for-the-fed/2019/07/11/b044a072-a418-11e9-bd56-eac6bb02d01d_story.html.

10. Alan Greenspan, "Gold and Economic Freedom," reprinted from *The Objectivist*, July 1966, in Ayn Rand, *Capitalism: The Unknown Ideal* (New York: New American Library, 1966), 95.

11. Author's personal email correspondence, July 12, 2019.

12. "Nominations of Judy Shelton and Christopher Waller," 19.

13. "Nominations of Judy Shelton and Christopher Waller," 35–36.

Introduction

1. See Alan Greenspan, "Gold and Economic Freedom," reprinted from *The Objectivist*, July 1966, in Ayn Rand, *Capitalism: The Unknown Ideal* (New York: New American Library, 1966), 89–95.

2. Greenspan, "Gold and Economic Freedom," 95.

3. Milton Friedman and Robert Mundell, "One World, One Money?," *Policy Options*, May 2001, 10–30, part of a series of eight exchanges between Friedman and Mundell under the title "Nobel Money Duel," originally published in the *National Post* (Canada), December 2000.

4. John Cochrane, *The Fiscal Theory of the Price Level* (Princeton, NJ: Princeton University Press, 2023).

5. See interview with Olivier Fines, Rhodri Preece, and Paul McCaffrey, "Cochrane and Coleman: The Fiscal Theory of the Price Level and Inflation Episodes," *Enterprising Investor*, CFA Institute, June 22, 2022.

6. For an assessment of the net effect of the Federal Reserve's new operating regime involving interest on reserves, remittances, and tax receipts, see Brian P. Cutsinger and William J. Luther, "Seigniorage Payments and the Federal Reserve's New Operating Regime," AIER Sound Money Project, Working Paper No. 2023-01, revised January 20, 2023.

7. "Federal Reserve Board Announces Preliminary Financial Information for the Federal Reserve Banks' Income and Expenses in 2023," press release, Board of Governors of the Federal Reserve System, January 12, 2024, https://www.federalreserve.gov/newsevents/pressreleases/other20240112a.htm.

8. "What Does It Mean That the Federal Reserve Is 'Independent Within the Government'?," *FAQs*, Board of Governors of the Federal Reserve System, n.d., accessed June 18, 2024, https://www.federalreserve.gov/faqs/about_12799.htm.

9. Consumer Financial Protection Bureau website, https://www.consumerfinance.gov/.

10. Amy Howe, "Supreme Court Lets CFPB Funding Stand," Opinion Analysis, *SCOTUSblog*, May 16, 2024, https://www.scotusblog.com/2024/05/supreme-court-lets-cfpb-funding-stand/.

11. "OTC Derivatives Statistics at End-June 2023," Bank for International Settlements, November 16, 2023, https://search.app/fbUWfGH5edzAK76k6.

12. Gita Gopinath and Pierre-Olivier Gourinchas, "How Countries Should Respond to the Strong Dollar," *IMF Blog*, International Monetary Fund, October 14, 2022, https://www.imf.org/en/Blogs/Articles/2022/10/14/how-countries-should-respond-to-the-strong-dollar#:~:text=Given%20the%20significant%20role%20of,inflation%20close%20to%20its%20target.

13. "Tariff Rate, Applied, Weighted Mean, All Products (%)," World Bank Open Data, n.d., accessed June 18, 2024, https://search.app/69FoaXpYT4gzPiT7A.

14. Robert Mundell, *Monetary Theory: Interest, Inflation and Growth in the World Economy* (Santa Monica, CA: Goodyear Publishing Co., 1971), http://robertmundell.net/major-works/monetary-theory-interest-inflation-and-growth-in-the-world-economy/.

15. Jacques de Larosiere, "Bretton Woods and the IMF in a Multipolar World?," keynote speech, "Bretton Woods at 70" conference, Workshop No. 18, *Oesterreichische National-bank* (February 28, 2014), in *Workshops: Proceedings of OeNB Workshops, Oesterreichische Nationalbank (OeNB)* (Vienna: Oesterreichische Nationalbank, 2014), 180–85, https://www.econstor.eu/handle/10419/264853.

16. See "Farewell to 'Greatest Central Banker Who Ever Lived'," *Mail and Guardian*, February 1, 2006, http://mg.co.za/article/2006-02-01-farewell-to-greatest-central-banker-who-ever-lived.

17. "Alan Greenspan on Central Banks, Stagnation, and Gold," interview with Gillian Tett, C. Peter McColough Series on International Economics, *Council on Foreign Relations*, October 29, 2014, https://www.cfr.org/event/alan-greenspan-central-banks-stagnation-and-gold-0.

18. Christopher Bellamy, "MoD Makes a Mint from the Sale of Gulf War Gold Coins," *Independent*, May 30, 1996, https://www.independent.co.uk/news/mod-makes-a-mint-from-the-sale-of-gulf-war-gold-coins-1349915.html.

Chapter 1: Central Planning Doesn't Work

1. See Judy Shelton, *The Coming Soviet Crash: Gorbachev's Desperate Pursuit of Credit in Western Financial Markets* (New York: Free Press, 1989), 29–51.

2. Edwin J. Feulner, Jr., foreword to Friedrich A. Hayek, *The Road to Serfdom*, in an abridgment privately printed by the Heritage Foundation with permission of the University of Chicago Press, 1994. To read the original article by Hayek, written as a rebuttal to econo-mists who endorsed central planning, see "The Use of Knowledge in Society," *American Economic Review* 35, no. 4 (September 1945), 519–30.

3. Aimee Picchi, "The Federal Reserve Holds Interest Rates Steady. Here's the Impact on Your Money," *Moneywatch*, CBS News, March 20, 2024, https://www.cbsnews.com/news/federal-reserve-meeting-rate-decision-march-2024/#.

4. See Antoine Martin and Sam Schulhofer-Wohl, "How Do the Fed's MBS Purchases Affect Credit Allocation?" *Liberty Street Economics*, Federal Reserve Bank of New York, August 6, 2018, https://libertystreeteconomics.newyorkfed.org/2018/08/how-do-the-feds-mbs-purchases-affect-credit-allocation/.

5. Thomas Jefferson, "Notes on the Establishment of a Money Unit, and of a Coinage for the United States," April 1784, in *The Works of Thomas Jefferson*, Federal Edition, vol. 4 (New York: G. P. Putnam's Sons, 1904–5).

6. "Review of Monetary Policy Strategy, Tools, and Communications: 2020 Statement on Longer-Run Goals and Monetary Policy Strategy," Board of Governors of the Federal Reserve System, adopted effective January 24, 2012, as amended effective August 27, 2020, https://www.federalreserve.gov/monetarypolicy/review-of-monetary-policy-strategy-tools-and-communications-statement-on-longer-run-goals-monetary-policy-strategy.htm.

7. "Introduction: Primary Objective," European Central Bank / Eurosystem, 2024, https://ecb.europa.eu/mopo/intro/html/index.en.html.

8. "Introduction: The Treaty," 2024, European Central Bank / Eurosystem, http://www.ecb.europa.eu/mopo/intro/html/index.en.html.

9. See speech by Mary C. Daly (president and CEO, Federal Reserve Bank of San Francisco), "Climate Risk and the Fed: Preparing for an Uncertain Certainty," June 22, 2021, https://www.frbsf.org/news-and-media/speeches/mary-c-daly/2021/06/climate-risk-and-the-fed-preparing-for-an-uncertain-certainty/.

10. Vladimir I. Lenin, *Collected Works* (Moscow, 1960), vol. 26, 106, quoted in George Garvy, *Money, Financial Flow and Credit in the Soviet Union* (Cambridge, MA: Ballinger, 1977), 21; emphasis in original.

11. This analysis comes from Shelton, *Coming Soviet Crash*, 3–27.

12. Ben R. Craig and Matthew Koepke, "Excess Reserves: Oceans of Cash," *Economic Commentary*, Federal Reserve Bank of Cleveland, February 12, 2015, https://www.cleveland-fed.org/publications/economic-commentary/2015/ec-201502-excess-reserves-oceans-of-cash.

13. See "Liabilities and Capital: Other Factors Draining Reserve Balances: Reserve Balances with Federal Reserve Banks: Wednesday Level," Economic Research, *FRED*, Federal Reserve Bank of St. Louis, April 17, 2024.

14. See "Interest Rate on Reserve Balances," *Economic Data*, Federal Reserve Bank of St. Louis, April 18, 2024.

15. See Judy Shelton, "Fed Policy Is Smothering Private Lending," *Wall Street Journal*, March 8, 2021, https://www.wsj.com/articles/fed-policy-is-smothering-private-lending-11615250626.

16. See Judy Shelton, "The Soviet Banking System—and Ours," *Wall Street Journal*, July 24, 2012, https://www.wsj.com/articles/SB10000872396390444025204577545522816187642.

17. Steve H. Hanke and Kurt Schuler, "A Monetary Constitution for Argentina: Rules for Dollarization," *Cato Journal* 18, no. 3 (Winter 1999), 411, https://www.cato.org/sites/cato.org/files/serials/files/cato-journal/1999/1/cj18n3-11.pdf.

18. "Stock Markets All Around the World Broke Records," *CNNMoney*, February 24, 2015, http://money.cnn.com/2015/02/24/investing/stocks-market-dow-record-high/.

19. Karma Allen, "Yardeni: Markets All Rigged, It Is What It Is," CNBC, March 19, 2015, http://www.cnbc.com/id/102519784.

20. "Current High Levels of Financial Repression Create Significant Costs and Lower Long-Term Investors' Ability to Channel Funds into the Real Economy, a New Swiss Re Study Shows," Swiss Re Group, March 26, 2015, https://www.swissre.com/media/press-release/2015/nr_20150326_financial_repression.html.

21. George A. Selgin, "The Futility of Central Banking," *Cato Journal* 30, no. 3 (Fall 2010), 465–73, https://ciaotest.cc.columbia.edu/journals/cato/v30i3/f_0019763_16834.pdf.

22. John B. Taylor, "Discretion Versus Policy Rules in Practice," *Carnegie-Rochester Conference Series on Public Policy* 39 (December 1993), 195–214.

23. Quoted in Binyamin Appelbaum, "House Republicans Intensify Attacks on Federal Reserve," *New York Times*, February 25, 2015, https://www.nytimes.com/2015/02/26/business/economy/house-republicans-press-janet-yellen-on-stimulus-campaign.html.

24. Transcript of Hearing Before the U.S. House of Representatives Committee on Financial Services, February 28, 2001, in "The Alan Greenspan-Ron Paul Congressional

Exchanges (2000–2002)," USAGold, http://www.usagold.com/cpmforum/greenspan-paul-hearingsrecord2000-2002/.

25. See "Alan Greenspan on Fox Business Network," YouTube video, October 15, 2007, https://m.youtube.com/watch?v=ZjMQG3qUFK0.

26. "Statement of Ben S. Bernanke, Chairman, Board of Governors of the Federal Reserve System, before the Joint Economic Committee, United States Congress," April 2, 2008, https://www.jec.senate.gov/archive/Hearings/04.02.08%20Econ%20outlook/040208_%20JointEconomicCommittee.pdf.

27. "Meeting of the Federal Open Market Committee on April 29–30, 2008," transcript, 47–48, https://www.federalreserve.gov/monetarypolicy/files/FOMC20080430meeting.pdf.

28. See Judy Shelton, "The Case for Monetary Regime Change," *Wall Street Journal*, April 21, 2019, https://www.wsj.com/articles/the-case-for-monetary-regime-change-11555873621.

29. Oliver Bush, Katie Farrant, and Michelle Wright, "Reform of the International Monetary and Financial System," Financial Stability Paper No. 13, Bank of England, December 2011, 11.

30. Sean Hanlon, "Sovereign Debt—US vs. the World," *Forbes*, December 14, 2023, https://www.forbes.com/sites/seanhanlon-1/2023/12/14/sovereign-debt--us-vs-the-world/?sh=46e323146d54.

31. Joseph Adinolfi, "Wall Street's 'Fear Gauge' Surges as Volatility Reawakens Across Markets," *Market Watch*, April 17, 2024, https://www.marketwatch.com/story/wall-streets-fear-gauge-surges-as-volatility-reawakens-across-markets-f7e37ab4?mod=mw_quote_news.

32. Ralph Atkins, "Yellen Battles Draghi in Euro-Dollar Drama," *Financial Times*, March 19, 2015, https://www.ft.com/content/64dde7b2-ce0f-11e4-9712-00144feab7de.

33. Tommy Stubbington and Chiara Albanese, "Forex Market Erupts on Central-Bank Moves," *Wall Street Journal*, March 19, 2015, https://www.wsj.com/articles/forex-market-erupts-on-central-bank-moves-1426773181.

34. Claudio Borio, Robert McCauley, and Patrick McGuire, "Dollar Debt in FX Swaps and Forwards: Huge, Missing and Growing," *BIS Quarterly Review*, December 2022, https://www.bis.org/publ/qtrpdf/r_qt2212h.pdf.

35. See Judy Shelton, "The Federal Reserve at War," *Wall Steet Journal*, October 31, 2023, https://www.wsj.com/articles/the-federal-reserve-at-war-gaza-monetary-policy-market-turmoil-1c020ce9.

36. Anmol Karwal, "US Consumer Giants Suffer $4bn Headwind as the Dollar Strengthens," *EuroFinance*, May 31, 2022, https://www.eurofinance.com/news/us-consumer-giants-suffer-4bn-headwind-as-the-dollar-strengthens/.

37. Paul Volcker and Toyoo Gyohten, *Changing Fortunes: The World's Money and the Threat to American Leadership* (New York: Times Books, 1992), 21.

38. "National Debt by Country/Countries with the Highest National Debt 2024," World Population Review, n.d., http://worldpopulationreview.com/country-rankings/countries-by-national-debt.

39. Review & Outlook, "The Slow-Growth Fed," *Wall Street Journal*, April 29, 2015, https://www.wsj.com/articles/the-slow-growth-fed-1430350138.

40. Karen Petrou, *Engine of Inequality: The Fed and the Future of Wealth in America* (Hoboken, NJ: John Wiley & Sons, Inc., 2021), 187.

41. For an analysis of the repercussions of liquidity injections and credit allocation by central banks and how interest groups form to capture those benefits, see Louis Rouanet and Peter Hazlett, "The Redistributive Politics of Monetary Policy," *Public Choice* 194 (2023), 1–26.

42. John Weinberg, "The Great Recession and Its Aftermath," *Federal Reserve History*, Federal Reserve Bank of St. Louis, November 22, 2013, https://www.federalreservehistory. org/essays/great-recession-and-its-aftermath.

43. See Phil Gramm, Robert Ekelund, and John Early, *The Myth of American Inequality: How Government Biases Policy Debate* (Lanham, MD: Rowman & Littlefield, 2022).

44. Ben S. Bernanke, *21st Century Monetary Policy: The Federal Reserve from the Great Inflation to COVID-19* (New York: W.W. Norton & Company, 2022), 329.

45. Ben S. Bernanke, "WSJ Editorial Page Watch: The Slow-Growth Fed?" *Commentary*, Brookings Institution, April 30, 2015, https://www.brookings.edu/blog/ben-bernanke/2015/04/30/wsj-editorial-page-watch-the-slow-growth-fed/.

46. James Madison, "Notes for Speech Opposing Paper Money, [ca. 1 November] 1786," *Founders Online*, https://founders.archives.gov/documents/Madison/01-09-02-0066.

47. George Bancroft, *History of the United States of America, Complete Volumes 1–6: From the Discovery of the Continent*, vol. 6 (November 20, 2018), loc. 2850, Kindle.

48. Thomas Jefferson, "IV. Notes on Coinage, [March–May 1784]," *Founders Online*, https://founders.archives.gov/documents/Jefferson/01-07-02-0151-0005.

49. Thomas Jefferson, "Plan for Establishing Uniformity in the Coinage, Weights, and Measures of the United States," communicated to the House of Representatives, July 13, 1790," *The Avalon Project: Documents in Law, History and Diplomacy*, Lillian Goldman Law Library, Yale Law School, https://avalon.law.yale.edu/18th_century/jeffplan.asp.

50. George Washington, "Third Annual Message, United States, October 25, 1791," *The Avalon Project: Documents in Law, History and Diplomacy*, Lillian Goldman Law Library, Yale Law School, https://avalon.law.yale.edu/18th_century/washs03.asp#:~:text=An%20 uniformity%20in%20the%20weights,conducive%20to%20the%20public%20convenience.

51. Roger Sherman, "A Caveat Against Injustice, or an Inquiry into the Evil Consequences of a Fluctuating Medium of Exchange," 1752, http://www.rogershermansociety. org/caveat.htm.

52. Juliana Menasce Horowitz, Ruth Igielnik, and Rakesh Kochhar, "Most Americans Say There Is Too Much Economic Inequality in the U.S., but Fewer than Half Call It a Top Priority," Pew Research Center, January 9, 2020, https://www.pewresearch.org/social-trends/2020/01/09/most-americans-say-there-is-too-much-economic-inequality-in-the-u-s-but-fewer-than-half-call-it-a-top-priority/.

53. Janet Yellen, "Perspectives on Inequality and Opportunity from the Survey of Consumer Finances," speech given at the Conference on Economic Opportunity and Inequality, Federal Reserve Bank of Boston, Boston, Massachusetts, October 17, 2014, http://www. federalreserve.gov/newsevents/speech/2014speech.htm.

54. F. A. Hayek, *The Constitution of Liberty* (Chicago: University of Chicago Press, 1960), 338–39.

Chapter 2: Stable Money Fosters Productive Growth

1. "Measuring the Economy: A Primer on GDP and the National Income and Product Accounts," Bureau of Economic Analysis, U.S. Department of Commerce, December 2015, 1, https://bea.gov/sites/default/files/methodologies/nipa_primer.pdf.

2. "How Happy Is the Planet?," Wellbeing Economy Alliance, October 2021, https://happyplanetindex.org/wp-content/themes/hpi/public/downloads/happy-planet-index-briefing-paper.pdf.

3. Stephen G. Cecchetti and Enisse Kharroubi, "Reassessing the Impact of Finance on Growth," BIS Working Paper No. 381, Bank for International Settlements, July 2012, https://www.bis.org/publ/work381.pdf.

4. Cecchetti and Kharroubi, "Reassessing the Impact of Finance on Growth," 14.

5. Stephen G. Cecchetti and Enisse Kharroubi, "Why Does Financial Sector Growth Crowd Out Real Economic Growth?," BIS Working Paper No. 490, Bank for International Settlements, February 2015, 14, http://www.bis.org/publ/work490.pdf.

6. "FX Survey 2020: Press Release," *Euromoney*, June 25, 2020, http://www.euromoney.com/article/b1lp5n97k4v6j0/fx-survey-2020-press-release.

7. Michael Collins, "How the Financialization of America Hurt Workers and the Economy," *Industry Week*, October 5, 2022, http://www.industryweek.com/the-economy/public-policy/article/21252236/how-the-financialization-of-america-hurt-workers-and-the-economy.

8. Mathias Drehmann and Vladyslav Sushko, "The Global Foreign Exchange Market in a Higher-Volatility Environment," *BIS Quarterly Review*, Bank for International Settlements, December 5, 2022. https://search.app/VukLXjwTA3oGk2ePA.

9. Jacques de Larosiere, *Putting an End to the Reign of Financial Illusion: For Real Growth* (Paris: Odile Jacob, 2022), 29.

10. Ozgur Orhangazi, "Financialisation and Capital Accumulation in the Non-financial Corporate Sector: A Theoretical and Empirical Investigation on the US Economy: 1973–2003," *Cambridge Journal of Economics* 32, no. 6 (2008), 863–86, https://papers.ssrn.com/sol3/papers.cfm?abstract_id=1297129.

11. Julie M. Zauzmer, "Where We Stand: The Class of 2013 Senior Survey," *Harvard Crimson*, May 28, 2013, https://www.thecrimson.com/article/2013/5/28/senior-survey-2013/.

12. Jian Cai, Kent Cherny, and Todd Milbourn, "Compensation and Risk Incentives in Banking and Finance," *Economic Commentary*, Federal Reserve Bank of Cleveland, September 24, 2010, https://fcic-static.law.stanford.edu/cdn_media/fcic-docs/2010-09-14%20Cai-Cherny-Milbourn%20Compensation%20and%20Risk%20Incentives.pdf.

13. Jack Kelly, "Wall Street Bonuses at JPMorgan, Goldman Sachs and Morgan Stanley Are Under Scrutiny by U.S. Regulators," *Forbes*, April 22, 2024. https://search.app/7gfzQ5bEBmEsz9JC9.

14. Donald Tomaskovic-Devey and Ken-Hou Lin, "Financialization: Causes, Inequality Consequences, and Policy Implications," *North Carolina Banking Institute* 18, no. 1 (2013), article 17, 167, https://scholarship.law.unc.edu/cgi/viewcontent.cgi?referer=-&httpsredir=1&article=1365&context=ncbi#:~:text=Financialization%20distorts%20economic%20investment%20and,standard%20of%20living%20to%20citizens.

15. Tomaskovic-Devey and Lin, "Financialization," 194.

16. Harriet Agnew, "Millennials Look to Tech Stars as Finance Careers Leave Them Cold," *Financial Times*, November 7, 2014, https://www.ft.com/content/0b344c28-6673-11e4-8bf6-00144feabdco.

17. Melissa Korn, "Elite Grads in Business Flock to Tech," *Wall Street Journal*, November 6, 2013, https://www.wsj.com/articles/DJFVW00020131106e9b6anknf.

18. Debra Skodack, "In Evolving Landscape, Community Banks Remain Vital to Customers and the Economy," *Ten Magazine*, Federal Reserve Bank of Kansas City, October 7, 2021, https://www.kansascityfed.org/ten/2021-fall-ten-magazine/in-evolving-landscape-community-banks-remain-vital-to-customers-and-the-economy/.

19. Scott Shane, "How the Decline in Community Banks Hurts Small Business," *Entrepreneur*, April 2, 2015, https://www.entrepreneur.com/money-finance/how-the-decline-in-community-banks-hurts-small-business/244573.

20. Brian Domitrovic, "My Presentation to Janet Yellen," *Forbes*, March 1, 2015, https://www.forbes.com/sites/briandomitrovic/2015/03/01/my-presentation-to-janet-yellen/?sh=4e0bd3196d9c.

21. Brian Domitrovic, "Inequality Is the Child of Fiat Money," *Forbes,* October 25, 2012, https://www.forbes.com/sites/briandomitrovic/2012/10/25/inequality-is-the-child-of-fiat-money/?sh=135cb3476ec3.

22. Janet L. Yellen, "Communication in Monetary Policy," speech at the Society of American Business Editors and Writers 50th Anniversary Conference, Washington, D.C., April 4, 2013, https://www.federalreserve.gov/newsevents/speech/yellen20130404a.htm.

23. "Transcript of Chair Yellen's Press Conference, March 19, 2014," https://www.federalreserve.gov/mediacenter/files/FOMCpresconf20140319.pdf.

24. Caroline Baum, "Twenty-Five Basis Points That Could Shake the World," *Commentary*, Manhattan Institute, September 1, 2015, https://manhattan.institute/article/twenty-five-basis-points-that-could-shake-the-world.

25. "Transcript of Chair Powell's Press Conference, July 27, 2022," https://www.federalreserve.gov/mediacenter/files/FOMCpresconf20220727.pdf.

26. Michelle W. Bowman, "Forward Guidance as a Monetary Policy Tool: Considerations for the Current Economic Environment," speech at the Money Marketeers of New York University, New York, October 12, 2022, https://www.federalreserve.gov/newsevents/speech/bowman20221012a.htm.

27. Bowman, "Forward Guidance as a Monetary Policy Tool."

28. Sarah Foster, "Survey: Fed Seen Aggressively Hiking Rates About 5% in 2023," *Bankrate*, January 4, 2023, https://www.bankrate.com/banking/federal-reserve/economic-indicator-survey-interest-rates-january-2023.

29. Bendix Anderson, "Slowing Rent Growth Hits Apartments, but Investors Have Not Lost Interest," Wealth Management.com, January 9, 2023, https://www.wealthmanagement.com/multifamily/slowing-rent-growth-hits-apartments-investors-have-not-lost-interest.

30. Kate Duguid and Harriet Clarfelt, "Investors Price in Growing Chance of Another Federal Reserve Interest Rate Rise," *Financial Times*, April 23, 2024, https://www.ft.com/content/8c5da64b-766e-4993-86f5-aac95342432a.

31. "BIS Global Liquidity Indicators at End-December 2023," Bank for International Settlements, April 30, 2024. https://search.app/neqUBLk8PF2BraQD8.

32. Claudio Borio, Robert N. McCauley, and Patrick McGuire, "Dollar Debt in FX Swaps and Forwards: Huge, Missing and Growing," *BIS Quarterly Review*, December 5, 2022, https://www.bis.org/publ/qtrpdf/r_qt2212h.htm.

33. Karen Brettell, "Dollar Dips as Powell Says Rate Hikes May Slow," Reuters, November 30, 2022, https://www.reuters.com/markets/currencies/dollar-near-one-week-high-traders-prepare-powell-payrolls-tests-2022-11-30/.

34. Dan McCrum, Robin Wigglesworth, and Elaine Moore, "Fed's Decision to Hold Rates Adds to the Uncertainty," *Financial Times*, September 25, 2015, https://www.ft.com/content/b65c519c-6355-11e5-97e9-7f0bf5e7177b.

35. Paul A. Volcker and Toyoo Gyohten, *Changing Fortunes: The World's Money and the Threat to American Leadership* (New York: Times Books, 1992), 239–40.

36. Adam Smith, *The Wealth of Nations* (New York: Modern Library, 1937), 424.

37. Volcker and Gyohten, *Changing Fortunes*, 246.

38. Articles of Agreement of the International Monetary Fund, article IV: "Obligations Regarding Exchange Arrangements," section 2(b), July 22, 1944, https://www.imf.org/external/pubs/ft/aa/index.htm.

39. "Hensarling Calls for More Transparent and Accountable Federal Reserve," press release, Financial Services Committee, U.S. House of Representatives, July 15, 2015, https://financialservices.house.gov/news/documentsingle.aspx?DocumentID=399364.

40. "Hensarling Opening Statement at Monetary Policy Hearing," press release, Financial Services Committee, U.S. House of Representatives, June 22, 2016. https://search.app/HYwBhJJoTbDZBoAX8.

41. John B. Taylor, "Rules Versus Discretion: Assessing the Debate over the Conduct of Monetary Policy," Working Paper 24149, National Bureau of Economic Research, December 2017, 5, https://www.nber.org/papers/w24149.

42. Taylor, "Rules Versus Discretion," 10.

43. "Monetary Policy and the State of the Economy," Hearing Before the Committee on Financial Services, U.S. House of Representatives, February 25, 2015, https://www.govinfo.gov/content/pkg/CHRG-114hhrg95048/html/CHRG-114hhrg95048.htm.

44. Sam Fleming, "Janet Yellen Defends US Central Bank Independence," *Financial Times*, February 25, 2015, https://www.ft.com/content/6016b23c-bd06-11e4-b523-00144feab7de.

45. "Challenges Associated with Using Rules to Make Monetary Policy," *Monetary Policy Principles and Practice*, Board of Governors of the Federal Reserve System, updated

March 8, 2018, https://www.federalreserve.gov/monetarypolicy/challenges-associated-with-using-rules-to-make-monetary-policy.htm.

46. "Challenges Associated with Using Rules to Make Monetary Policy."

47. Gillian Tett, "An Interview with Alan Greenspan," *Financial Times*, October 25, 2013, https://www.ft.com/content/25ebae9e-3c3a-11e3-b85f-00144feab7de#axzz2j3lkZYmf.

48. Alan Greenspan, *The Map and the Territory: Risk, Human Nature, and the Future of Forecasting* (New York: Penguin Press, 2013), 131.

49. Norbert Michel, "Why Congress Should Institute Rules-Based Monetary Policy," Heritage Foundation, February 22, 2015, https://www.heritage.org/monetary-policy/report/why-congress-should-institute-rules-based-monetary-policy.

Chapter 3: Money Should Work Across Borders

1. Constantinos C. Markides and Norman Berg, "Manufacturing Offshore Is Bad Business," *Harvard Business Review*, September 1988, https://hbr.org/1988/09/manufacturing-offshore-is-bad-business.

2. Robert E. Scott, Valerie Wilson, Jori Kandra, and Daniel Perez, *Botched Policy Responses to Globalization Have Decimated Manufacturing Employment with Often Overlooked Costs for Black, Brown, and Other Workers of Color*, Economic Policy Institute, January 31, 2022.

3. "The Nobel Memorial Prize in Economics 1999: Press Release from the Royal Swedish Academy of Sciences," *Scandinavian Journal of Economics* 102, no. 2 (June 2000), 193, https://www.jstor.org/stable/3440637.

4. Greg Palast, "Robert Mundell, Evil Genius of the Euro," *The Guardian*, June 26, 2012, https://www.theguardian.com/commentisfree/2012/jun/26/robert-mundell-evil-genius-euro.

5. "White House Report on the Program for Economic Recovery, February 18, 1981," Ronald Reagan Presidential Library and Museum, https://www.reaganlibrary.gov/archives/speech/white-house-report-program-economic-recovery-0.

6. See the pioneering article by Robert A. Mundell, "Capital Mobility and Stabilization Policy Under Fixed and Flexible Exchange Rates," *Canadian Journal of Economic and Political Science* 29, no. 4 (1963), 475–85.

7. Laura Wallace, "Ahead of His Time," *Finance and Development* 43, no. 3 (September 2006), https://www.imf.org/external/pubs/ft/fandd/2006/09/people.htm.

8. Robert A. Mundell, *Monetary Theory: Inflation, Interest, and Growth in the World Economy* (Pacific Palisades, CA: Goodyear Publishing Company, 1971), 2.

9. Judy Shelton, "Currency Chaos: Where Do We Go from Here?" (interview with Robert Mundell), *Wall Street Journal*, October 16, 2010, https://www.wsj.com/articles/SB10001424052748704361504575552481963474898.

10. Terence Corcoran, "'A Couple of Prima Donnas': Managing Mundell-Friedman," *Policy Options*, May 1, 2001, https://policyoptions.irpp.org/magazines/one-world-one-money/a-couple-of-prima-donnas-managing-mundell-friedman/.

11. Milton Friedman with Robert Mundell, "Nobel Money Duel: Do We Want a World Currency?," *National Post* (Canada), December 16, 2000, D11, in *The Collected Works of Milton Friedman*, comp. and ed. Robert Leeson and Charles G. Palm, Hoover Institution, https://miltonfriedman.hoover.org/internal/media/dispatcher/214964/full.

12. Friedman and Mundell, "Nobel Money Duel: Do We Want a World Currency?"

13. Milton Friedman with Robert Mundell, "Nobel Money Duel: Fixed or Flexible Exchange Rates?," *National Post* (Canada), December 11, 2000, in *The Collected Works of Milton Friedman*, comp. and ed. Robert Leeson and Charles G. Palm, Hoover Institution, https://miltonfriedman.hoover.org/internal/media/dispatcher/214958/full.

14. Michael D. Bordo, "The Bretton Woods International Monetary System: A Historical Overview," in *A Retrospective on the Bretton Woods System: Lessons for International Monetary Reform*, ed. Michael D. Bordo and Barry Eichengreen (Chicago: University of Chicago Press, January 1993), 50, https://www.nber.org/system/files/chapters/c6867/c6867.pdf.

15. Wallace, "Ahead of His Time."

16. Shelton, "Currency Chaos."

17. "The Emerging New Monetarism," June 14, 2011 (from an interview on Bloomberg Television, *Taking Stock*, with Pimm Fox, May 26, 2011), *The Works of Robert Mundell*, https://robertmundell.net/2011/06/the-emerging-new-monetarism-gold-convertibility-to-save-the-euro/.

18. Shelton, "Currency Chaos."

19. Milton Friedman, "As Good as Gold: A Symposium," *National Review*, June 11, 1990, 28–31.

20. Milton Friedman and Robert Mundell, "One World, One Money?," *Policy Options*, May 1, 2001, https://policyoptions.irpp.org/magazines/one-world-one-money/one-world-one-money/.

21. Milton Friedman, "Free-Floating Anxiety," *National Review*, September 12, 1994, 32, 34, 36. https://miltonfriedman.hoover.org/internal/media/dispatcher/215018/full.

22. H. D. White, "Preliminary Draft Proposal for a United Nations Stabilization Fund and a Bank for Reconstruction and Development of the United and Associated Nations," April 1942, in J. K. Horsefield (ed.), *The International Monetary Fund, 1945–65: Twenty Years of International Monetary Cooperation,* vol. 3: *Documents* (Washington, DC: International Monetary Fund, 1996), 46–47.

23. Dave Herndon, "Dingell Speaks Out Against Fast Track Legislation," *Press and Guide* (Sterling Heights, MI), January 8, 2015, https://www.pressandguide.com/2015/01/07/dingell-speaks-out-against-fast-track-legislation/.

24. William Mauldin, "Currency Manipulation Has Emerged as the Big Sticking Point on Trade," *Wall Street Journal*, May 13, 2015, https://www.wsj.com/articles/BL-REB-32478.

25. Arthur B. Laffer, "Currency Manipulation and Its Distortion of Free Trade," Laffer Center at the Pacific Research Institute, December 1, 2014, https://www.pacificresearch.org/wp-content/uploads/2017/06/Laffer_Center_Template_Currency_Manipulation_Paper_Final_Draft.pdf.

26. Michael McAuliff, "Chuck Schumer Warns Obama His Trade Agenda Is Dead Without a China Currency-Manipulation Crackdown," *Huffington Post*, May 2, 2015, https://www.huffpost.com/entry/chuck-schumer-currency-trade-china_n_7192708.

27. Tim Sablik, "The Fed's Foray into Forex," *Econ Focus*, Federal Reserve Bank of Richmond, second quarter 2017, https://www.richmondfed.org/publications/research/econ_focus/2017/q2/federal_reserve.

28. See "Currency Then and Now: The Plaza Accord," Rice University's Baker Institute for Public Policy, September 17, 2015, https://www.bakerinstitute.org/research/plaza-accord, for conference agenda, proceedings, and papers.

29. Joseph E. Gagnon, "Foreign Exchange Intervention Since Plaza: The Need for Global Currency Rules," International Economics Working Paper, Rice University's Baker Institute for Public Policy, September 16, 2015, https://www.bakerinstitute.org/research/foreign-exchange-intervention-plaza-need-global-currency-rules.

30. "Foreign Exchange Operations," Federal Reserve Bank of New York, n.d., https://www.newyorkfed.org/markets/international-market-operations/foreign-exchange-operations.

31. Mathias Drehmann and Vladyslav Sushko, "The Global Foreign Exchange Market in a Higher-Volatility Environment," *BIS Quarterly Review*, December 5, 2022, https://www.bis.org/publ/qtrpdf/r_qt2212f.htm.

32. Julian Caballero, Alexis Maurin, Philip Wooldridge, and Dora Xia, "The Internationalisation of EME Currency Trading," *BIS Quarterly Review*, December 5, 2022, graph 2 (citing IMF, *Balance of Payments Statistics, World Economic Outlook*, national data, BIS Triennial Central Bank Survey, and authors' calculations), https://bis.org/publ/qtrpdf/r_qt2212g.htm#box-A.

33. Virginia Harrison and Mark Thompson, "5 Big Banks Pay $5.4 Billion for Rigging Currencies," *CNNMoney*, May 20, 2015, https://money.cnn.com/2015/05/20/investing/ubs-foreign-exchange.

34. Aruna Viswanatha, "Banks to Pay $5.6 Billion in Probes," *Wall Street Journal*, May 20, 2015, https://www.wsj.com/articles/global-banks-to-pay-5-6-billion-in-penalties-in-fx-libor-probe-1432130400.

35. Steve Forbes and Elizabeth Ames, *Money: How the Destruction of the Dollar Threatens the Global Economy* (New York: McGraw Hill, 2014), 25.

36. Robert A. Mundell, *Man and Economics* (New York: McGraw-Hill, 1968), 49.

37. William Blackstone, *Commentaries on the Laws of England: A Facsimile of the First Edition of 1765–1769*, vol. 3, article 1, section 8, clause 5, document 1 (Chicago: University of Chicago Press, 1979).

38. Thomas Jefferson, "Notes on the Establishment of a Money Mint, and of a Coinage for the United States," April 1784, in *The Works of Thomas Jefferson*, Federal Edition, vol. 4 (New York and London: G.P. Putnam's Sons, 1904–5), 4.

39. Jefferson, "Notes on the Establishment of a Money Mint," 4.

40. Jefferson, "Notes on the Establishment of a Money Mint," 4.

41. Jefferson, "Notes on the Establishment of a Money Mint," 4.

42. Satoshi Nakamoto, "Bitcoin: A Peer-to-Peer Electronic Cash System," November 1, 2008, https://bitcoin.org/bitcoin.pdf.

43. Gillian Tett, "Breathe Deep and Pay in Bitcoin," *Financial Times*, December 19, 2014, https://www.ft.com/content/351c928c-8560-11e4-ab4e-00144feabdc0.

44. Alan Greenspan, "Year End Q & A," Advisors Capital Management, January 2023, https://acmwealth.com/wp-content/uploads/2023/01/ACM_AG_Article_JAN_-2023.pdf.

45. Hannah Murphy, "Elon Musk Pushes Forward with Twitter Payments Vision," *Financial Times*, January 30, 2023, https://www.ft.com/content/9d84d534-b2dd-4cff-85d1-aee137b26a45.

46. Swathi Kashettar, "Ten Online and Offline Places to Spend Bitcoin," *Analytics Insight*, February 9, 2023, https://www.analyticsinsight.net/ten-online-and-offline-places-to-spend-bitcoin/.

47. Cheyenne Ligon, "Sen. Ted Cruz Wants Capitol Hill Vending Machines to Accept Crypto," *Policy*, CoinDesk, January 26, 2023, https://www.coindesk.com/policy/2023/01/26/sen-ted-cruz-wants-to-force-capitol-hill-vending-machines-to-accept-crypto/.

48. Patrick M. Byrne, "Overstock CEO: Why We're Accepting Bitcoins," CNBC, January 7, 2014, https://www.yahoo.com/lifestyle/tagged/health/overstock-ceo-why-were-accepting-133640241.html.

49. "Special Drawing Rights (SDR)," International Monetary Fund, updated January 2023, https://www.imf.org/en/About/Factsheets/Sheets/2023/special-drawing-rights-sdr.

Chapter 4: Fix What Broke

1. Ken Sweet, "Banks Are Paying Savers Again After Many Years of Low Rates," Associated Press, April 24, 2023, https://apnews.com/article/banks-savings-cds-money-markets-deposits-08cde0e6bb4263c9194fa6544851a78f.

2. Leland Crabbe, "The International Gold Standard and U.S. Monetary Policy from World War I to the New Deal," *Federal Reserve Bulletin*, Board of Governors of the Federal Reserve System, June 1989, 423–40, https://fraser.stlouisfed.org/files/docs/meltzer/craint89.pdf.

3. See Ronald McKinnon, "The Rules of the Game: International Money in Historical Perspective," *Journal of Economic Literature* 31, no. 1 (March 1993), 1–44, http://www.jstor.org/stable/2728149.

4. Michael David Bordo, "The Classical Gold Standard: Some Lessons for Today," *Research*, Federal Reserve Bank of St. Louis, May 1981, 7, https://research.stlouisfed.org/publications/review/81/05/Classical_May1981.pdf.

5. This description comes from George Selgin, "The Rise and Fall of the Gold Standard in the United States," Policy Analysis No. 729, Cato Institute, June 20, 2013, 2, https://www.cato.org/policy-analysis/rise-fall-gold-standard-united-states.

6. Nathan Lewis, "The 1870–1914 Gold Standard: The Most Perfect One Ever Created," *Forbes*, January 3, 2013, https://www.forbes.com/sites/nathanlewis/2013/01/03/the-1870-1914-gold-standard-the-most-perfect-one-ever-created/.

7. Lewis, "1870–1914 Gold Standard."

8. Arthur I. Bloomfield, *Monetary Policy Under the International Gold Standard: 1880–1914* (New York: Federal Reserve Bank of New York, 1959), cited in Lewis, "1870–1914 Gold Standard."

9. Barry W. Ickes, "Lecture Note on the Gold Standard," Portland State University, Fall 2006, https://studylib.net/doc/8204476/lecture-note-on-the-gold-standard.

10. Ickes, "Lecture Note on the Gold Standard," 4.

11. Selgin, "Rise and Fall of the Gold Standard," 3.

12. Alan Greenspan, "Remarks by Chairman Alan Greenspan at the 15th Annual Monetary Conference of the Cato Institute, Washington, D.C., October 14, 1997: Globalization of Finance," Federal Reserve Board, http://www.federalreserve.gov/boarddocs/speeches/1997/19971014.htm.

13. Alan Greenspan, "Remarks by Chairman Alan Greenspan at the Annual Meeting of the Securities Industry Association, Boca Raton, Florida, November 5, 1998: The Structure of the International Financial System," Federal Reserve Board, http://www.federalreserve.gov/boarddocs/speeches/1998/19981105.htm.

14. Selgin, "Rise and Fall of the Gold Standard," 9.

15. McKinnon, "Rules of the Game," 3.

16. See Donald N. McCloskey and J. Richard Zecher, "How the Gold Standard Worked, 1880–1913," in *The Monetary Approach to the Balance of Payments Theory*, ed. Jacob A. Frenkel and Harry G. Johnson (London: George Allen & Unwin, 1976).

17. Lawrence White, "Recent Arguments Against the Gold Standard," Policy Analysis No. 728, Cato Institute, June 20, 2013, 20, https://www.cato.org/policy-analysis/recent-arguments-against-gold-standard.

18. For an analysis of the government's commitment to restore gold convertibility of its currency at the original fixed rate after temporarily abandoning convertibility during a wartime emergency, see Michael D. Bordo and Finn E. Kydland, "The Gold Standard as a Rule: An Essay in Exploration," *Explorations in Economic History* 32, no. 4 (October 1995), 423–64, https://doi.org/10.1006/exeh.1995.1019.

19. Robert Mundell, "A Reconsideration of the Twentieth Century," Nobel Prize lecture delivered in Stockholm, Sweden, December 8, 1999, https://www.nobelprize.org/uploads/2018/06/mundell-lecture.pdf.

20. Michael D. Bordo and Hugh Rockoff, "The Gold Standard as a 'Good Housekeeping Seal of Approval," Papers Presented at the Fifty-Fifth Annual Meeting of the Economic History Association, *Journal of Economic History* 56, no. 2, June 1996, 389–428, http://www.jstor.org/stable/2123971.

21. John Maynard Keynes, *Indian Currency and Finance* (London: Macmillan and Co., 1913), 99.

22. Keynes, *Indian Currency and Finance*, 36.

23. J. Keith Horsefield, *The International Monetary Fund, 1945–1965: Twenty Years of International Monetary Cooperation*, vol. I: *Chronicle* (Washington, DC: International Monetary Fund, 1969), 14–15.

24. John Maynard Keynes, "Proposals for an International Clearing Union," draft dated April 1943, reproduced in Horsefield, *International Monetary Fund, 1945–1965*, vol. III, 19.

25. Horsefield, *International Monetary Fund, 1945–1965*, vol. I, 12.

26. Horsefield, *International Monetary Fund, 1945–1965*, vol. I, 12.

27. H. D. White, "Preliminary Draft Proposal for a United Nations Stabilization Fund and a Bank for Reconstruction and Development of the United and Associated Nations," draft dated April 1942, in Horsefield, *International Monetary Fund, 1945–1965*, vol. III, 46.

28. White, "Preliminary Draft Proposal," 40.

29. White, "Preliminary Draft Proposal," 38–39.

30. White, "Preliminary Draft Proposal," 44.

31. White, "Preliminary Draft Proposal," 44.

32. John Maynard Keynes, "Proposals," draft dated February 11, 1942, in Horsefield, *International Monetary Fund, 1945–1965*, vol. III, 6.

33. John Maynard Keynes, "My Early Beliefs," *The Collected Writings of John Maynard Keynes*, edited by Elizabeth Johnson and Donald Moggridge (London: Macmillan for the Royal Society, 1971), 447.

34. Harry Dexter White, "Preliminary Draft Proposal," in Horsefield, *International Monetary Fund, 1945–1965*, vol. III, 41.

35. Edward Bernstein, "Reflections on Bretton Woods," *The International Monetary System: Forty Years After Bretton Woods*, Federal Reserve Bank of Boston, May 1984, 18, https://www.bostonfed.org/news-and-events/events/economic-research-conference-series/the-international-monetary-system-forty-years-after-bretton-woods.aspx (download: conf28b.pdf).

36. Oliver Bush, Katie Farrant, and Michelle Wright, "Reform of the International Monetary and Financial System," Financial Stability Paper No. 13, Bank of England, December 2011, https://www.bankofengland.co.uk/-/media/boe/files/financial-stability-paper/2011/reform-of-the-international-monetary-and-financial-system.pdf.

37. *Economic Report of the President Together with the Annual Report of the Council of Economic Advisers*, transmitted to the Congress February 2015, https://www.govinfo.gov/content/pkg/ERP-2015/pdf/ERP-2015.pdf.

38. Thomas Piketty, *Capital in the Twenty-First Century* (Cambridge, MA: Belknap Press of Harvard University Press, 2014).

39. Bush, Farrant, and Wright, "Reform of the International Monetary and Financial System," 4.

40. Bush, Farrant, and Wright, "Reform of the International Monetary and Financial System," 23.

41. Bush, Farrant, and Wright, "Reform of the International Monetary and Financial System," 3.

42. Bush, Farrant, and Wright, "Reform of the International Monetary and Financial System"; see table A, panel A, 7.

43. Bush, Farrant, and Wright, "Reform of the International Monetary and Financial System"; see table A, panel B, 7.

44. Bush, Farrant, and Wright, "Reform of the International Monetary and Financial System"; see table A, panel C, 7.

45. Bush, Farrant, and Wright, "Reform of the International Monetary and Financial System"; see table A, panel C, 7.

46. Bush, Farrant, and Wright, "Reform of the International Monetary and Financial System," 8.

47. Bush, Farrant, and Wright, "Reform of the International Monetary and Financial System," 8.

48. Bush, Farrant, and Wright, "Reform of the International Monetary and Financial System"; see table A, panel A and panel C, 7.

49. Charles Kadlec, "An International Gold Standard Beats the Rules of the Governing Elite," *Forbes*, December 19, 2011, http://www.forbes.com/sites/charleskadlec/2011/12/19/an-international-gold-standard-beats-the-rule-of-the-governing-elite/?sh=58c2591e77a1.

50. *Economic Report of the President*, 29.

51. *Economic Report of the President*, 31.

52. *Economic Report of the President*, 33.

53. Piketty, *Capital in the Twenty-First Century*, 96.

Chapter 5: Golden Link to the Future

1. "Federal Debt: Total Public Debt," *FRED Economic Data*, Federal Reserve Bank of St. Louis, updated June 6, 2024, https://fred.stlouisfed.org/series/GFDEBTN.

2. Judy Shelton, "The Fed's Monetary Policy Tool Kit Needs an Overhaul," *Wall Street Journal*, June 13, 2023, https://www.wsj.com/articles/the-feds-monetary-policy-tool-kit-needs-an-overhaul-interest-rates-budget-ea23c68a.

3. *The 2023 Long-Term Budget Outlook*, Congressional Budget Office, June 28, 2023, https://www.cbo.gov/publication/59014#section2.

4. Govind Bhutata, "Here's How Central Banks Have Used Gold in the Last 30 Years: 30 Years of Central Bank Gold Demand," *Financial and Monetary Systems*, World Economic Forum, March 20, 2023. https://www.weforum.org/agenda/2023/03/heres-how-central-banks-have-used-gold-in-the-last-30-years/.

5. Annalyn Censky, "Central Banks Join Gold Rush," *CNNMoney*, June 18, 2010, https://money.cnn.com/2010/06/17/news/economy/gold_reserves/index.htm.

6. Munemasa Horio, "Gold Snatched Up by Central Banks at Fastest Pace in 55 Years," *Nikkei Asia*, February 1, 2023, https://asia.nikkei.com/Business/Markets/Commodities/Gold-snatched-up-by-central-banks-at-fastest-pace-in-55-years.

7. "Gold Demand Trends Full Year 2022," *Central Banks*, World Gold Council, January 31, 2023, https://www.gold.org/goldhub/research/gold-demand-trends/gold-demand-trends-full-year-2022/central-banks.

8. "As Market Matures Central Banks Conclude That a Formal Gold Agreement Is No Longer Necessary," press release, European Central Bank, July 26, 2019, https://www.ecb.europa.eu/press/pr/date/2019/html/ecb.pr190726_1-3eaf64db9d.en.html.

9. Harry Dempsey, "ECB's Gold Sales Deal with European Central Banks Lapses," *Financial Times*, July 26, 2019, https://www.ft.com/content/49e8178c-afc6-11e9-8030-530adfa879c2.

10. "Gold-Report: Status Report of U.S. Government Gold Reserve," Bureau of the Fiscal Service, U.S. Department of the Treasury, February 28, 2021, https://www.fiscal.treasury.gov/reports-statements/gold-report/21-02.html.

11. Richard N. Cooper, "Toward an International Commodity Standard?," *Cato Journal* 8, no. 2 (Fall 1988), 315–38, https://www.cato.org/sites/cato.org/files/serials/files/cato-journal/1988/11/cj8n2-5.pdf.

12. Douglas Burns, "Tie Value of Dollar to Corn, Beans, Ag Commodities, Presidential Candidate Vivek Ramaswamy Says," *Iowa Capital Dispatch*, August 16, 2023, https://iowacapitaldispatch.com/2023/08/16/tie-value-of-dollar-to-corn-beans-ag-commodities-presidential-candidate-vivek-ramaswamy-says/.

13. Daniel Indiviglio, "Ron Paul Asks Ben Bernanke: How Do You Define a Dollar?," *The Atlantic*, March 2, 2011, https://www.theatlantic.com/business/archive/2011/03/ron-paul-asks-ben-bernanke-how-do-you-define-a-dollar/71944/.

14. See Roger Sherman (writing as *Philoeunomos*), "A Caveat Against Injustice, or An Inquiry into the Evils of a Fluctuating Medium of Exchange," 1752, https://www.scribd.com/document/437575042/Roger-Sherman-Caveat.

15. Treasury bills are short-term government securities with maturities ranging from a few days to fifty-two weeks. Bills are sold at a discount from their face value.

16. "U.S. Treasury Monthly Statement of the Public Debt (MSPD)," *Fiscal Data*, U.S. Department of the Treasury, updated June 6, 2024, https://fiscaldata.treasury.gov/datasets/monthly-statement-public-debt/summary-of-treasury-securities-outstanding.

17. Spencer Kimball, "Costco Sold More Than $100 Million in Gold Bars Last Quarter," CNBC, December 15, 2023, https://www.cnbc.com/2023/12/15/costco-sold-more-than-100-million-in-gold-bars-last-quarter.html.

18. Judy Shelton, "Currency Chaos: Where Do We Go from Here?" *Wall Street Journal*, October 16, 2010, https://www.wsj.com/articles/SB10001424052748704361504575552481963474898.

19. "Treasury Inflation Protected Securities (TIPS)," Treasury Marketable Securities, *TreasuryDirect*, U.S. Department of the Treasury, n.d., https://www.treasurydirect.gov/marketable-securities/tips/.

20. "How TIPS Protects You Against Inflation," *TreasuryDirect*, U.S. Department of the Treasury, n.d., https://treasurydirect.gov/marketable-securities/tips/#id-how-tips-protects-you-against-inflation-796810.

21. "Savings Bonds/EE Bonds," *TreasuryDirect*, U.S. Department of the Treasury, n.d., accessed June 22, 2024, https://treasurydirect.gov/savings-bonds/ee-bonds/.

22. The official price of gold in dollars was raised from $38.02 in December 1971 to $42.22 in February 1973. The U.S. government holds 261,498,926.241 fine troy ounces of gold for a total book value of $11,041,059,957.90, based on book value per fine troy ounce calculated at the statutory rate of $42.2222. See "Financial Statements of the United States Government for the Fiscal Years Ended September 30, 2023, and 2022," Balance Sheets/

Table/Assets: Cash and Other Monetary Assets (Note 2) https://search.app/TjoHV5UJn-WMnMWpm8 and "Notes to the Financial Statements, Note 2. Cash and Other Monetary Assets," 82, accessed June 22, 2024, https://search.app/VAAj9PocDTz66uscA.

23. Maggie Haberman, "Donald Trump Says He Favors Big Tariffs on Chinese Exports," *New York Times*, January 7, 2016, https://archive.nytimes.com/www.nytimes.com/politics/first-draft/2016/01/07/donald-trump-says-he-favors-big-tariffs-on-chinese-exports/.

24. Team Fix, "6th Republican Debate Transcript, Annotated: Who Said What and What It Meant," *Washington Post*, January 15, 2016, https://www.washingtonpost.com/news/the-fix/wp/2016/01/14/6th-republican-debate-transcript-annotated-who-said-what-and-what-it-meant/.

25. Tom Mitchell and Shawn Donnan, "China Currency is 'No Longer Undervalued', Says IMF," *Financial Times*, May 26, 2015, https://www.ft.com/content/11e96e1e-03a7-11e5-b55e-00144feabdco.

26. *Report to Congress on International Economic and Exchange Rate Policies*, U.S. Department of the Treasury, Office of International Affairs, April 9, 2015, 3, https://home.treasury.gov/system/files/206/Report%20to%20Congress%20on%20International%20Economic%20and%20Exchange%20Rate%20Policies%2004092015.pdf.

27. Sandy Levin, "The Need to Address Currency Manipulation in TPP, and Why U.S. Monetary Policy Is Not at Risk," *Huffington Post*, February 6, 2015, https://www.huffpost.com/entry/the-need-to-address-curre_b_6631514.

28. Levin, "The Need to Address Currency Manipulation in TPP."

29. "Currency Manipulation 101: What Is It and How Does It Affect American Jobs?," American Automakers, American Automotive Policy Council (AAPC), n.d., accessed June 22, 2024, https://www.americanautomakers.org/currency-manipulation-101.

30. *Report to Congress on International Economic and Exchange Rate Policies*, 2.

31. "Gold Spot Prices," *Goldhub*, World Gold Council, June 10, 2024, https://www.gold.org/goldhub/data/gold-prices.

32. Pallavi Rao, "Visualizing 30 Years of Imports from U.S. Trading Partners," *Visual Capitalist*, November 23, 2023, https://www.visualcapitalist.com/30-years-imports-us-trading-partners/.

33. "Treasury Releases Report on Macroeconomic and Foreign Exchange Policies of Major Trading Partners of the United States," press release, U.S. Department of the Treasury, November 10, 2022, https://home.treasury.gov/news/press-releases/jy1094.

34. "Treasury Releases Report on Macroeconomic and Foreign Exchange Policies."

35. *Report to Congress*: *Macroeconomic and Foreign Exchange Policies of Major Trading Partners of the United States*, U.S. Department of the Treasury, Office of International Affairs, November 2022, https://home.treasury.gov/system/files/206/November_2022_FXR_FINAL.pdf, 3.

36. "Treasury Designates China as a Currency Manipulator," press release, U.S Department of the Treasury, August 5, 2019, https://home.treasury.gov/news/press-releases/sm751.

37. "US Reverses China 'Currency Manipulator' Label," *BBC News*, January 14, 2020, https://www.bbc.com/news/business-51098294.

38. William C. Dudley, Jennifer Roush, and Michelle Steinberg Ezer, "The Case for TIPS: An Examination of the Costs and Benefits," *FRBNY Economic Policy Review*, Federal Reserve Bank of New York, July 2009, 12, https://www.newyorkfed.org/medialibrary/media/research/epr/09v15n1/0907dudl.pdf.

39. Dudley, Roush, and Ezer, "Case for TIPS," 12–13.

40. Robert Zoellick, "The G20 Must Look Beyond Bretton Woods II," *Financial Times*, November 7, 2010, https://www.ft.com/content/5bb39488-ea99-11df-b28d-00144feab49a.

41. For a thoughtful consideration of important questions related to the market price of gold relative to an appropriate reentry parity, as well as potential costs in adopting gold redeemability, see Brian P. Cutsinger, "On the Feasibility of Returning to the Gold Standard," *Quarterly Review of Economics and Finance* 78 (2020), 88–97.

42. "World Official Gold Holdings," *International Financial Statistics*, World Gold Council, February 2024. https://www.gold.org//goldhub/data/gold-reserves-by-country#from-login=1 (download: "Latest World Official Gold Reserves").

43. *Report to the Congress of the Commission on the Role of Gold in the Domestic and International Monetary Systems*, vol. 1, March 1982, https://images.procon.org/wp-content/uploads/sites/23/gold_comission_report_1982.pdf.

44. Alan Greenspan, "Can the U.S. Return to a Gold Standard?" *Wall Street Journal*, September 1, 1981, https://newworldeconomics.com/alan-greenspan-wsj-1981-can-the-u-s-return-to-a-gold-standard/.

45. Greenspan, "Can the U.S. Return to a Gold Standard?"

46. Greenspan, "Can the U.S. Return to a Gold Standard?"

47. Greenspan, "Can the U.S. Return to a Gold Standard?"

48. Greenspan, "Can the U.S. Return to a Gold Standard?"

49. Greenspan, "Can the U.S. Return to a Gold Standard?"

50. Greenspan, "Can the U.S. Return to a Gold Standard?"

51. "Gold: The Ultimate Insurance Policy," interview with Alan Greenspan, *Gold Investor*, World Gold Council, February 2017, 13, https://www.gold.org (download: Gold_Investor_February_2017.pdf).

52. "Gold and the IMF," International Monetary Fund, updated September 2022, https://www.imf.org/en/About/Factsheets/Sheets/2022/Gold-in-the-IMF.

53. "The IMF at a Glance," *The Challenges of Growth, Employment and Social Cohesion: Joint ILO-IMF Conference in Cooperation with the Office of the Prime Minister of Norway*, International Monetary Fund, September 13, 2010, https://www.imf.org/external/NP/seminars/eng/2010/oslo/imf.htm.

54. Peter T. Kilborn, "Baker Hints at Gold as Guide on Policy," *New York Times*, October 1, 1987, http://www.nytimes.com/1987/10/01/business/baker-hints-at-gold-as-guide-on-policy.html.

55. Kilborn, "Baker Hints at Gold."

56. Hobart Rowen, "Baker's Gold Gambit," *Washington Post*, October 18, 1987, https://www.washingtonpost.com/archive/business/1987/10/18/bakers-gold-gambit/bo2da6db-b624-4e69-9516-41c80b8973b7/.

57. George Zornick, "Rep. Mike Pence Suggests that the U.S. Return to the Gold Standard," *Think Progress*, November 29, 2010, https://archive.thinkprogress.org/rep-mike-pence-suggests-that-the-u-s-return-to-the-gold-standard-4f207559c1f7/.

58. "Federal Reserve's First Monetary Policy Report for 2011," Hearing Before the Committee on Banking, Housing, and Urban Affairs, U.S. Senate, 112th Congress, First Session on Oversight on the Monetary Policy Report to Congress Pursuant to the Full Employment and Balanced Growth Act of 1978, March 1, 2011, 38, https://www.govinfo.gov/content/pkg/CHRG-112shrg65824/pdf/CHRG-112shrg65824.pdf.

59. H.R.2435—Gold Standard Restoration Act, 118th Congress (2023–24), https://www.congress.gov/bill/118th-congress/house-bill/2435/text?s=3&r=17q=%7B%22search%22%3A%5B%22%22%5D57D.

60. Sound Money Defense League, "Three Congressmen Introduce Gold Standard Bill to Stabilize the Dollar's Value," *Accesswire*, April 4, 2023, https://finance.yahoo.com/news/three-congressmen-introduce-gold-standard-015000789.html.

Chapter 6: The Leadership Imperative

1. Annie Linskey and Aaron Zitner, "'Stop Printing Money.' How Voters Would Solve the Debt-Ceiling Standoff," *Wall Street Journal*, May 10, 2023, https://www.wsj.com/articles/stop-printing-money-how-voters-would-solve-the-debt-ceiling-standoff-96e36a03?mod=hp_lead_pos4.

2. Jeffrey M. Jones, "Americans Lack Confidence in Major Economic Leaders," Gallup, May 9, 2023, https://news.gallup.com/poll/505478/americans-lack-confidence-major-economic-leaders.aspx.

3. "Currency Composition of Official Foreign Exchange Reserves (COFER)," *IMF Data: Access to Macroeconomic and Financial Data*, International Monetary Fund, updated March 29, 2024, https://data.imf.org/?sk=e6a5f467-c14b-4aa8-9f6d-5a09ec4e62a4.

4. "We Believe in America: 2012 Republican Platform," August 27, 2012, American Presidency Project, University of California, Santa Barbara, https://www.presidency.ucsb.edu/documents/2012-republican-party-platform.

5. "Republican Platform 2016," July 18, 2016, 7, https://prod-cdn-static.gop.com/media/documents/DRAFT_12_FINAL [1] -ben_1468872234.pdf.

6. H.R. 3189, 114th Congress, 1st Session, November 30, 2015, section 16, https://www.congress.gov/114/bills/hr3189/BILLS-114hr3189rds.pdf.

7. S. 1786: Centennial Monetary Commission Act of 2015, 114th Congress (2015–2016), July 16, 2015, https://www.congress.gov/bill/114th-congress/senate-bill/1786/text.

8. Clerk, U.S. House of Representatives, 114th Congress, 1st Session, Roll Call 641, Bill Number: H.R. 3189, November 19, 2015, https://clerk.house.gov/Votes/2015641; cosponsors are listed at https://www.congress.gov/bill/114th-congress/house-bill/3189/all-info#cosponsors-content.

9. "What Economic Goals Does the Federal Reserve Seek to Achieve Through its Monetary Policy?," *FAQs*, Board of Governors of the Federal Reserve System, updated August 27, 2020, https://www.federalreserve.gov/faqs/what-economic-goals-does-federal-reserve-seek-to-achieve-through-monetary-policy.htm.

10. January 2021 to May 2024, "CPI Inflation Calculator," U.S. Bureau of Labor Statistics, U.S. Department of Labor, n.d., accessed June 22, 2024, https://data.bls.gov/cgi-bin/cpicalc.pl.

11. Federal Open Market Committee, "Statement on Longer-Run Goals and Monetary Policy Strategy," *Review of Monetary Policy Strategy, Tools, and Communications*, Board of Governors of the Federal Reserve System, reaffirmed effective January 30, 2024, https://www.federalreserve.gov/monetarypolicy/files/FOMC_LongerRunGoals.pdf.

12. "Meeting of the Federal Open Market Committee, July 2–3, 1996," transcript, *Historical Materials by Year*, Board of Governors of the Federal Reserve System, https://www.federalreserve.gov/monetarypolicy/files/fomc19960703meeting.pdf.

13. "Meeting of the Federal Open Market Committee," 43.

14. "Meeting of the Federal Open Market Committee," 44.

15. "Meeting of the Federal Open Market Committee," 45.

16. "Meeting of the Federal Open Market Committee," 51.

17. "Meeting of the Federal Open Market Committee," 51.

18. "Meeting of the Federal Open Market Committee," 52.

19. "Economy and Trade," Office of the United States Trade Representative, Executive Office of the President, n.d., accessed June 22, 2024, https://ustr.gov/issue-areas/economy-trade#:~:text=America%20is%20the%20world's%20largest,the%20development%20of%20American%20prosperity.

20. "Dollar Dominance Monitor," from the Atlantic Council's GeoEconomics Center, Atlantic Council, December 11, 2023. For an in-depth analysis of current trends regarding the U.S. dollar's usage worldwide and its ongoing role in monetary and trade transactions, see https://www.atlanticcouncil.org/programs-geoeconomics-center/dollar-dominance-monitor/.

21. Jordan Finneseth, "Ditch the Dollar Movement Grows as Moscow Calls for the Creation of a Common BRICS Currency," *HotCopper*, March 31, 2023, https://hotcopper.com.au/threads/gold.2750023/page-118320?post_id=67082054.

22. Diego Lasarte, "Putin Is Strengthening the Yuan's Role as Russia's Foreign Currency of Choice," *Yahoo!Money / Quartz*, March 21, 2023, https://money.yahoo.com/putin-strengthening-yuan-role-russia-212300796.html.

23. Joe Leahy and Hudson Lockett, "Brazil's Lula Calls for End to Dollar Trade Dominance," *Financial Times*, April 13, 2023, https://www.ft.com/content/669260a5-82a5-4e7a-9bbf-4f41c54a6143.

24. Chen Aizhu, "Vast China-Russia Resources Trade Shifts to Yuan from Dollars in Ukraine Fallout," Reuters, May 10, 2023, https://www.reuters.com/markets/currencies/vast-china-russia-resources-trade-shifts-yuan-dollars-ukraine-fallout-2023-05-11/.

25. Meaghan Tobin, Lyric Li, and David Feliba, "Move Over, U.S. Dollar. China Wants to Make the Yuan the Global Currency," *Washington Post*, May 16, 2023, https://

www.washingtonpost.com/world/2023/05/16/china-yuan-renminbi-us-dollar-currency-trade/.

26. "Saudi Arabia Open to Trading in Currencies Besides the US Dollar," *Middle East Eye*, January 17, 2023, https://www.middleeasteye.net/news/saudi-arabia-open-trading-currencies-besides-us-dollar.

27. Wahid Pessarlay, "France's BNP Paribas Partners with Bank of China to Promote Digital Yuan Usage," *Coingeek*, May 11, 2023, https://coingeek.com/france-bnp-paribas-partners-with-bank-of-china-to-promote-digital-yuan-usage/.

28. Bruce Stokes, "Republicans, Especially Trump Supporters, See Free Trade Deals as Bad for U.S.," Pew Research Center, March 31, 2016, https://www.pewresearch.org/short-reads/2016/03/31/republicans-especially-trump-supporters-see-free-trade-deals-as-bad-for-u-s/.

29. Mohamed Younis, "Sharply Fewer in U.S. View Foreign Trade as Opportunity," *Politics*, Gallup, March 31, 2021, https://news.gallup.com/poll/342419/sharply-fewer-view-foreign-trade-opportunity.aspx.

30. For example, "Transcript of Chair Powell's Press Conference, March 22, 2023," Federal Open Market Committee, *Transcripts and Other Historical Materials*, Federal Reserve Board of Governors, 1, https://www.federalreserve.gov/mediacenter/files/FOMCpresconf20230322.pdf.

31. Rachel Siegel and Jeff Stein, "World Watches in Disbelief and Horror as U.S. Nears Possible Default," *Washington Post*, May 19, 2023, https://www.washingtonpost.com/business/2023/05/19/world-watches-us-debt-ceiling-worries-default/.

32. Christopher Condon, "Yellen Says Debt Default Would Hurt US International Leadership," *Economics*, Bloomberg, May 11, 2023, https://www.bloomberg.com/news/articles/2023-05-11/yellen-says-debt-default-would-hurt-us-international-leadership.

33. Alex Gangitano, "Biden Warns 'the Whole World Is in Trouble' if US Defaults on Debts," *The Hill*, May 10, 2023, https://thehill.com/homenews/administration/3998249-biden-warns-the-whole-world-is-in-trouble-if-us-defaults-on-debts/.

34. "Countries Using the Euro," European Union, accessed June 22, 2024, https://european-union.europa.eu/institutions-law-budget/euro/countries-using-euro_en.

35. Kevin Brown, "Zoellick Urges G20 to Heed Gold Price," *Financial Times*, November 10, 2010, https://www.ft.com/content/54a44c3e-ec7c-11df-ac70-00144feab49a.

36. "United States–Mexico–Canada Trade Fact Sheet: Modernizing NAFTA into a 21st Century Trade Agreement," Office of the U.S. Trade Representative, Executive Office of the President, accessed June 22, 2024, https://ustr.gov/trade-agreements/free-trade-agreements/united-states-mexico-canada-agreement/fact-sheets/modernizing.

37. "United States–Mexico–Canada Trade Fact Sheet."

38. "Trade in Goods with China, 2023," U.S. Census Bureau, n.d., accessed June 22, 2024, https://www.census.gov/foreign-trade/balance/c5700.html.

39. "Economic and Trade Agreement Between the Government of the United States of America and the Government of the People's Republic of China," chapter 5, article 5.2(3), p. 5-2, https://ustr.gov/countries-regions/china-mongolia-taiwan/peoples-republic-china/phase-one-trade-agreement/text.

40. "Yi Says China Largely Ended Currency Intervention in Market Tilt," *Economics*, Bloomberg, April 15, 2023, https://bloomberg.com/news/articles/2023-04-15/yi-says-yuan-set-by-market-pboc-basically-stopped-intervention.

41. "Exchange Rates and Currency Manipulation," Congressional Research Service, updated June 11, 2024, https://sgp.fas.org/crs/misc/IF10049.pdf.

42. "Theresa May at Davos 2017: Her Speech in Full," World Economic Forum, January 19, 2017, https://www.weforum.org/agenda/2017/01/theresa-may-at-davos-2017-her-speech-in-full/.

43. Stephen Fidler, Te-Ping Chen, and Lingling Wei, "China's Xi Jinping Seizes Role as Leader on Globalization," *Wall Street Journal*, January 17, 2017, https://www.wsj.com/articles/chinas-xi-jinping-defends-globalization-1484654899.

44. Doug Palmer, "New IMF Report Doesn't Back Trump's Currency Manipulation Charge Against China," *Politico*, August 9, 2019, https://www.politico.com/story/2019/08/09/imf-report-trump-currency-manipulation-1653096.

45. "The Role of Gold," *Gold and the IMF*, International Monetary Fund, updated September 2022, https://www.imf.org/en/About/Factsheets/Sheets/2022/Gold-in-the-IMF.

46. Richard M. Nixon, "Address to the Nation Outlining a New Economic Policy: The Challenge of Peace," August 15, 1971, Papers of Richard M. Nixon, *FRASER / Discover Economic History*, Federal Reserve, https://fraser.stlouisfed.org/archival-collection/papers-richard-m-nixon-1173/address-nation-outlining-a-new-economic-policy-3390.

47. "President Ronald Reagan Commercial on the Gold Standard," YouTube video, posted September 4, 2017, https://www.youtube.com/watch?v=M-T6sv6slWM.

48. Ron Paul, "The Secret Ronald Reagan Told Me About Gold and Great Nations," *New York Sun*, August 14, 2021, https://www.nysun.com/article/national-the-golden-secret-ronald-reagan-told-me-about.

49. Clara Nugent and Michael Stoff, "Javier Milei Takes Office Pledging Deep Spending Cuts for Argentina," *Financial Times*, December 10, 2023, https://www.ft.com/content/ebe8382e-57b2-478e-984b-057b01ec7f5f.

50. Hernan Nessi, "Argentina Annual Inflation Tops 211%, Highest Since Early 90s," *Macro Matters*, Reuters, January 11, 2024, https://www.reuters.com/markets/argentina-annual-inflation-tops-211-highest-since-early-90s-2024-01-11/.

51. Michael Stoff, "The Nightmare Economic In-Tray Awaiting Argentina's Javier Milei," *Financial Times*, December 8, 2023, https://www.ft.com/content/4213be36-a122-4649-9214-4e763b098dc7.

52. "What to Read About Argentina," *The Economist*, November 17, 2023, https://www.economist.com/the-economist-reads/2023/11/17/what-to-read-about-argentina.

53. "Income, Poverty and Health Insurance Coverage in the United States: 2022," Press Release Number CB23-150, U.S. Census Bureau, September 12, 2023. https://search.app/egRcKT8eESJSrewj7.

54. Filip De Mott, "Argentina's New President Is Dragging His Feet After Promising to Use the US Dollar More," *Business Insider / Yahoo! Finance*, February 6, 2024, https://finance.yahoo.com/news/argentinas-president-dragging-feet-promising-022036901.html.

55. "Official Dollarization in Emerging-Market Countries," Joint Hearing, Committee on Banking, Housing, and Urban Affairs, U.S. Senate, April 22, 1999.

56. Miguel A. Kiguel, "The Argentine Currency Board," CEMA Working Papers: Serie Documentos de Trabajo, Universidad del CEMA, July 1, 1999, https://api.semantic-scholar.org/CorpusID:153264962.

57. "Official Dollarization in Emerging-Market Countries," 3.

58. "Official Dollarization in Emerging-Market Countries," 6–7.

59. "Official Dollarization in Emerging-Market Countries," 15.

60. "Official Dollarization in Emerging-Market Countries," 26.

61. "Official Dollarization in Emerging-Market Countries," 49–50.

62. Murray N. Rothbard, *What Has Government Done to Our Money? and The Case for a 100 Percent Gold Dollar* (Auburn, AL: Ludwig von Mises Institute, 2005).

63. Satoshi Nakamoto, "Bitcoin: A Peer-to-Peer Electronic Cash System," Bitcoin.org, n.d., accessed June 23, 2024, https://bitcoin.org/en/bitcoin-paper.

64. Nakamoto, "Bitcoin: A Peer-to-Peer Electronic Cash System."

65. Satoshi Nakamoto, "Bitcoin Open Source Implementation of P2P Currency," P2P Foundation, February 11, 2009, http://p2pfoundation.ning.com/forum/topics/bitcoin-open-source.

66. "Key Findings," Central Bank Digital Currency Tracker, Geoeconomics Center, Atlantic Council, updated May 2024, https://www.Tatlanticcouncil.org/cbdctracker/.

67. Sarah Wynn, "US Lawmakers Introduce 'First Bipartisan Bill' Blocking a CBDC," *Cryptonews*, May 19, 2023, https://cryptonews.com/news/us-lawmakers-introduce-first-bipartisan-bill-blocking-a-cbdc.htm.

68. "Central Bank Digital Currency (CBDC)," Board of Governors of the Federal Reserve System, updated April 20, 2023, https://www.federalreserve.gov/central-bank-digital-currency.htm.

69. "Central Bank Digital Currency (CBDC): Frequently Asked Questions," question 6, Board of Governors of the Federal Reserve System, updated April 11, 2023, https://federalreserve.gov/cbdc-faqs.htm.

70. George Kingslay, "6 Best Gold-Backed Crypto in 2024," *CoinCodex*, March 21, 2024, https://coincodex.com/article/29449/gold-backed-crypto/.

71. Samuel Haig, "Australian Startup Offers New Spin on Tokenized Gold Trading," *Coin Telegraph*, April 1, 2020, https://cointelegraph.com/news/australian-startup-offers-new-spin-on-tokenized-gold-trading.

72. John P. Mangudya, "Issuance and Usage of Gold-Backed Digital Tokens," press statement by governor of Reserve Bank of Zimbabwe, April 28, 2023, http://www.rbz.co.zw/documents/press/2023/April/Press_Statement_-_Issuance_of_Gold-backed_Digital_Tokens_1.pdf.

73. "Zimbabwe Introduces New Gold-Backed Currency to Tackle Inflation," *Al Jazeera*, April 5, 2024, https://www.aljazeera.com/news/2024/4/5/zimbabwe-introduces-new-gold-backed-currency-to-tackle-inflation.

74. Chris Muronzi, "Zimbabwe's New Gold-Backed Digital Currency: All You Need to Know," *Al Jazeera*, May 9, 2023, https://www.aljazeera.com/news/2023/5/9/zimbabwes-new-gold-backed-digital-currency-all-you-need-to-know.

75. Peter Aitken, "Russia, China May Be Preparing New Gold-Backed Currency, but Expert Assures US Dollar 'Safest' Currency Today," *Fox Business*, October 29, 2022, https://www.foxbusiness.com/economy/russia-china-may-be-preparing-new-gold-backed-currency-expert-assures-us-dollar-safest-currency-today.

76. Kwasi Kwarteng, "A Chinese Gold Standard?" *New York Times*, July 24, 2014, https://www.nytimes.com/2014/07/25/opinion/a-chinese-gold-standard-renminbi.html.

77. Hogan Gore, "Digital Currency Built on Texas Gold? Here's What's Being Proposed," *Austin American-Statesman*, May 9, 2023, https://eu.statesman.com/story/news/politics/state/2023/05/09/texas-senate-bill-2334-proposal-new-digital-currency-texas-gold-purchase-everyday-goods/70195299007/.

78. Jeff Stein, Rachel Siegel and Tony Romm, "As Funds Run Short, Treasury Asks Agencies If Payments Can Be Made Later," *Washington Post*, May 23, 2023, https://www.washingtonpost.com/business/2023/05/23/debt-ceiling-later-payments/.

79. In April 2024, U.S. Senators Kirsten Gillibrand and Cynthia Lummis introduced bipartisan legislation aimed at protecting consumers by requiring stablecoin issuers to maintain one-to-one reserves; unbacked, algorithmic stablecoins would be prohibited. The legislation seeks to create a regulatory framework that gives roles to both federal and state agencies for chartering and enforcement with the objective of preventing illicit or unauthorized use of stablecoins by issuers and users. In announcing the legislation, the sponsors emphasized that it would protect American interests:

- Passing payment stablecoin legislation will support the dollar as the medium of digital exchange. In 2021, the President's Working Group on Financial Markets recognized the promise of well-regulated stablecoins to improve the speed and efficiency of the existing financial system while promoting dollar dominance.
- Codifying standards for compliant U.S-issued stablecoins will counter foreign ambitions to establish alternative settlement systems and enshrine American values and the dollar as the base currency for the $4.5 trillion digital economy.
- Will create healthy competition and a race to create compliant stablecoins among American companies including banks, payments, and financial technology companies. Malign actors will no longer have the option to use unregulated foreign stablecoins, and consumers will benefit by knowing they are using safe, compliant U.S. payment instruments.

"Lummis, Gillibrand Introduce Bipartisan Landmark Legislation to Create Regulatory Framework for Stablecoins," press release, Cynthia Lummis, Senator for Wyoming, April 17, 2024, http://www.lummis.senate.gov/press-releases/lummis-gillibrand-introduce-bipartisan-landmark-legislation-to-create-regulatory-framework-for-stablecoins/.

Epilogue

1. Grover Cleveland, "Special Session Message," August 8, 1893, American Presidency Project, University of California, Santa Barbara, https://www.presidency.ucsb.edu/documents/special-session-message-0.

2. Victoria Guida, "Fed's Powell Cites Top Barrier to Taming Inflation—Workers' Wages," *Politico*, November 30, 2022, https://www.politico.com/news/2022/11/30/feds-powell-inflation-workers-wages-00071403.

3. "Distribution of Household Wealth in the U.S. Since 1989," *DFA: Distributional Financial Accounts*, Board of Governors of the Federal Reserve System, updated March 24, 2023, https://www.federalreserve.gov/releases/z1/dataviz/dfa/distribute/chart/#quarter:126;series:Corporate%20equities%20and%20mutual%20fund%20shares;demographic:networth;population:1,3,5,7;units:levels;range:2006.1,2021.1.

4. For an analysis of the association between individual-level automation anxiety and insomnia among workers, see Seong-Uk Baek, Jin-Ha Yoon, and Jong-Uk Won, "Association Between Workers' Anxiety over Technological Automation and Sleep Disturbance: Results from a Nationally Representative Survey" (Paul B. Tchounwou, academic editor), *International Journal of Environmental Research and Public Health* 19, no.16 (August 2022), https://www.ncbi.nlm.nih.gov/pmc/articles/PMC9408459.

5. George Gilder, *Microcosm: The Quantum Revolution in Economics and Technology* (New York: Simon & Schuster, 1989).

6. George Gilder, *The Scandal of Money: Why Wall Street Recovers but the Economy Never Does* (Washington, DC: Regnery Publishing, 2016), 162–63.

7. Gilder, *Scandal of Money*, 161–63.

8. George Gilder, "Three Steps to Save America from Collapse," *Economics*, Discovery Institute, July 1, 2019, https://www.discovery.org/a/three-steps-to-save-america-from-collapse/.

9. Gilder, "Three Steps to Save America."

10. Gilder, "Three Steps to Save America."

11. Jack Kemp speech excerpted in "Faith at Work: Morality and Ethics Undergird Capitalism and Prosperity," *Washington Times*, May 11, 2016, https://www.washingtontimes.com/news/2016/may/11/faith-at-work-morality-and-ethics-undergird-capita/.

12. Jack Kemp, "Is There a Political Consensus for Monetary Reform?," remarks at U.S. Congressional Summit on Exchange Rates and the Dollar, Washington, D.C., November 13, 1985.

Index

46; independence of, 6, 19, 79, 178, 226; and inflation, 111–112, 132, 193–194, 230; and interest rates, 38, 226; as lender of last resort, 5, 40, 81, 128; and maximum employment, 21; paying interest on reserves, 25–26; power of, 19, 68, 78; relationship with the Treasury, 5–7; and stable price, 21; and Treasury debt, 5, 25, 40–41

Federal Reserve regional banks, 4, 25, 71; Bank of Cleveland, 25, 62, 195; Bank of New York, 104, 175–176; Bank of St. Louis, 123, *161*

Federal Reserve Reform Act (1977), 21

FedNow, 213

Feulner, Edwin, 18–19

financial booms, 59

financial derivatives. *See* derivatives

financial services, 60, 62–63

financialization, 61, *61*, 61–64, 66, 82

Finland, 124

Fisher, Irving, 21

FOMC. *See* Federal Open Market Committee (FOMC)

Forbes, Steve, 108

foreign exchange market (forex/FX), 105–107

Foundation for Economic Education, 186

France, 124

francs, 166

free trade, 10–11, 12, 39, 76, 85, 89, 94, 99, 100, 102, 123, 170, 200, 204

freedom: economic, 9, 14, 35, 64, 226; individual, 19, 35, 51, 190; political, 64

Friedman, Milton, 2, 89, 90–91, 94–99, 103, 145

FTX, 114, 115

Furer, Guido, 29

FX (foreign exchange market), 105–107

G

Gagnon, Joseph, 104

GDP. *See* gross domestic product (GDP)

Germany: deutsche mark, 98, 103, 104; economic policies, 171; gold reserves, 124; government debt, 38; stock markets, 28; after World War I, 133; and World War II, 135

Gilder, George, 227–229

Global Exchange Rate Assessment Framework, *172*

global financial crisis, 25, 40, 46, 62, 80–81, 119, 126, 150, 151

globalization, 86, 126, 204

gold: as benchmark, 153, 166, 174, 212; as collateral, 178, 179; dollar linked to, 152–153, 186–187, 191, 206; dollar price of, 156, 157, 162,

167; futures contracts, 177; held by the IMF, 184; held by the U.S. government, 159–160; linked to Treasury Trust Bonds, 155–156; as monetary asset, 202; as money, 109; price in euros, 167, *168*; price of, 152, 167–174, *169–172*, 184; public confidence in, 160; as reserve asset, 96, 97; as safe-haven asset, 151; state bullion depository, 217; *see also* gold standard

gold coins, 13–14, 50, 111, 125–126

Gold Commission, 184

gold convertibility: advantages of, 31, 32, 90, 122, 128, 182; in Argentina, 209; and the Bretton Woods system, 67, 77, 96, 132, 178, 197; in Britain, 121; as discipline, 150, 174, 181–182; of the dollar, 77, 88–90, 96, 139, 140, 206, 228; in earlier monetary systems, 78, 120–121, 221; and the gold standard, 122, 125, 129, 131, 132; and international trade 106, 127, 128, 131, 133; of sovereign debt instruments 178, 179, 183, 205, 212; and Treasury Trust Bonds, 152, 156, 175, 178, 180, 191, 183, 206, 217–218, 224, 225, 231

Gold Reserve Act (1934), 140

gold standard, 1, 12–13, 37, 67, 77, 97, 120, 122–132, 186, 192; automaticity of, 126–127; benefits of, 1, 8, 99; compared to Bretton Woods system, 141–148; Greenspan's support for, 31–32; international, 1, 88, 120, 128; and international trade, 128–131; as monetary system, 123–125; return to, 181; vulnerability to war, 131

Gold Standard Restoration Act, 186

GoldCoin, 216

Gorbachev, Mikhail, 17, 24

Gosbank, 23–25

government: economic interventions by, 87–88, 89, 189–190, 219; and the gold standard, 129–131; limiting the role of, 64; policies of, 54–55; restoring confidence in, 191–197, 226

government debt, 4, 38, 130, 149–150, 175

Graham, Benjamin, 154

Great Depression, 121

Great Recession, 46

Greenspan, Alan, 1–2, 13, 31–32, 80–81, 114, 126, 129, 181–183, 186, 194, 195, 208

gross domestic product (GDP), 53–56, 59, 60, 105, 150, *172*, 192

Group of Seven, 201

Guatemala, 57–58

Gulf War, 13

Gyohten, Toyoo, 41

About the Author

JUDY SHELTON is an economist who specializes in global finance and monetary issues. She is a senior fellow at Independent Institute. She was former chair of the National Endowment for Democracy and former U.S. director of the European Bank for Reconstruction and Development. She has provided expert testimony before the Senate Banking Committee, Senate Foreign Relations Committee, House Financial Services Committee, House Committee on Foreign Affairs, and the Joint Economic Committee. She has been consulted on international economic and financial issues by national security officials at the White House and Pentagon and received the Distinguished Service Award from the Treasury Department. She served on the transition team for the Trump administration as lead advisor on international affairs at the Treasury Department and was nominated by President Trump for the Board of Governors of the Federal Reserve.

Shelton won the Trefftzs Award for outstanding scholarly achievement from the Western Finance Association and received a postdoctoral fellowship from the Hoover Institution at Stanford University as a public affairs fellow. She is the author of *The Coming Soviet Crash* (1989) and *Money Meltdown* (1994). Her opinion articles have been published by the *Wall Street Journal, Financial Times, New York Times, Washington Post,* and *The Hill.* She served as an advisor for the National Commission on Economic Growth and Tax Reform chaired by Jack Kemp and was a founding member of the board of directors of Empower America.